W9-BBW-308

THE STORY OF THE JEWISH PEOPLE

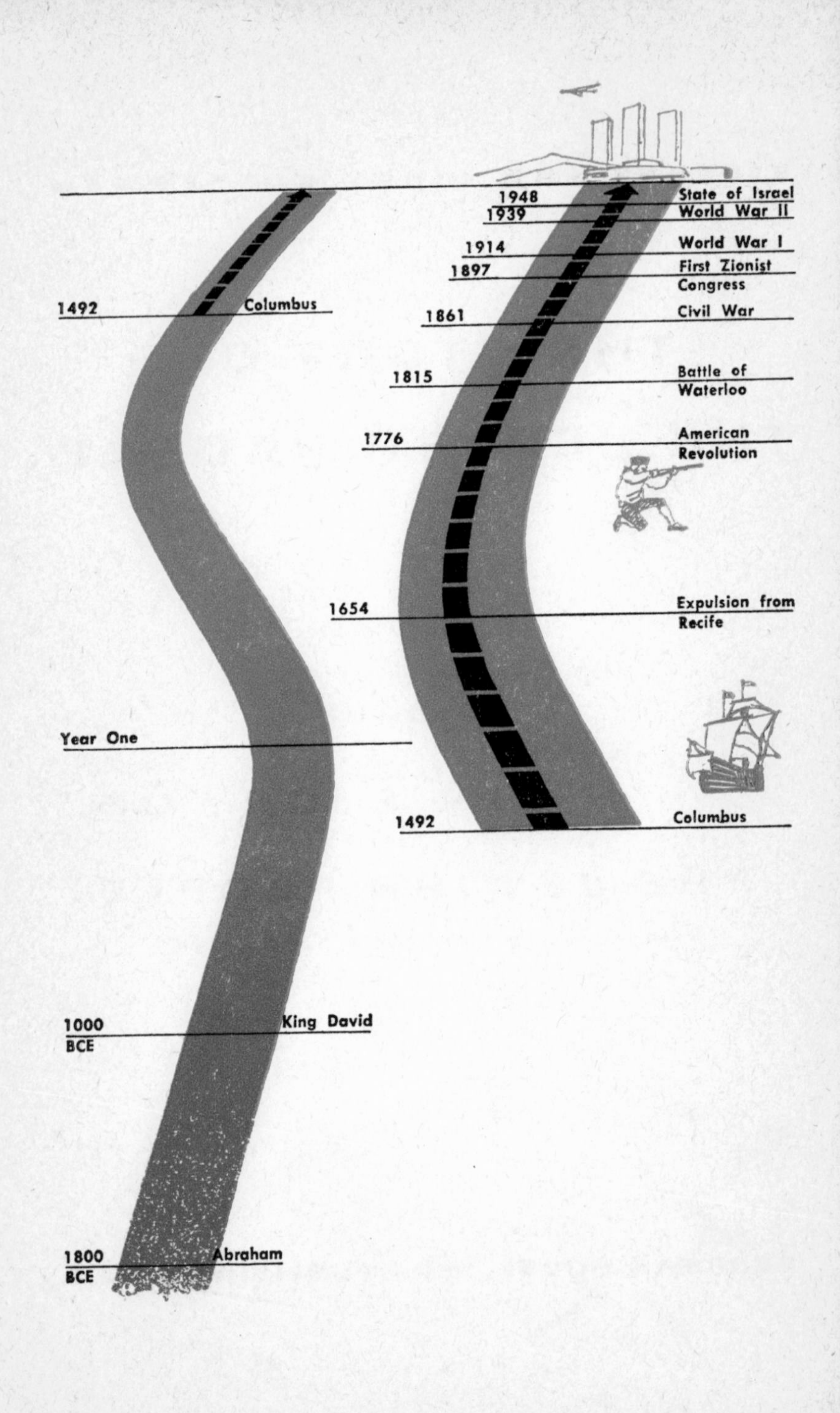
1948
State of Israel
1939
World War II
1914
World War I
1897
First Zionist Congress
1861
Civil War
1815
Battle of Waterloo
1776
American Revolution
1654
Expulsion from Recife
1492
Columbus
1492
Columbus
Year One
1000 BCE
King David
1800 BCE
Abraham

GILBERT AND LIBBY KLAPERMAN

THE STORY OF THE JEWISH PEOPLE

VOLUME FOUR

From the Settlement of America through Israel Today

Illustrated by LORENCE F. BJORKLUND

BEHRMAN HOUSE, INC. • PUBLISHERS • N.Y.

Published by Behrman House, Inc.
1261 Broadway, New York 1, N.Y.
Manufactured in the United States of America
Library of Congress Catalog Card Number: 56-12175

Preface

It is with profound gratification that we have brought this final volume of *The Story of the Jewish People* to completion. For even though the history of our people is a deep sea of experience and "to the writing of books there is no end," this series, nevertheless, forms a self-contained and comprehensive picture of Jewish life and faith from ancient days.

It is our hope that these volumes will serve as an introduction to the values of Judaism and a stimulation to the further study of its unique and inspirational qualities.

All four books in the series benefited greatly from the advice and assistance of a patient and painstaking editor to whom the smallest phrase was as dear as the loftiest thought. Throughout, Frances Long has helped shape the structure of our material and mold the presentation of our ideas. To her and to our publisher, Jacob Behrman, whose good taste and unerring judgment we owe more than we can express, our fondest thanks and appreciation.

GILBERT and LIBBY KLAPERMAN

For our beloved mother

FRIEDA RUBINSTEIN KLAPERMAN

who built her house with Wisdom

CONTENTS

CONTENTS (concluded)

GOD'S ROAD TO TOMORROW

Up until this time, for the most part, we have studied Jewish history from a great distance and have seen how it developed in strange lands. Now, we will come closer to home and study it as it took place in our own land and in the new-born State of Israel.

As we come nearer to the present time, to the "Now," we will not see Jewish history in the garb of the Chassidim or of ancient Palestine. We will not find it written in Aramaic or in the foreign languages of Europe. We will study the history of our people as it unfolds before our very eyes, as it speaks our language and wears the same kind of clothes we do.

We will see how the golden thread of Torah which formed the Jews as a people throughout their existence is the most important factor which keeps them alive today. You will see how the Torah and the Talmud, our language and our customs, our beliefs and our practices, are like the banks of the river we spoke about in Volume 3, uniting our people, and directing their lives.

Abraham, the father of monotheism, Moses, the Lawgiver, David, the Psalmist and king, Isaiah the teacher and prophet, the sages of the Talmud, the Gaonim that followed, and the spiritual leaders of the European interlude, all were inspired by God to guide the people of Israel in their mission of bringing the message of religion to the world.

The existence of each of these spiritual leaders was a miracle of God's interest in the welfare and survival of His people. By them the people of Israel were taught to respect and believe the words of the Torah and the ideals of ethics and universal decency and kindness which the Torah teaches.

But our holy Torah was not only the source of those great spiritual values which gave strength and beauty to our people throughout the ages. It also was the fountainhead from which all civilization learned the dignity and rights of man and the virtues of morality, goodness, and peace.

However, in the 20th century, the spiritual values which the Jew and the Torah had given to the world were threatened as never before. In this volume you will see how in modern times the world was called upon to wage the fiercest and greatest war in history against the godless armies of Nazism and the materialistic philosophies of communism. Unfortunately, in the struggle between these evil forces and the forces of righteousness represented by the Jewish people and the teachings they have given to the Christian and Moslem worlds, six million of our brethren were cruelly slain as helpless victims and martyrs during Nazi German attacks alone. Thousands of others have fallen in the endless attacks against religion in the Communist countries, and more than three million are still prisoners in the lands behind the Iron Curtain.

Then, when Jewish fortune seemed at its darkest, God's miracle revived the remnant of our people and fulfilled the promise He had made to Abraham, to bring them to Canaan, the land of milk and honey. We may not be able to see this as a miracle because it is too close to us, but the establishment of the State of Israel is the work of God's hand, writing the history of our people today, just as it did in years gone by.

God's concern for the people of Israel is in itself a continued miracle. It does not end with the Gaonim or the Golden Age of Spain or with the establishment of the State of Israel. By studying Jewish history, by learning Hebrew, by knowing the Torah and by practicing the mitzvoth, you will better be able to feel and understand how God shapes our destiny and the future of the world.

This is the most important thing to remember, as you study the history of the Jews in America and in Israel. Look for the thread of the Torah. Look for God's will in all that happens.

Some boy or girl, living one thousand years from today, might be able to see God's will in today's events better than you can, just as you were able to see God's hand in the days of the Judges better than the boy or girl who lived in that time.

But if you try, and if you have faith, you will see it as well and will have the courage to live a good and worth-while life.

Gilbert and Libby Klaperman

UNIT ONE:

FROM COLUMBUS TO LINCOLN

The year that most people think of joyously as the date of the discovery of America, is for American Jews a sad one too, for 1492 was the year in which Queen Isabella and King Ferdinand expelled the Jews from Spain.

Have you ever wondered in what ways Jewish history might have been very different if this expulsion had not taken place? We will never know. Fortunately, we can say that while 1492 was a year of great calamity for Jews, it was also a year of great blessing for the world, since in that year Columbus and his men discovered the Western Hemisphere in which democracy was to grow and flourish. Here in this New World, too, was the land in which the greatest Jewish community in history was later to find a home. This land, of course, was America.

From your social studies courses, you have learned a great deal about American history. Now you will be able to fit Jewish life into this general picture. You will learn about Jews on Columbus' ship, and Jews in Washington's army. You will learn about Jews in pre-Colonial days, in the Revolutionary War, and in the Civil War. You will become acquainted with the part they played in the development and growth of our country.

You will see how the Torah, the Bible of the Jews, inspired the founders of the United States and how the constitution and government of this new country—the very concept of democracy, of the equality of man—came originally from the Torah and from Judaism. The teachings of the prophets calling for righteousness and honesty are gradually being fulfilled in America today.

You will discover that God's word has helped to shape American life and make it what it is today.

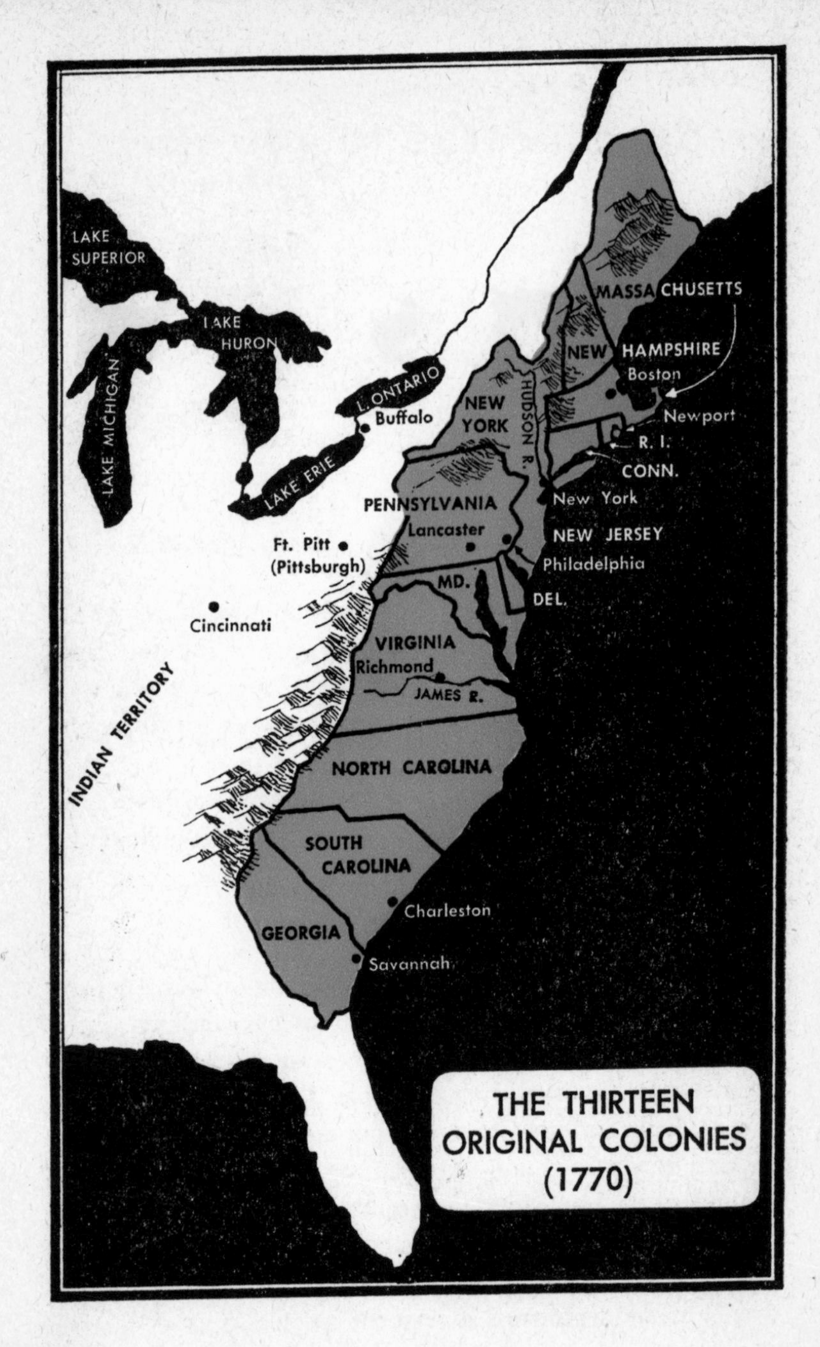
LAKE SUPERIOR
LAKE HURON
LAKE MICHIGAN
L. ONTARIO
LAKE ERIE
Buffalo
NEW YORK
HUDSON R.
MASSACHUSETTS
NEW HAMPSHIRE
Boston
Newport
R. I.
CONN.
New York
NEW JERSEY
Philadelphia
DEL.
PENNSYLVANIA
Lancaster
Ft. Pitt
(Pittsburgh)
MD.
Cincinnati
VIRGINIA
Richmond
JAMES R.
INDIAN TERRITORY
NORTH CAROLINA
SOUTH CAROLINA
Charleston
GEORGIA
Savannah
THE THIRTEEN ORIGINAL COLONIES (1770)

CHAPTER ONE

THE VOYAGE TO A NEW LAND

The year 1492 is one of the most important dates in the history of man, for it marks the discovery of the new land, America. It is most important because in America a new way of life, the democratic way of life, was developed for all peoples of the world to imitate.

We have said that the year 1492 was a sad one for Jews, since it was also the year in which they were driven from Spain by the evil Inquisition.

What was the Inquisition?

Just to refresh your memory, the Inquisition was a department of the Church in Spain set up to discover disloyal Christians. The judges of the Inquisition, even though they were clergymen, were cruel, vicious people. They were determined to make Spain entirely Christian, without exception. To achieve this end they forced non-Christians to accept their faith. The methods of the Inquisition were methods of torture. The bones of the victims were broken on diabolic torture racks. Arms and legs were burned or cut off. Often, poor innocent men and women would be burned alive at the stake.

How was the Inquisition brought to the New World?

In Spain, most victims of the Inquisition were Jews. In the new land, however, the terror of the Inquisition affected Indians as well. The Spanish explorers were a vicious and greedy lot, who respected neither people nor their traditions.

Cortez, the conqueror of Mexico, and Pizarro, the conqueror of Peru, with their guns and armor and their cruel dealing, destroyed a great part of the native population. Entire villages and cities were wiped out, and their population burned or fed to the dogs. In Mexico, the natives of many villages preferred to die by their own hands rather than to face the Spanish invaders. A Spanish missionary of the time estimated that twenty million natives were slain by his countrymen.

So you see that even as Columbus planted the flag of Spain on the island which he called San Salvador in the West Indies he opened a new territory for the religious fanaticism of the Church's Inquisition. Soon its tortures and cruelty were to be felt by natives and Marranos alike.

How did Jews help Columbus?

It is interesting to note that with Columbus there came a number of Jews, who helped contribute to the success of his undertaking. These probably undertook the dangerous voyage because they had no other choice, having been expelled from Spain. They may also have been prompted by their desire for knowledge of the world at large, and by their adventurous spirits.

Other Jews who were not actually members of Columbus' expedition were even more helpful because, to begin with, they had created many of the navigational aids used on the journey. Among these aids were the maps devised by Judah Crescas, who was known as the "map Jew" and the "compass Jew." Crescas was the director of the nautical school of Portugal and was famous for his maps and navigational instruments. A photograph of one of his maps still exists and can be found in *The Jewish Encyclopedia* (Vol. 3, opp. p. 678).

Abraham Zacuto, another Jew, was also represented on this important trip, for it was his almanacs and astronomical tables that were used by Columbus. Zacuto was an unusual person. He served as a professor in a Spanish university, and was the author of many books in Hebrew on astronomy and Jewish history. He was the man who recommended Columbus to Ferdinand and Isabella to be head of the expedition. Later, he helped another famous explorer, Vasco de Gama. When Zacuto had to flee from Spain as a refugee from the Inquisition, he went to Portugal, and helped de Gama in his journey from that land to India.

Still other Jews helped to make Columbus' voyage possible. Among them were Isaac Abrabanel, Abraham Senior, Luis de Santangel, and Gabriel Sanchez, a relative of Rodrigo Sanchez, one of Columbus' crewmen. All these prominent Spanish Jews were instrumental in raising the money that was needed to equip the expedition. They served in different capacities as financial aides, treasurers, and tax officials in Spain, who raised or advanced the money themselves in order to finance the trip. A good deal of the money, too, came from the confiscated possessions of Jewish victims of the Inquisition.

Who were the Jews in Columbus' crew?

The two doctors of Columbus' small fleet, Bernal and Marco, and two of his crew, Rodrigo Sanchez and Luis de Torres, were Jews. Luis de Torres, as it happened, was the first European to set foot on San Salvador. He was an interpreter, and in addition to knowing many European tongues, spoke Hebrew, Aramaic, and Arabic fluently. He was the first man to land on San Salvador because Columbus hoped that he might be able to converse with the natives who lived there. Luis de

Torres was so impressed with the New World that he settled in Cuba, the second stopping place of Columbus' expedition.

These Jewish members of the crew had been baptized, because no Jews were permitted to set foot on the deck of a Spanish ship, just as none were allowed to set foot on Spanish soil. However, their baptism did not really mean that in their hearts they had accepted Christianity. We do know, for example, that the physician Bernal had been punished for practicing Judaism in secret. This devotion to Judaism might well have characterized the others as well.

Some historians believe that Columbus himself was the descendant of a Jewish family that had been forced into Christianity. While this belief has never been fully proved, there is considerable evidence to support it.

We see, then, that the Jews had a great deal to do with the discovery of the New World and that Columbus himself might have been of Jewish descent. But this was just the beginning of the great contribution that the Jewish spirit would make to the American way of life.

How did the Inquisition create Indian Marranos?

Twenty years after Columbus' first voyage, the Inquisition was established in the New World. Within a short time it was cruelly enforced in all South and Central America and in the southern part of North America, all of which were held by Spain or Portugal. This time, however, the Inquisition applied not only to Jews but to natives as well. A great many of the natives were forced to practice Christianity in their public life, while secretly they remained true to their ancient faiths. In this way Indian Marranos were created, like the Jewish Marranos of the Iberian Peninsula. Just as the Jews learned to hate the Inquisition, so did the natives of America. As one historian put it, "The Inquisition taught the savages of America to shudder at the name of Christianity."

What struggle took place in Recife?

If Spain and Portugal had succeeded in holding the entire Western Hemisphere under their control, it is doubtful whether Judaism could have remained alive in the New World.

Fortunately, the French, English, and Dutch governments were also seeking a foothold in the New World. In 1621, the Dutch West India Company was founded, and by 1630 it had captured from the Portuguese the Atlantic coastal town of Recife, or Pernambuco, in Brazil. The Dutch, who had adopted protestantism, were not too kindly disposed toward the Catholic Church. As a result they had been hospitable to the Marranos who fled to Holland, and they now practiced similar tolerance in Recife. Jews from all parts of the continent flocked to Recife, and by 1642 about six hundred more Jews had come from Europe to join their brethren in South America.

However, the flourishing Jewish community of Recife was short-lived. In 1645, the Portuguese set siege to Recife in order to reconquer it. After nine bloody years of war, the city, starved and broken, was forced to surrender to the Portuguese besiegers.

Again an expulsion followed. The Portuguese Governor, glad to be rid of the Jews, assembled a fleet of 16 ships, loaded almost all the Jews of Recife upon them, and sent them forth to their various destinations. Many returned to Holland. Some found their way to London. The majority, however, continued on to other Jewish settlements that had been founded in the New World. These were in several cities of Dutch Guiana; the islands of Curaçao, Jamaica, and Barbados; and in Guadaloupe and Martinique in the French West Indies. There the Jews engaged in trade, in the development of plantations, and in the search for natural resources.

Who were the first Jews to come to the United States?

Of those who set out from Recife in 1654, 23 men, women, and children aboard a French ship, the *St. Charles*, left for New Amsterdam, the Dutch colony which later developed into New York City. They were the first Jews to land in what is now the United States of America.

The woebegone, pitiful group of refugees came in September of that year, with almost no baggage or household furnishings, to start life anew. Their money had long since been spent, and what meager possessions they still owned had to be auctioned off in order to pay for their passage.

But dismal as the moment must have been for them, coming penniless to a new land, it was also a happy moment because they were thankful to have escaped alive from the persecution of the Inquisition to the comparative friendliness of a Dutch colony. Because they had faith that God would not forsake them, they found new strength and courage to keep their tiny band together. Little did they dream that from their new settlement would grow the largest, the most resourceful and important, Jewish community in the Western World, and later, in the entire world.

What civil rights did Jews lack?

Jewish life under the Dutch in New Amsterdam was not as free as Jewish life in the United States today. It was a thousand times better than in the Spanish possessions, because of course, there was no Inquisition in New Amsterdam to hang over the Jews like a sword ready to strike. But it was not crowned with the full rights and privileges that other citizens enjoyed.

As a matter of fact, Peter Stuyvesant, the Director General of New Netherlands, was quite put out by the arrival of the Jews of Recife. He was rude to them and called them members of "a deceitful race." He even wrote to the West India Company in Holland for permission to exclude the Jews from all the company's lands in the New World. He showed his open distrust of the poor immigrants by keeping three of the twenty-three new arrivals as hostages for several weeks until the Jews completed paying for their passage on the *St. Charles*.

In the colony, the Jews were not allowed to own land. They paid a higher tax rate than their neighbors. They could not trade in certain locations, and while they were not forced to accept Christianity, neither were they permitted to practice their religion publicly by having a synagogue or by worshiping in an organized religious service. Even after a year, when the Jews had bought a plot of ground for the express purpose of building a synagogue, permission was still refused them.

The most important civil right denied to the Jews was the privilege of becoming burghers, or citizens, or serving in the militia. This meant they could not fight shoulder to shoulder with the other colonists in defense of their homes. In addition, even though the authorities refused to allow them to fight, they were forced to pay a special tax simply because they did not "keep watch and ward like other burghers."

The New Amsterdam Jews, under the leadership of Asser Levy and Jacob Barsimson, were a hardy and proud group. They refused to be content with this second-rate citizenship. They wanted the privileges of burghers and were eager and happy to accept the responsibilities that come with citizenship. Again and again they petitioned Stuyvesant, his Council, and the West India Company to grant them full citizenship on equality with the other colonists, full freedom to trade, and the right to bear arms in the defense of their city.

With great contempt, Stuyvesant in effect told the Jews that if they did not like the conditions under which they were permitted to live in New Amsterdam, "consent is hereby given to them to depart whenever and whither it pleases them."

But Asser Levy and Jacob Barsimson would not give up. They continued the fight for the rights that should have been theirs. Diligently they worked, building up good will and enlisting the aid of their fellow colonists. Finally their efforts were crowned with success. The Jews of New Amsterdam were allowed to obtain the "burgher's certificate," the cherished right to be full-fledged citizens.

What principle did Asser Levy strive to establish?

One highly important thing came out of Jewish living in New Amsterdam. This was the principle established by the West India Company in its reply to Peter Stuyvesant, when he wrote them and asked that Jews be excluded from the new colonies.

We do not know whether the West India Company was moved by the suffering of the Jews under the Portuguese in Brazil, or whether it was influenced by the large holdings of Amsterdam Jews in the Dutch West India Company, which controlled New Amsterdam. At any rate, Stuyvesant was told that he must admit the Jews. He was also instructed that he must "not force people's consciences, but allow everyone to have his own belief, as long as he behaves quietly and legally."

This was the first time in the New World that the rights of individuals to worship as they saw fit was clearly expressed. If for nothing else, Jews and other minorities are to be thankful for the period of Dutch rule in New Netherlands during which time this privilege was established.

The rights to hold citizenship, to own land, to trade freely, and to bear arms are all taken for granted today in our advanced democratic society. But these rights had never before been enjoyed by Jews in the Diaspora except in Holland itself. The establishment of the principle that these rights belonged to all, regardless of religious faith, represented a very important step towards complete freedom and equality. Furthermore, this was a precedent established for the entire New World. Thus Asser Levy and Jacob Barsimson in their fight for Jewish rights had won a fight for all minorities.

When did New Amsterdam become New York?

Ten years after the bedraggled refugees arrived in the Dutch colony of New Amsterdam, an English naval group forced the surrender of the city. In September of 1664, scarcely 40 years from the time that Peter Minuit had bought Manhattan Island from the Indians for trinkets and goods worth less than $25, all of New Netherlands became a possession of England, and New Amsterdam became New York.

When the English took over the rule of the Dutch colony, the rights of the Jews remained in force, but the prohibition against public worship was also retained. This meant that the Jewish community still could not build its synagogue or pray together.

Later, Jews were allowed to be naturalized without taking the oath of citizenship which included the objectionable phrase "upon the true faith of a Christian." In 1776, the Constitution of the State of New York gave Jews full and complete equality.

The freedom of the Jews in New York undoubtedly brought some additional Jewish settlers to that city. They had been trickling in even during the Dutch period, but the Jewish settlement grew slowly. It is estimated that by 1664, of the two million Jews in the world, only about three hundred were in North America. So far, the new country had not attracted them in large numbers.

Things to Remember

1. New Words: Inquisition, almanac, astronomy, burgher.
2. How did Jews help Columbus in his journey to the New World? Name at least two Jews in your answer.
3. What did Asser Levy fight for in New Amsterdam?
4. What principle did the Dutch West India Company establish in its letter to Peter Stuyvesant?

Things to Think About

1. Your text says that God's will can be seen in many of the events that occur in modern history. What was God's will, do you think, in the expulsion of the Jews from Recife?
2. In their struggle with Peter Stuyvesant, do you think Asser Levy and Jacob Barsimson were right to insist that Jews be allowed to stand watch and serve in the militia? Why? Wasn't it safer just to pay a tax? Give reasons for your answer.
3. In what respect did the Dutch West India Company help to establish an underlying principle of democracy?

CHAPTER TWO

LIVING AS A JEW IN EARLY AMERICA

Why were most early Jewish settlers Sephardic?

Settlers in the New World, in the beginning of American history, were drawn across the Atlantic by exciting reports of new opportunities in America. Trading companies like the Dutch West India Company furnished information about America and encouraged and helped them to make the hazardous voyage and find a place to live. However, there was no company to help Jews make the expensive trip and to settle in America. Furthermore, there were very few Jews who knew much of what was happening in America. Only those who lived near the seaports of the Western European lands and saw the ships and the traffic with the New World, were aware of the prospects which America had to offer. The Sephardic Jews of Holland, as well as the Sephardic descendants of the Spanish and Portuguese Marranos who had found their way to England and France, were most informed of the discoveries taking place in the New World. These Jews had either themselves traveled a great deal or had seen seafarers come and go from the busy ports of Western Europe. For them an ocean voyage was not as frightening as it was for the Jews of central and Eastern Europe, those who lived in Poland or in Russia, for example. As a result, it was the Jews of Sephardic descent who first came to America.

How did the first Jews live in America?

From the time that New Amsterdam became New York in 1664, the Jewish population in the colonies continued its slow and hesitant growth. By 1776, there were about 2500 Jews in the original Thirteen Colonies, but they were concentrated in only 5 communities: New York, Newport, Philadelphia, Savannah, and Charleston. In each of these cities, the Jews represented a very small fraction of the population, but their contribution to the American way of life was great.

Unlike their fellows in the ghettos of Europe, Jews in the New World were free to move, to travel, and to mingle with the people who lived around them. Wherever they lived, they quickly adopted the customs, interests, language, and general social pattern of the other colonists. Even as the Jews adopted the culture and language of the new land, the Americans got to know them too, and to learn that they were fine, hard-working citizens.

The contacts between Jews and non-Jews were widened also by the diversity of Jewish activity. Many Jews were engaged in shipping and in outfitting ships. Others were skilled craftsmen working with metals, wood, and leather. Still others were candlemakers, shoemakers, silversmiths, tailors, storekeepers, and peddlers. Some became plantation owners in the South, while some became fur-traders in the trading posts of the North and West.

Among the Jews were also those who engaged in slave trade, the buying and selling of slaves, a business that was considered quite respectable in those days. There were Jews, too, who because they had connections with family and friends in the European ports, were able to export cargoes of wheat and lumber. They also arranged for the import of finished textile products and other goods which a growing America could use. In this fashion, they helped industry and commerce thrive in the New World.

Who were some prominent Jews of that time?

As trade and commerce developed, many Jewish merchants became very wealthy. Among them was Hayman Levy of New York, who at one time was the employer of John Jacob Astor. Jacob Franks, a brother-in-law of Hayman Levy, became one of the chief suppliers of the British army in the French and Indian War.

In New York, too, there was the well-known Seixas family. Benjamin Seixas was a founder of the New York Stock Exchange. His brother, Gershom Mendes Seixas, was the religious leader in turn of Mikveh Israel, the first Jewish synagogue in Philadelphia, and of Shearith Israel, the first Jewish congregation in New York.

In Philadelphia, there was the famous Gratz family. One member of the family endowed Gratz College in that city. It still exists today, and is the oldest institution for the training of Jewish religious schoolteachers in the United States. Another member of the Gratz family served in the Pennsylvania legislature. Rebecca Gratz, a noted beauty and great wit, became famous as an educator and a public servant. Some believe that she was the model for Rebecca, the daughter of Isaac of York, in Walter Scott's *Ivanhoe.*

Haym Salomon, the wizard financier whom George Washington called upon to help finance the American Revolution, also came from the city of Philadelphia. Another important supplier of the Continental Army came from Philadelphia, too. His name was Joseph Simon. Simon later left Philadelphia to settle with other Jews in Lancaster, and to start a thriving Jewish community there.

Newport was the home of Aaron Lopez, considered to be

one of the leading merchants in the Colonies. He and his father-in-law, Jacob Rivera, were among the largest manufacturers of candles in the entire continent. In the famous diary of Dr. Ezra Stiles, the president of Yale University, Rivera was described as "a merchant of First Eminence for Honor and Extent of Commerce probably surpassed by no merchant of America."

When was the first Jewish synagogue established?

Even though these prominent Jewish families and other Jewish settlers made easy and free contact with their non-Jewish neighbors, and adopted the language and ideas of the colonies, they nevertheless retained a deep allegiance to their faith. They knew that they needed a strong religious life to help them survive in a land that was rough and unformed. They looked to God for guidance and support in these difficult days of early settlement. They never gave up their desire for a synagogue in which to pray, and in which their children might be educated in their ancient faith. At home they spoke Spanish, Portuguese, German, Yiddish, or whatever language had been their own before coming to America. But they insisted on learning and studying Torah. This was their way of keeping contact with their past. Almost all of them tried to teach their children personally or by hiring tutors so that they would know the Hebrew language and the Torah.

Although the Dutch had banned a Jewish house of worship in New York City, by the end of the 17th century, under the English, the situation had changed. The Jews were permitted to worship publicly in a building on Beaver Street. Later, in 1730, the Congregation, known as Shearith Israel, was permitted to have its own house of worship on Mill Street. The colonists could now come out in the open, establish a school for their children, and pray with a *minyan*, the necessary quorum of ten men for public worship. Shearith Israel was the first Jewish synagogue in the new land.

How was the Jewish community of Newport immortalized?

In Newport, Rhode Island, a colony had been founded by Roger Williams in order to give complete religious freedom to all who sought refuge from persecution. Here another famous synagogue was erected. The Jewish community of Newport was founded in 1658, only shortly after the one in New Amsterdam. Because of the religious freedom offered by Roger Williams, the Jewish community of Newport attracted many new settlers and became the center of the Jewish population of colonial America. In 1768, a beautiful synagogue was built. By this time, more than 1000 Jewish souls lived in the city. They represented almost half of all the Jews in the Thirteen Colonies, and they held a prominent position in the financial circles of the town. Visiting rabbis from Europe and Israel came there to find help for the institutions and communities they represented.

Jews earned their livelihood in this beautiful seaport town in much the same way as their Christian neighbors. Ships owned by Jews of Newport touched at harbors all along the Atlantic coast. Jewish sea traders visited the islands in the West Indies, exchanging copper pans and silver for sugar and molasses.

The Revolution of 1776, however, put an end to the importance of Newport and of its Jewish community. The British captured the city and confiscated the ships of the Jewish merchants who were loyal to the colonists. Most of them were forced to flee. Few ever returned. Today, Newport has only a relatively small Jewish community, but it has splendid memories. Henry Wadsworth Longfellow wrote a beautiful poem called "The Jewish Cemetery in Newport," which is dedicated to the courage and faith of the Jews of Newport. Also cherished to this very day is a letter sent to the Jewish Congregation of Newport by President George Washington in 1790. In this letter Washington stated that the government of the United States recognized no differences between its citizens, nor would it support any form of persecution. All the President asked was that all the inhabitants of the country act as good and loyal citizens.

Newport's synagogue is now the oldest existing synagogue building in the United States, even though it was the third synagogue to be built by the colonists.

Was there anti-Semitism in the Colonies?

Generally speaking there was no specific anti-Jewish feeling in the Colonies before and immediately after the Revolutionary War. There were too few Jews to be of any significance. By and large they were tolerated, although they were not permitted to vote or hold office in most of the Colonies.

These restrictions against the civil rights of Jews existed not because the colonists were anti-Semitic but because the early settlers were all Protestants and looked with suspicion on every non-Protestant, particularly Catholics. Most often the Jews suffered because in their dislike of the Catholics, the colonists included all non-Protestants.

How did the Jews fare in Massachusetts and Connecticut?

It should be pointed out that while individual Jews did settle in all the colonies, there were no Jewish communities in several colonies, among them Massachusetts and Connecticut. These two colonies were Pilgrim colonies formed in the Puritan religious tradition. The Puritan tradition was a very narrow one, which left no room for other beliefs. In fact, the Puritans were called such because they wished to "purify" their Protestant faith of all non-Protestant, mainly Catholic, influence. As a result, the Protestants were cruelly severe with all who did not follow their way of thought. For this reason, Jews, like Quakers, Catholics, and even non-Puritan Protestants were forbidden to settle in Puritan colonies. Only members of the Puritan church were welcome. It seems strange that those who first fled England because of the religious persecution against them should now, when they were free, practice religious persecution against others.

Why were there no Jewish communities in Maryland or Virginia?

Jews were not tolerated in Maryland or Virginia, either. In Maryland, an "Act of Toleration" had been accepted; but it created "tolerance" only for Protestants, and no Jew openly professing his faith was admitted into the Colony. Maryland was one of the last states to cancel laws discriminating against Jews.

Virginia too recognized none but the Christian religion. Just as Jews could not enter England without special permission, so they were barred from entering Virginia. It was not until after the Revolution that Jews were admitted.

How were conditions in Georgia different?

Georgia, which was founded in 1732, had a more liberal attitude towards Jews. James Oglethorpe, the founder, who had received a grant from the King of England to establish the colony, admitted the Jews on a technicality. The charter of the colony prohibited Catholics from entering, but did not mention Jews, and consequently Oglethorpe argued that Jews might legally settle in Georgia.

As a result, 40 well-to-do Jews of Spanish and Portuguese extraction came to the colony. After them came several impoverished German Jewish families, who were helped by English Jews to settle in Georgia. Together, they gradually began to build a Jewish community.

In 1740, there was a split in the colony on the question of slavery, which was opposed by the trustees, or owners, who lived in England. Many Christians and Jews left Georgia at this time. A large number of Jews moved to Charleston, South

Carolina. When the slavery issue in Georgia was settled, some Jews returned to that colony. In 1774, they founded the Savannah congregation, the fourth oldest in the United States.

Who was Francis Salvador?

The most liberal of the Southern colonies was South Carolina. We know of Jews in the colony as early as 1695. With the influx of Jews from Georgia in 1740, the settlement of Charleston was enlarged. The first synagogue in the state was built there in 1749. It was known as Beth Elohim. The congregation is still in existence, although the original synagogue building itself has long since been destroyed.

Among the famous Jews of Charleston, the most prominent by far was Francis Salvador, a member of the Provincial Assembly. He was a wealthy English Jew, who owned a large plantation in South Carolina. He was a very bright and promising young man, and when the Revolution broke out against the English, he was among the first to go into battle. His bravery and courage were unparalleled, and he became a legend in his time. Unfortunately, while he was defending the border against Indian raids, Francis Salvador was killed and scalped, in 1776, by a group of Cherokee Indians who had been incited by the British.

How did the Jews retain their identity?

We have seen that the Jewish settlers in America before the American Revolution were mainly Sephardic Jews who came from Spanish, Portuguese, and Dutch centers in Europe. Those who came from England held the Sephardic tradition as well. There were virtually no immigrants from Eastern Europe.

We have also seen that the Jewish settlers in America adopted the same forms of business and commerce as their Christian neighbors. They learned to speak the English language in addition to their native tongue. But they did not give up their religious traditions. Of course, there were some who lived all alone in outposts in the West or South who married Christian women and gradually gave up their Judaism.

The great majority of the Jews in America, however, remained true to their faith. They did not lose their true sense of values in the face of the uncontrolled exploitation of man and land which was beginning to take place in America. The Jews who held fast to the religion of Abraham, Isaac, and Jacob helped to discipline themselves and the community about them. They emphasized the importance of humility, of love of their fellow man. By spreading the words of Torah and of man's dependence on God, they strengthened the responsibility of each individual man to live decently and properly.

Many of the Jewish pioneers did no work on the Sabbath. The famous Gratz family in Philadelphia kept their business closed on the Sabbath. A Jewish concern in Lancaster, Pennsylvania, advertised regularly that its place of business was closed on Saturday. This was true of many, many others in colonial America. It was no mean accomplishment, for the Jew

was risking his livelihood by voluntarily giving up one day's business and by calling attention to his Jewishness.

The important factor in the religious strength of the pioneers was the synagogue. There were only five synagogues before the Revolution. We have seen how these five developed in New York, Newport, Philadelphia, Savannah, and Charleston. Fortunately, these five synagogues were centrally located for the twenty-five hundred or so Jewish settlers of that time.

All Jews who professed the faith of Judaism were Orthodox. Orthodox Judaism not only gave the early Jewish settlers a very strong tie to their past and to all other Jews in the world, it also gave them the powerful courage needed for the future.

Things to Remember

1. Why were most of the early Jewish settlers Sephardic?
2. What were the cities in which the first five synagogues were built?
3. What is most important about each of the following?
   a. Rebecca Gratz
   b. Haym Salomon
   c. Francis Salvador
4. Why were there no Jewish communities in Massachusetts and Connecticut?

Things to Think About

1. Why was it that the Jews did not find complete freedom in the Thirteen Colonies, even though the founders themselves had been victims of persecution?
2. Do you think Jews made an important contribution to America in its early stages? Document your answer.
3. Your text says that keeping the Sabbath for the Jew was no "mean accomplishment." Explain what this means. Do you think it holds true today, as well?

CHAPTER THREE

THE FIGHT FOR FREEDOM

The Jews in the American colonies before the Revolution had very little influence on the course of American politics and government. They were too few in number to have any great weight, and their Christian neighbors thought too little of them to take their thinking into account. Only in five of the Thirteen Colonies, New York, Rhode Island, Pennsylvania, Georgia, and South Carolina—were there any large Jewish communities. In Massachusetts, Connecticut, Delaware, Maryland, and Virginia there were no organized Jewish communities, only an occasional individual Jewish settler or small group of settlers. There were none in New Hampshire, New Jersey, and North Carolina.

Jews as individuals could not influence the destiny of American democracy and the great American republic that was to come forth from the Revolution, but their history, their culture, and their Bible did.

How did Judaism influence American thought?

It is no exaggeration to say that the Hebrew Bible played a major role in shaping the thinking of the American colonists. New England, the center of the Puritans, was most responsive to the Bible. While the Puritans themselves were not liberal people and did not fully understand the precepts of the Bible which taught that "Thou shalt love Thy neighbor as Thyself," they tried to guide themselves by the letter of the Bible, if not by its spirit. The constitution and the laws of Plymouth Colony, of Massachusetts, and Connecticut, were based on the teachings of the Torah. The Mosaic Law was adopted in the Connecticut Code of 1650 and half of the statutes in the Code of 1658 for the colony of New Haven contained references to the Bible. To such an extent was early colonial practice based on the Torah that it was said of the Puritans that "they may be considered as Jews and not as Christians. Their God was the God of the Old Testament; their laws were the laws of the Old Testament; their guides to conduct were the characters of the Old Testament."

The Puritans imitated the model of the Jewish holidays. Thanksgiving was patterned after the Festival of Succoth, which as we have learned, is the feast of the harvest and the occasion for thanksgiving to God.

Biblical names abounded in New England, and Hebrew was taught at Harvard College in 1655. In New Haven, it was taught even in the public schools. The leading men of these colonies studied and knew Hebrew well.

The Puritans found in the story of the Exodus from Egypt a parallel to their own attempt to find religious freedom in the New World. Even the motto engraved on the Liberty Bell, "Proclaim liberty throughout the land unto all the inhabitants thereof," was taken from the Book of Leviticus of the Bible. Franklin, Jefferson, and John Adams had gone so far as to suggest that the seal of the United States should show a picture of the children of Israel crossing the Red Sea.

The colonists also found in the stories of the prophets, who denounced the kings of their day, encouragement to discredit King George III, whom they detested. They considered the ancient Jewish form of government, on the other hand, "a perfect republic." It was from all these evidences that a historian later concluded that "Hebraic mortar cemented the foundations of American democracy."

What role did Jews play in the Revolution?

The Jews, like their neighbors the Christians, were divided between loyalty to England and devotion to the Continental Army and the Revolutionists. By and large, they sided with the majority of the rest of the Americans. Even though they were for the most part businessmen, and consequently well-to-do, they nevertheless risked their wealth and fortunes in favor of the patriots.

As against the few Jews who were opposed to the Revolution, there was a vast majority who fought in the ranks of the Continental Army. The most distinguished Jewish leader was Francis Salvador, whom we have already discussed. He was killed at the very outbreak of the rebellion. Another Southerner was Mordecai Sheftall, of Georgia, one of the leaders of Savannah Jewry. He was considered, by the British, to be one of the leading rebels of the South. When Savannah was captured, the British took Sheftall and his son as prisoners. They were held first on a prison ship, and then in the West Indies for several years. After the war, Sheftall was granted permission to return to Georgia, where he again took up a leading position in public affairs.

Many Jews had the rank of lieutenant-colonel in the colonial Army. Among these, to mention only a few, were David S. Franks, Isaac Franks, and Solomon Bush. George and Louis Bush and Benjamin Nones held the rank of major. After the war, Nones became the president of Philadelphia's Congregation Mikveh Israel. There were many other Jewish officers and enlisted men in the colonial Army, all too many to mention. All acquitted themselves well in the service of their country.

How did Jews help behind the scenes?

It was not only on the fighting front that Jews were active. They, together with the other revolutionaries, joined in drawing up resolutions against King George and against the unfair taxation exercised by England in that day. Bernard and Michael Gratz were among a number of prominent Philadelphia Jewish businessmen who signed a Non-importation Resolution. This was a pledge not to buy British goods until the repeal of the Stamp Act. Other Jewish men, at the risk of harming their own business, were equally loyal.

In addition, the Continental government needed vast financing in order to survive the critical period of war, and the difficult years that followed. Here again, Jews were very helpful. Joseph Simon and Aaron Levy of Lancaster, Pennsylvania, made direct gifts and loans to pay the troops, as did the Sheftall and Minis families of Savannah, Georgia. Isaac Moses of Philadelphia, too, helped the struggling government as much as his finances would allow. The most prominent of these financiers, however, was a Jewish immigrant from Poland named Haym Salomon.

Why is Haym Salomon revered today?

Haym Salomon was born in a small town in Poland about 1740. He traveled for several years in Europe before coming to New York in 1772. There he began to help Robert Morris, the financier of the American Revolution, to supply the necessary funds for the Colonial Army. He helped raise the money through obtaining loans from others and from the sale of government securities. He personally endorsed bills of exchange of the wavering government, thus risking his own credit. In this fashion, he was able to bring in hundreds of thousands of dollars for the government. He also advanced his own money to delegates to the Continental Congress. These delegates did not receive expense money from their own states to attend the Congress, and many of them might not have been able to attend if it were not for Salomon. Among them were Jefferson, Madison, and Monroe—all destined to become presidents of the United States. About Salomon, Madison wrote:

> I have been a pensioner for some time on the favor of Haym Salomon. The kindness of our friend near the coffee house is a fund that will preserve me from extremities, but I never resort to it without great mortification, as he obstinately rejects all recompense. To necessitous delegates, he always spares them supplies.

In 1776, Haym Salomon was arrested by British soldiers in New York, tried, and sentenced to die. After two years in prison, he managed to escape to Philadelphia where he arrived penniless and destitute. The years that he had given of himself

so freely had taken their toll. He died in 1785, only 45 years of age, and he left his widow and four little children in great poverty. His heirs tried several times to recover the great sums of money that he had loaned to the government, but without success. The family was doomed to poverty.

Although his money was never repaid, Haym Salomon received the warm admiration and thanks of the government. More than any other Jew, and more than most other colonists, the modest Polish Jewish immigrant had been instrumental in making the American Revolution successful.

After his death, Congress, at different times, described his work in glowing terms. They described him as one who "gave great assistance to the government by loans of money and by advancing liberally of his means to sustain the men engaged in the struggle for independence." They said that one should "consider Haym Salomon as one of the truest and most efficient friends of the country at a very critical period of its history."

In 1941, a memorial to Haym Salomon was erected in Chicago. It is a monument showing General Washington flanked by Robert Morris on his left and Haym Salomon on his right. All the funds for the project were raised by later admirers of Haym Salomon, the unusual personality who was the most important single Jewish contributor to the success of the Revolutionary War.

What freedoms did the citizens of early America enjoy?

The newly won victory in the Revolutionary War against England brought complete independence for the Thirteen Colonies, now known as the United States of America. It did not, however, bring complete independence for all its citizens.

We who live in the United States today rightfully consider our country to be a model of freedom and democracy for all its inhabitants. Legally, every adult, regardless of his race, religion, or color, has the right to vote and to run for office in the government. This right was not granted, however, immediately upon the close of the war against England. British tyranny had been directed politically and economically against the colonists, but it had not affected the lives of Jews, Catholics, and Quakers as religious minority groups. The rights, privileges, or lack of privileges, of these groups had been governed by the individual colonies. When the Revolution was over, the states retained the same attitudes towards these minorities that they had held before as colonies.

The new Federal government left the qualifications for voting and holding office to each individual state. The only protection against discrimination was offered in the Constitution, Article VI, Section 3. Here the founding fathers stated: "No religious test shall ever be required as a qualification to any office or public trust under the United States."

To this, they added the guarantee expressed in the first of the ten amendments to the Constitution which we call the Bill of Rights. This amendment provided only that "Congress shall make no law respecting an establishment of religion, or prohibiting the free exercise thereof." Actually, neither of these guarantees for religious freedom limited the individual states from doing as they pleased. The new states coming into the Union after 1787 would be bound to live up to the requirements of the Constitution, but the States that initially made up the Union still had their own jurisdiction in such matters.

What was the status of the Jews?

We have already pointed out that Jews enjoyed wide religious freedom in the new land. That is, they were free to remain Jews if they wished to do so, without pressure from the Church or the state to convert them to Christianity. So great was the spirit of American liberty that among the marchers in a parade held to celebrate the Constitutional Convention in Philadelphia were "the clergy of the different Christian denominations with the rabbi of the Jews walking arm in arm." Nevertheless, the Jews found that if they remained Jews they were not granted the right to vote or to run for office in most of the states. To put it simply, Jews at the time of the Constitutional Convention of 1787 enjoyed religious freedom but not political freedom.

The Jews were not unhappy under these conditions, because they knew that in the European countries from which they came their lot was even worse. In central and Eastern Europe, Jews were still outcasts; and even in England where they had wealth and influence, Jews were still without political rights.

After the Revolution, morever, the very climate of the colonies changed, and hopes for universal political freedom ran high.

How was legal discrimination defeated in Virginia?

Virginia had the sad distinction of being the state that discriminated most against Jews. Jews were made so uncomfortable in that colony that we have no record that any Jew lived there on a permanent basis until after the Revolution. The colonists of Virginia believed in the Church of England, which was the official religion of their homeland. This religion, which was against the Catholic Pope, was also opposed to Judaism. Because in England it was the exclusive and official church of the state, efforts were made to install this religion as the only one in Virginia as well. Such an attempt was made in 1784. Happily, James Madison, who may have been influenced by his friendly relationship with Haym Salomon, fought against the proposal and caused its defeat. Two years later, Thomas Jefferson joined Madison and George Mason, another Virginia liberal, in passing the "Virginia Law to Establish Religious Freedom." By the terms of this law, all religious discrimination in Virginia was abolished. Thomas Jefferson was so proud of this achievement that he asked that this accomplishment be listed on his tombstone as one of his great services to the people of America. In 1790, only four years after the passage of the Law, a Jewish congregation was formed in Richmond, Virginia.

New York had adopted a religious freedom law in 1777, and after Virginia's action, Georgia, Pennsylvania, South Carolina, and Delaware followed with laws to outlaw all forms of religious intolerance. Maryland got on the bandwagon in 1826, and North Carolina finally followed in 1868.

What debt do Jews owe to Thomas Kennedy?

In Maryland, credit for the passage of an anti-discrimination law goes to a Scotsman named Thomas Kennedy. Kennedy had come to Maryland from Scotland. In 1822, as a member of the legislature of Maryland, he fought for the passage of a bill to give equal political rights to Jews. The bill was passed, but Maryland statutes required that it pass the legislature a second time in order that it become law.

In the next election for the legislature, Kennedy was defeated and his "Jew bill" as it was called, was defeated with him. But in 1826, the doughty champion of liberty stood for office again, was victorious, and brought the bill through the legislature.

Kennedy made a statement about Jewish rights which affects all minorities:

> There are no Jews in the country from which I come, nor have I the slightest acquaintance with any Jew in the world.... There are few Jews in the United States; in Maryland there are very few; but if there were only one, to that one we ought to do justice.

How was the discrimination law tested in North Carolina?

An interesting test of North Carolina's discriminatory laws came in 1809 when a Jew, Jacob Henry, who had been elected to the legislature, found that his election was being contested on the grounds that he was a Jew. Jacob Henry made a magnificent defense of his faith. His stirring appeal, a call for equality and religious liberty, became a classic. It was printed widely and was referred to and quoted in Maryland in the battle for freedom in that state. Henry was permitted to keep his seat in the legislature, thereby establishing another precedent, gaining another victory against discrimination. In 1868 North Carolina finally outlawed all religious requirements for voting and office holding.

New Hampshire was the last to fall into the pattern of democracy, not adopting the principle of religious freedom until well after the Civil War, in 1897. However, even before that all restrictions had already become meaningless and were not enforced.

How did religious freedom compare with that of Europe?

The progress of religious emancipation in the United States was more fruitful, more predictable, and swifter than that of the European states. In Europe, only France itself, after a bloody Revolution, proclaimed in its National Assembly of 1791 that "the Jews in France enjoy the rights of full citizens."

But the Jews of central and Eastern Europe were still without the elementary guarantees of protection of their lives. They were subjected to brutality and murder, often with the connivance of the governments themselves. In Volume 3 you saw how in England, Germany, Italy, and Austria, Jewish rights were still withheld.

In comparison, even the Jews of those American states in which there were no laws guaranteeing equal rights possessed a degree of dignity and freedom that existed in no other land.

Things to Remember

1. New Words: reiterate, recompense, minority, discrimination, status.
2. How did Judaism help to shape the American way of life?
3. Who was Haym Salomon? What did he accomplish?
4. What did Jacob Henry and Thomas Kennedy have in common?

5. How did the conditions of the Jews in America differ from the conditions under which Jews lived in Europe?

Things to Think About

1. Your text says that the Puritans were considered by many "as Jews and not as Christians." Do you agree or disagree with that view of the Puritans? Give reasons for your answer.
2. Do you think that Haym Salomon deserved a statue in his memory? Give reasons for your answer.
3. Why do you think Madison and Jefferson fought against the adoption of a state religion in Virginia? How would it have affected our lives today if they had lost their fight?
4. Do you agree or disagree with Thomas Kennedy's statement that even if there is only one person in a minority, we have to do justice to that minority? Give reasons for your answer.

CHAPTER FOUR

NEW IMMIGRANTS IN A NEW LAND

The intolerance and persecution of the European countries played a major role in the development of the Jewish community of the United States. Just as the small band of refugees from Recife came to New Amsterdam because of Portugese persecution, so later waves of Jewish immigrants came to America because of war or persecution in the lands of their birth. Who knows if there would have ever been Jews living in the New World if not for the intolerance of the European governments!

How did Napoleon's defeat affect Jewish immigration?

In 1791, an edict of the National Assembly of France, giving equal rights to all Jews, was joyfully received. Later, Napoleon Bonaparte, who had become Emperor of France, brought the emancipation to all the countries that he had conquered–those countries which are now known as Germany, Austria, Hungary, and Czechoslovakia. But Napoleon was defeated at the Battle of Waterloo in 1815, and all his reforms that improved Jewish living were canceled.

Many thousands of individuals living in the countries that had fallen to Napoleon had felt the breath of freedom which he offered them. They refused to go back to the dark days of the pre-Napoleonic monarchies. They began underground revolutionary actions which were quelled time and time again.

After each defeat, many revolutionaries left Europe to find a new life in America. Among the foremost of these fighters were Jews. It was no wonder, then, that by 1840 there were 15,000 Jews in America in comparison to the 3000 Jews who were there at the beginning of the 19th century.

In 1848, the revolutionary movement once again broke out violently. The outbreaks started in Paris and spread to Austria, Hungary, Prussia, and Italy. These rebellions also were crushed, and another large wave of emigration to America resulted. Among these immigrants to the United States, who were called the "Forty-eighters" because of the year of their arrival, there were large numbers of Jews. You can imagine in what numbers they came, if by 1850 there were 50,000 Jews in the United States, and by 1860 their number had risen to 150,000.

Historians refer to the immigration of colonial days as the First Wave of Jewish Immigration. They call the period beginning with 1815 or 1820 the Second Wave of Jewish Immigration.

The Jews of the "First Wave" were mostly Sephardic. They were of Spanish or Portuguese descent, coming from Spain or Portugal where they had been Marranos, living secretly as Jews, or coming from England or Holland where their forefathers had sought refuge. Although there were exceptions among them, like Haym Salomon, who came from Poland, and the Franks family, who came from Germany via England, they were for the most part Sephardim. That is why we call this early period of immigration the Sephardic period. Naturally, the synagogues they built in America followed the Sephardic ritual.

In the 1800s, because of the bloody revolutions in northern and Eastern Europe, Ashkenazic Jews began to come to America. They, of course, founded their synagogues according to their own ritual. The earliest Ashkenazic synagogues were Rodeph Sholom, which was founded in Philadelphia in 1802, B'nai Jeshurun, which was founded in New York City in 1825, and Anshei Chesed, organized in that same city a few years later.

Why was peddling important in those days?

In the 19th century, American settlement was rapidly expanding towards the West. The new Jewish settlers joined the other pioneers who were founding settlements beyond the seaport cities. They moved into the Ohio Valley and beyond, creating new and growing centers of population.

Very few of the immigrants of this first half of the 19th century came with much money. They were escaping from their unhappy lands, and generally were able to take little more than the clothes on their backs. Those who knew a trade may have been able to get jobs in the new land, but those who had no profession or trade were temporarily lost.

Many of these economically misplaced immigrants soon discovered a new occupation—that of the peddler. The peddler formed the bridge between the city and the farm, bringing goods from the city to the pioneer at the edge of the wilderness. His was an important occupation, for there were many isolated settlements which were being hacked out in the vast, uncultivated areas of the United States. These settlements had no direct, regular contact with the big cities, and so they found great difficulty in getting the supplies they needed. A blanket, a kettle, soap, a shirt, or baby furniture were impossible to buy outside of the big cities. Some settlements were three or four days' ride from the cities and were often snowed in during the winter. The average farmer or fur-trapper could not afford to spend time to make such a long and hazardous journey to buy the odds and ends of household needs. For him, the peddler was a godsend. He served as a combination general store, mail-order house, traveling salesman, and banker.

Why did the immigrants turn to peddling?

Peddling was an attractive trade for the immigrant because there were not too many people engaged in it. Peddling did not require too much money to start, and it certainly did not require any special skill or experience.

Very often, only days after landing in America, the immigrant would set out with a pack or trunk on his back or a heavy valise in his hands. He was ready to bring goods and supplies to small hamlets and farms that were off the beaten track. Tracing the trails through the forests and mountains, sometimes blazing trails of his own, he made his way westward. Like the mailman, the peddler was not fazed by snow, rain, frost, cold, or sleet. He plodded, often as many as 25 miles a day, selling a tablecloth, several dishes, a bolt of silk, some yards of ribbon, or a writing tablet and pencils at half a dozen different isolated farms.

At night, if he was fortunate, the hardy peddler slept in a rickety bed in some generous homesteader's hut. More often than not, he was forced to sleep in an abandoned cabin or under the open sky. After a week or two on the road, having disposed of his wares and taken orders for other merchandise, he would return to the city to replenish his stock.

This was not the pleasantest sort of life. The peddler could have no real home, no regular hours, and he could hardly build a family. His religious observances often suffered because of the difficulties of finding kosher food, of maintaining the Sabbath, and of praying with a minyan in the synagogue.

But the peddlers were tough and courageous people. They refused to be defeated by weather or circumstances. They maintained their faith, their courage, and their hopes. They moved through Illinois, Ohio, Indiana, Missouri, Louisiana,

Kansas, Nevada, and Oregon. They traveled throughout the northeastern states, and moved as far north as Montreal.

How did Americans learn to know the Jews?

Often the peddlers were the first Jews ever to come to a city. They were the first Jews ever to be seen by farmers and lonely settlers. These Christians may have thought that Jews were different from other people, but the peddler soon created a warm and friendly relationship between them.

A story is told by Joseph Jonas in his memoirs which illustrates this point. He was the first Jew to come to Cincinnati, Ohio, about 1817. When the news was spread that a Jew had come to the city, people came from all over to look at him. One old Quaker woman said to him:

"Thou art a Jew?...Wilt thou let me examine thee?"

When she had turned him around, and looked at him closely she stepped back and said in a surprised voice:

"Well, thou art no different to other people!"

Joseph Jonas was not a peddler, but a watchmaker born in England. Not all the Jewish immigrants were peddlers. They entered into the same occupations that their Christian neighbors entered. They became blacksmiths, cobblers, horse-traders, fur-traders, tailors, and carpenters. Wherever they settled, they helped to convince the Christian world that Jews were like all other people with the same feelings, the same desires, and the same appearance.

A story similar to that told by Joseph Jonas is told about Julius Meyer, a storekeeper in Omaha. Here, however, the impression was made upon the Pawnee Indians, who traded with him. They recognized him as a man of great integrity and honesty, whom they could always trust. In order to show what they thought of him, they adopted him and gave him an Indian name which, translated into English, meant "Curly Headed White Chief with One Tongue." This was their way of saying that they appreciated the fact that Julius Meyer never lied and always kept his word to them.

How did Levi pants get their name?

Another early tale tells how a Jewish name was given to a popular type of apparel, in the days of the Old West. Levi Strauss, a Jewish peddler, came to a mining town in the West carrying a load of burlap to sell. He found no buyers for the material, but he did discover that the miners were looking for strong trousers that would not easily tear against the rough walls of the mines.

Strauss was highly enterprising. He seized the opportunity to go into partnership with another immigrant tailor to make pants out of his burlap. By riveting them to the trousers, the pockets of the pants were made extra strong, in order to be able to hold the tools and the chunks of ore which the miners carried. The new pants sold quickly and were soon in great demand. The miners called the trousers "Levis" after their designer and manufacturer, Levi Strauss. Levis have remained popular all over America, even to this very day.

How were some great stores founded?

Joseph Jonas, Julius Meyer, and Levi Strauss were among the early immigrants and peddlers whose descendants became the most successful merchants and financiers in the United States. Meyer Guggenheim, founder of the famous Guggenheim family, which did so much for philanthropic organizations, began his career as a peddler of spices, needles, and stove polish in the mining towns of Pennsylvania. The father of the great financiers Isidor, Oscar, and Nathan Strauss, was also a peddler. He settled in a small village in Georgia. Later his family founded Macy's and Abraham and Strauss, both great department stores in New York City.

Other large department stores, like Bloomingdale's, B. Altman's, and Gimbel's, also grew out of the little stores started by immigrant peddlers. So you see, the American economy was strengthened and developed partly through the efforts of these new immigrants in their new land.

Why were some communities named after Jews?

Not only peddlers and small merchants moved on across the mountains and plains of our vast country. Jews of another type struck out across the West at almost the same time as the "Forty-eighters." They were among the thousands of Americans who rushed to California when gold was discovered in that state in 1849.

The Jews in the Gold Rush of 1849 toiled over weary, endless trails, flat hot lands, and jagged mountain peaks to join others in the search for wealth. So quickly did they reach California that in the very year that the Gold Rush began, Yom Kippur services were held in a tent in San Francisco. By 1850, two congregations were organized in that city, and temporary congregations met for services in almost a score of mining camps, lasting as long as the camps themselves did.

Jews were among the first to settle several communities in the Far West. Because of this, or because of the respect in which they were held, many sites were named after them. Among these were Solomonsville, Levy, and Altman in California, and Weiss Bluff in Texas. A similar practice was followed in the East, where, for example, Aaronsburg, Pennsylvania, was named after Aaron Levy, its founder.

How did Jews retain their Jewishness in the New Land?

All the new Jewish immigrants and pioneers developed a simple formula to follow in order to preserve their religious way of life. Wherever Jews settled, they tried almost at once to form a congregation. The congregation was the organization of the Jewish community, a religious corporation that consecrated a cemetery, built a synagogue, provided a religious school for the children, and instituted a society for charity and help to the less fortunate.

The congregation was established promptly because this was the symbol of their way of life and the institution in which Jews joined to express their common religious feelings. Here they found strength in identification with each other. Here they discussed their common interests and their common problems. Often they were not able to build a synagogue immediately because of the great financial expenditure that was involved. In Cincinnati, where Joseph Jonas helped found the Jewish community, a congregation had been formed in 1824. Their meetings and religious services were held in the houses of various members. A dozen years later, the 24 members of the congregation realized that they simply did not have the resources to build a synagogue for themselves. Nevertheless, there was an urgent need for one, since there was not a Jewish house of worship within 500 miles. Finally, in desperation, they wrote to synagogues in the East begging for help, and finally succeeded in building their synagogue.

A similar situation existed in Baltimore, Maryland, where services were held in a private home as early as 1829. Before a synagogue was built, the congregation organized a burial society in 1832, and a charity society in 1846. A cemetery had been founded as early as 1786.

In New Orleans, Louisiana, the same procedure took place. The first burial ground was mapped out in 1828. The synagogue came later.

The same pattern was followed in Richmond, Virginia. There are records of Jews having settled there before the Revolution, but the first synagogue was not built until 1822. The cemetery, on the other hand, dates back to 1791.

Frequently the cemetery came first because it was more vitally needed. A Jew could live without a synagogue, but when he died, he could not be buried in any but a Jewish cemetery. The existence of the physical structure of a synagogue was not necessary, since worshipers could pray together in each other's homes, or in a rented store or basement, on the Sabbaths and the Holidays.

How did the religious schools differ from ours today?

The religious school was of great importance. The first Hebrew school was originated by the Sephardic congregation of New York, Shearith Israel, as early as 1731. Here religion and the reading and writing of Hebrew were taught. Since the free public school system had not yet been introduced in America, the religious schools often taught secular subjects like English, arithmetic, and in the case of the Sephardic synagogue, Spanish, as well.

Sometimes Christian children attended these schools, since the absence of public schools made education very hard to come by. On the other hand, where there were no Jewish religious schools, Jewish children often attended Christian religious schools, and had to depend on their parents' instruction for their Jewish religious education.

Where there was a Jewish religious school, the teacher was generally the "hazzan," who led the services of the Sephardic congregation. The hazzan, moreover, not only led the services, but often acted as "shochet" too. The shochet slaughtered the cattle and fowl according to the kosher requirements of the Torah. Since professional teachers were not to be had, nor were there many men qualified to act in the role of a shochet, the hazzan often assumed all three duties. As a result, the hazzan was not the best teacher a child could have and the students received only the beginnings of a religious training. However, this was the best the early settlers could manage; and what they lacked in formal knowledge they made up for in faith and devotion.

How did the supplementary Jewish education program develop?

When broad public secular education was finally introduced, Jewish religious schools suffered even more. The schools which had taught both secular and religious subjects lost their reason for existence when free secular education became available for all. Children began to attend the public schools, and the religious all-day schools collapsed. A few of them, like the Shearith Israel school in New York City, continued with their religious training program. Their classes were now held in the afternoons, after public school hours. This is the pattern for our own Hebrew schools and Talmud Torahs, and is called the "supplementary Jewish education program."

How did Sunday Schools develop?

Unfortunately, most Jewish schools were reduced to meeting only once a week on Sunday mornings. Rebecca Gratz, of the famous Gratz family of Philadelphia, who was active in many charitable and benevolent organizations, was the founder of the first Jewish Sunday School in America. For 26 years, she served as its president and active head. Since there were no textbooks in English, Rebecca Gratz wrote out weekly lessons to be used as the text for the classes. As the Sunday School idea spread, her lessons were used by other schools as well.

In Charleston, South Carolina, a Sunday School was founded by the famous Jewish poetess, Penina Moise. Although Penina Moise was blind for the last 24 years of her life, she continued her dedicated work. Rebecca Gratz sent the weekly lessons which she used in Philadelphia to Penina Moise in Charleston where they were copied by the teachers and used in the Charleston school.

Sadly enough, although the intentions of its founder were lofty, the Sunday Schools began to exert a weakening effect on Jewish life. In the supplementary Jewish education program, students met every afternoon for several hours a day, but how much religion, writing, and language could one learn in one morning a week? The noble venture which Rebecca Gratz started so enthusiastically was better than nothing for those who would otherwise have received no religious training at all. But it was not the most desirable solution to the problem of Jewish education.

Why did Sephardic influence wane?

The Sephardic Jews, who made up the most of the Jewish population in the United States until the start of the 18th century, unfortunately left little to our American Jewish heritage. The Sephardim were generally rich and cultured, and they brought a proud history to this country. However, they were hurt by the two great wars, the Revolutionary War and the War of 1812, and they were altogether too small in number to make a lasting impression. Many of them intermarried with the Ashkenazic Jews, even though they looked down upon them socially as less cultured people and as immigrants who could not even speak the English language. Others intermarmarried with Christians, thereby losing their Jewish identity completely.

The German Ashkenazic immigrants who came in the beginning of the "Second Wave," were mostly from Bavaria, and were, in the main, poor workmen and merchants. Escaping from European tyranny, they purposefully sought to make a new life for themselves in the United States. The "Forty-eighters," when they came, were a more educated and worldly group of immigrants. They were wealthy professionals and well-read liberals, who had been most active in the revolt for freedom. These Ashkenazic Jews were able to make a more lasting contribution than the Sephardic Jews, because they came in larger numbers and because they maintained their identity for a longer period of time.

How did Ashkenazic immigration differ from Sephardic?

Even though the German Ashkenazic immigrants represented a variety of cultural types and backgrounds, they all had a love for liberty and a desire to become part of American life. They had a fierce determination to learn the language of their new land and to instruct their children. Generally, as soon as they became financially secure, they began to provide for the educational needs of their offspring. Their sturdy, sober attitude towards work was rewarded in that their children or grandchildren received the finest education that our colleges could give.

The striving of these immigrants for financial success and their desire for education, which they considered the prize possession, came out of their traditional love for learning, which had been part of the Jewish way of life throughout the centuries. This natural desire for learning was now heightened by their need for security, a security that they had not enjoyed in Europe. In this powerful yearning they were different from their predecessors, the Sephardic Jews. The Sephardic Jews in the United States were few in number and were settled in little compact communities. They were not under as much pressure to be successful as were the more numerous immigrants who came after the War of 1812, and spread out over the width and breadth of the country. The Sephardic Jews were more confident in themselves, and felt more secure among their Christian neighbors. In a sense, the German Jews worked more desperately, and were pushed harder to become self-reliant, self-supporting, and self-confident.

What was the Hebrew Benevolent Society?

The self-sufficiency that the new immigrant so much desired was not always easy to attain, and he sometimes had to rely on his neighbors and friends for help. Jews had always accepted the responsibility of giving help to all those who needed it. This was the commandment of Tzedakah, of charity, which the Torah and the Talmud repeated many times over. This was the commandment on which the Jews were nurtured—to take care of the sick, the poor, and the needy.

In the Middle Ages, even in the darkness of the ghetto, self-help organizations flourished. In the United States, too, each little Jewish community, almost as soon as it came into being, formed an organization for mutual help, generally called the Hebrew Benevolent Society. Sometimes a poor immigrant, alone and without relatives in this country, became sick or lost his job and had no one to turn to for his next meal. Or a new immigrant, just arrived, needed a home and perhaps a loan to get started in business. The Hebrew Benevolent Societies, which were supported by membership dues, were in a position to extend a loan, and to help in every way to make the adjustment of the new arrival easier.

Long before unemployment insurance became part of our American way of life, these societies also paid out a small weekly amount to members who were temporarily out of work. They gave a lump sum of money to the family of a member who died and left his loved ones impoverished. Members of the societies also visited the sick, sat up with the dead, and generally provided for all the needs that might beset a struggling newcomer in a strange land.

In time, as the immigrants became more firmly established, the need for financial aid decreased. The Hebrew Benevolent Societies became social and fraternal organizations, lodges to which members went for relaxation and recreation, to meet their friends, and to hear interesting programs.

How did the B'nai B'rith develop?

The charitable work of the lodges, however, was not given up, for the work which they had once done only for their own members was now directed towards other needy individuals and worth-while projects. They began to provide food and clothing for the poor of the community. They distributed holiday baskets and gave free loans to the needy, so that they could become self-supporting. Soon their interests extended even across the ocean to their native lands in Europe, and to the pious Jews in Palestine.

Such a mutual-help society formed by 12 men in 1843 in the city of New York was the beginning of the B'nai B'rith organization now famous throughout the world. Today, the B'nai B'rith serves many needs of the Jewish community, helping the sick and the poor, and working for the land of Israel. By 1860, there were four other such national fraternal orders, the two best-known of these being the Independent Order of the Sons of Abraham and the Free Sons of Israel.

What was the "Damascus affair"?

American Jews, then, were growing—growing as Jews and as free citizens of a free country. As they gained strength, they banded together to protect their civil rights and their honor, and also the rights of their brethren in other countries. Long ago the great prophets had inspired the Jewish people to lift up their voices for right and for justice. This inspiration now guided their descendants as a frightful and unjust accusation was leveled against them.

In the year 1840 the shocking news was heard that the Jewish community in Damascus, Syria, had been accused of murdering a Christian monk for the purpose of using his blood in the preparation of the Passover matzohs. This was the old false medieval legend and "blood libel" coming to life again in the 19th century.

Shortly after the disappearance of the monk, 3 rabbis, 13 community leaders and 60 Jewish children in Damascus were arrested and brutally tortured to make them "confess." At the same time, the Catholic and reactionary press in France, Italy, and Belgium began a violent campaign against the Jews. The brilliant French Jewish lawyer, Adolphe Cremieux, and the distinguished Jewish philanthropist, Moses Montefiore, of England, interested their governments to protest. The entire matter was finally dropped, and the Jews in prison were proved blameless and released.

While European Jews were exercising all their efforts on behalf of the Jews of Damascus, representatives of American Jewry also met in the B'nai Jeshurun Synagogue, in New York City, to adopt a resolution calling on President Martin Van Buren to intervene in the "Damascus affair."

The motive of the American Jews was primarily to save the lives of the arrested Jews in Damascus and to protect them against future attacks. At the same time, they realized that such unjust attacks might still take place in any part of the world, as they had in the past, if action was not taken to prevent and forestall them. In short, they felt the need for an organization that would always be ready to protect Jewish rights.

This organization came into being when another terrible event shook the Jewish world.

What famous case caused the organization of the "Board"?

In 1858, a six-year-old Jewish child, Edgar Mortara, of Bologna, Italy, was ordered by the Pope to be torn from his parents and placed in a convent. The Pope maintained that the child had been baptized by his Christian nurse four years earlier, and as a result, no longer belonged to his parents but to the Church.

Again, all over the world, a cry of outrage and anguish was raised by Jew and non-Jew alike. But unfortunately, this time it was to no avail. The boy was never released by the Catholic Church.

In France, this terrible experience led to the formation by Adolphe Cremieux of the *Alliance Israelite Universelle*, whose main purpose it was "to defend the honor of the Jewish name wherever it is attacked."

In America, it led to the formation of the Board of Delegates of American Israelites, which was dedicated to the same purpose. Its founders used almost the same language as the Alliance in defining their aim. The Board, they said, was "a national organization for the purpose of securing and maintaining civil rights at home and abroad."

The Board also planned to promote Jewish education, create a union of all the Jews of the United States, and to keep records and statistics concerning them. The most important function of the Board was to protect Jewish rights.

The American government recognized the Board as a spokesman for the Jews. A representative of the Board was always in Washington to bring the attention of the government to Jewish persecutions when they occurred. In this way the United States was often alerted to raise its voice in behalf of the unfortunate victims.

Although the Board did not represent all the Jews, it was

the first national body ever created by Jews in America. Today there are many national bodies, representing the American Jewish community in areas of anti-discrimination, education, philanthropy, religion, and Zionism. But for the Jews of the 19th century, the Board was a remarkable achievement. It was a step in the right direction. It showed that the Jews of America could be united on a common issue.

Things to Remember

1. Who were the Forty-eighters?
2. Why did some Jewish immigrants become peddlers? What important need did peddlers fill?
3. Why is the Hebrew Benevolent Society important?
4. What important lesson did the Mortara affair teach Jews?

Things to Think About

1. Would a peddler in the days of the Old West be looked down upon? Give reasons for your answer. Was he different from a peddler today? How?
2. Do you think the Ashkenazic Jews were right in organizing the Hebrew Benevolent Societies? Give reasons for your answer.
3. What important fact do the Damascus affair and the Mortara case bring home to you? Have things changed today? Can anything like this happen in our time?

CHAPTER FIVE

MEN OF PRINCIPLE

While America was growing in size, while Americans were learning to walk in freedom and democracy, while pioneers were trickling into wildernesses and forests, while villages and settlements were springing up everywhere, the Jewish population was also making its contribution. Jews were scattered all over America, venturing forth with the hardy to explore the wild lands, fighting Indians to protect the homesteads, and doing the day-to-day tasks as well. Jews were in the new settlements and in the old. They represented a cross section of American life, living in every geographic location and taking part in very kind of activity.

During this time, there were many Jews who were concerned with the growth of Judaism itself. We have seen, for example, how Rebecca Gratz's concern led her to develop a Sunday School curriculum. Other Jews became active in protecting Jewish rights and the Jewish reputation. They did this as individuals or as members of the Board of Delegates of American Israelites. Still others devoted their time to philanthropy, towards helping their fellow Jews become adjusted to the new land.

Every Jew raised on the teachings of the Torah and the Talmud felt the responsibility for his fellow-Jew. Those who were blessed with great wealth and affluence were able to assume this responsibility to a greater extent. We have already mentioned one of the outstanding Jewish philanthropists of this time. His name was Judah Touro.

How did Judah Touro become wealthy?

Judah Touro was the first recorded Jew to come to New Orleans, Louisiana. Judah was the son of the rabbi of the famous congregation in Newport, Rhode Island. He came to New Orleans in 1802, when it was still a French territory and not part of the United States. But Judah never forgot those early years spent under the peaceful influence of the Newport synagogue. Later, he would show his people how much those years meant to him.

In New Orleans, Judah Touro opened a small store, importing his goods from the New England region where he was born, and selling them in Louisiana. He was a good businessman, and people admired and respected him. As his sales brought him profits, Touro wisely invested the extra money in property and in ships. For 50 years he worked steadily. Slowly, by careful control of his business and by the many intelligent investments he made, Touro became very wealthy.

How did Touro become a philanthropist?

Touro was not a miser. He did not get pleasure just out of owning property or ships or great amounts of money. He wanted his wealth to be used in helping others. There were always needy people about his home or place of business, and Touro never turned anyone away.

Never having married, Judah Touro had no wife or children. He poured all his love upon his country and his people. A staunch patriot, he was ready to fight for his country at any time. In 1815, at the age of 40, when most men felt they were too old to fight, Judah Touro volunteered to join

the ranks of Gen. Andrew Jackson in the defense of New Orleans against the British. He was badly wounded, and actually left for dead on the field of battle. By a stroke of good fortune, a young soldier found him, carried him back, and helped nurse him back to health.

Now plans had been made to erect the Bunker Hill monument to heroes of the Revolutionary War, but these plans were not being carried out, since there were not enough funds available. When Touro learned of this situation, he sent a gift of $10,000 to match a similar amount offered by a Boston gentleman named Amos Lawrence. The sponsors of the monument were able to go ahead with their original plans, and in 1843 the monument was dedicated thanks to the magnificent gift from the Jew of the Southwest. The famed orator Daniel Webster spoke on that occasion, lauding the two principal donors. Now Judah Touro realized the great pleasures his money could bring him by doing good for others! Verses which were recited in his honor on that occasion became popular throughout the country.

This was in truth the first interfaith venture which received wide publicity and universal acclaim.

During his lifetime, Judah Touro made many great gestures that showed his love for liberty and his understanding of the coming American way of life. The soldier who had saved him on the New Orleans battleground was a young Virginian by the name of Rezin Davis Shepherd. Touro and Shepherd became good friends, after the harrowing experience which they had shared. Through his gentle influence, Touro convinced the Virginian that he should free all his household slaves. He himself, of course, freed the single slave he owned as soon as he realized the indignity of slavery and what it was doing to the South. As if this were not enough, Judah Touro bestowed enough funds upon the freed slaves to provide for their future. He, too, envisioned an America where all citizens would be equal, regardless of race, color, or creed.

This was a brave and handsome act to make in a Southern community which was committed to slavery. But Judah Touro faced up to his responsibility.

How did Touro help his people?

Throughout his life, Touro extended aid to Jew and non-Jew alike. Many of his gifts were made secretly so as not to embarrass the recipient or bring thanks to Touro. As a result, many of them have never become known. This was indeed the highest form of charity, to give in secret.

Just as his feelings for the new America were warm and strong, so his feelings for Judaism and for the Jewish people were strong. He was the founder of the Jewish congregation in New Orleans, and donated a huge sum of money so that a building should be purchased as a House of Worship. In addition, his generosity helped establish a Jewish hospital in New Orleans.

Touro remembered lovingly the synagogue at Newport where he had been brought up. He sent great sums of money to that congregation to maintain the synagogue. To this very day, the synagogue in Newport is known as the Touro Synagogue. In 1947, President Harry S. Truman proclaimed the Touro Synagogue a National Historic Shrine.

Judah Touro helped almost every Jewish congregation and charitable society in the United States, because at one time or another, they all came to him for money.

At a time when Palestine was in shambles and its Jewish inhabitants in poverty, Judah Touro, through his friendship with the great English philanthropist, Sir Moses Montefiore, sent financial aid to that country for the purpose of establishing colonies and settlements in the Holy Land.

How is Judah Touro remembered?

Judah Touro died, endeared to all who loved freedom and greatness of soul. He left a heritage of charity, of goodness, and of decency. His friends remembered him by naming streets after him both in Newport and New Orleans. The synagogues in each of these cities carry his name as well.

He was the first great Jewish American philanthropist. The following epitaph which is inscribed on his tombstone in the Newport Cemetery, is a true picture of this man of principle:

By righteousness and integrity he collected his wealth;
In charity and for salvation he dispensed it.
The last of his name, he inscribed it in the book of philanthropy
To be remembered forever.

Who was Mordecai Manuel Noah?

Another prominent Jew who lived in America at about the same time as Judah Touro was Mordecai Manuel Noah. He was the son of an officer in the Revolutionary War, and in many ways, as you will see, Noah turned out to be probably one of the most colorful Jews of the 19th century.

Noah was a highly talented man. He had a varied career as reporter, founder and editor of several leading New York newspapers, playwright and author. He was a forceful public speaker and active politician. At different times in his life, he was the high sheriff and a judge in New York City, surveyor of the Port of New York, and the United States consul to Tunis. He was also a major in the New York State Militia. Although he was so prominent in public affairs, Noah was an independent personality who was proud of being a Jew. He was most active in New York's Jewish congregation and served as president of its Jewish Charities. Noah took a back seat to no one in his loyalty to Judaism. An amusing tale is told about this when he assumed his duties as sheriff of New York.

An outraged political opponent complained bitterly that since Noah was the new sheriff, it was a pity that "Christians are to be hung by a Jew." Noah was unruffled. He quickly retorted, "What a pity that Christians should be so evil that they should have to be hung!"

His opponent could find no answer.

Why did Mordecai Manuel Noah want to establish a Jewish homeland?

Noah traveled throughout Europe on the way to assuming his duties as the United States consul at Tunis. During his journey he became deeply distressed by the unhappy life led by Jews in the European countries. This was, in fact, one of the reasons he had been so anxious to be appointed consul.

He wanted to see at first hand the conditions of his brethren in other parts of the world. The terrible impression that he received—the fact that Jews were not respected, were not allowed to practice every profession or enter every trade, and were denied equal rights as citizens—started this unusual man on his most spectacular lifework. He decided that the Jews needed their own land in order to find complete happiness.

What was Ararat?

This decision in itself was not an unusual one. From your study of Jewish history, you know how the people of Israel are tied to the land of Israel. Noah, for a while, had been toying with the idea of raising an army of Jews to take Palestine from the Turks by force. For many reasons, this dream was not feasible. With Palestine not available, Noah began to think seriously about finding a different homeland. He decided that it would be a good idea to create an independent Jewish state within the confines of the United States.

To advance this venture, the enterprising Jew consulted two past presidents, John Adams and Thomas Jefferson. Both replied in an encouraging manner. Adams even wrote his reply saying, "I wish the Jews again in Judea, an independent state."

Now Noah began to work seriously on his project. In 1825, he acquired a large parcel of about 17,000 acres on Grand Island in the Niagara River, opposite the city of Buffalo. This, he said, was to be the site of a Jewish settlement which he decided to call "Ararat." He chose this name because the Biblical Noah had landed his Ark on Mount Ararat after the great flood was over. Mordecai Manuel Noah, because of his own last name, saw the similarity between himself and the Biblical Noah. Just as Ararat was a refuge for those on the Ark in Biblical days, so the modern Ararat would be a refuge for Jews all over the world in his own time.

Noah planned and hoped that a successful Ararat would

be the steppingstone to ultimate Jewish colonization in Palestine. And in this sense we may call him the first Zionist in America.

Why did Ararat fail?

The dedication of the colony of Ararat took place in September of the year 1825 in a church in Buffalo. It was a festive and unusual gathering. Clergymen, state and federal dignitaries, mingled with military units and many colorfully bedecked Indians. Noah had personally invited these Indians, for he faithfully believed them to be members of the Lost Ten Tribes of Israel. He envisioned them reunited, now, with the rest of the Jewish people.

At the dedication, Noah, who was to be the "Governor and Judge of Israel," as well as head of the new settlement, was attired in a crimson robe of office, trimmed with ermine. The cornerstone was dedicated with great pomp and ceremony.

On the cornerstone, which was to mark the building of the new colony, were inscribed the words:

Hear O Israel, the Lord our God, the Lord is One.
Ararat
A City of Refuge for the Jews

When Mordecai Manuel Noah made his dedication speech, he explained his ideas about Ararat. To the large, distinguished assemblage he maintained his faith that Palestine would someday be the true and final Jewish homeland. He went on to maintain that "it is proper for me to state that the asylum is temporary....the Jews never should and never will relinquish the just hope of regaining possession of our ancient heritage."

Noah called upon all the Jews of the United States to support his project and to settle in Ararat. But his appeal fell on deaf ears. Many Jews could not think of uprooting themselves once again, especially when they were happy and content and earning a livelihood. Other Jews rightly felt that the only Jewish homeland they could ever accept was Palestine. They would move to go there but not to Ararat. A great many looked upon the entire scheme as though it were some crackpot idea. They even laughed at Noah. The project received greater support from the Protestants and their ministers than from the Jews.

What were Noah's accomplishments?

Because of the lack of Jewish enthusiasm for the project, Grand Island was never developed, and the cornerstone of Ararat remained a museum piece. It is now on display in the Buffalo Historical Society.

Although his hopes for a Jewish settlement in Ararat were shattered, Noah saw a glimmer of the truth. He saw his main idea, the creation of a Jewish national homeland, as a real and true possibility. As he met with more Jews, the truth was impressed upon him that that homeland could be established only in Palestine, the land that was promised to the children of Israel by God, the land of their forefathers.

Addressing a Protestant congregation in Philadelphia nearly 20 years after the dedication of Ararat, Noah made a moving and touching prediction.

"The time will come," he proclaimed, in discussing the hope for a Jewish state, "the time will come when the promise will be fulfilled."

Flamboyant and extroverted, Noah made a great impression on the social life of New York. His exciting personality won him many followers and friends.

But his greatest impression was made in the dream of a Jewish national homeland. Almost three-quarters of a century before Theodore Herzl initiated the movement of modern Zionism, Noah's imagination had captured this truth. Unfortunately, he was never able to make it real and meaningful for the thousands of Jews all over the world.

Mordecai Manuel Noah made another contribution, which he hardly realized. In undertaking to create a Jewish homeland, he had publicly expressed his devotion to this cause, even though he held high office in the American community. Yet nobody accused him of lacking patriotism to the United States. Nobody charged him with dual allegiance, of letting his loyalty to the Jewish homeland conflict with his patriotism to the United States. Everyone respected him the more for it.

This dual allegiance charge is sadly feared by many Jews living in our own day and is often used by the enemies of our people against the work of Zionism. What the Jews could learn from Mordecai Manuel Noah and what our enemies could learn from the enthusiasm and friendship of the Christians of his day!

Things to Remember

1. Why is Judah Touro the first great Jewish philanthropist?
2. Why did Mordecai Manuel Noah want to establish a Jewish homeland?
3. What was Ararat?
4. What is the charge of "dual allegiance"?

Things to Think About

1. Do you think that a Jewish homeland could ever be established in any other state besides Israel? Give reasons for your answer.
2. In what ways was Judah Touro an unusual man? Explain your answer by illustrations from his own life.
3. Who do you think made the more important contribution to American Jewish life—Judah Touro or Mordecai Manuel Noah? Why?
4. Your text say that many Jews today still fear the charge of "dual allegiance." Do you agree or disagree with this statement? Give reasons for your answer.

CHAPTER SIX

CRISIS IN THE CIVIL WAR

Slavery had existed in the United States from the very start of the nation. It was a cruel and inhuman thing to own the body and soul of another human being, and to take all his rights from him. Where slaves were kept, they were considered as so much cattle to be worked hard and fed little. Children of slaves were torn from their parents and sold to plantation owners by their masters. In most cases, these children never saw their parents again, or even heard their names. In the same way, husband and wife, and brother and sister were separated.

The United States, which had constantly been moving towards greater freedom for its inhabitants, could not long continue without facing the great moral issue of slavery. In the end, only a bloody war between brother and brother, and state and state, finally solved the problem.

Why did the South's economy require slavery?

The economy of the different sections of the country played a great role in determining who was to be for and who against slavery. At the beginning of the 19th century, even the Southern plantation owners were not all convinced that slavery should be maintained. As far back as pre-Revolutionary days, there was sharp sentiment among Southerners against slavery.

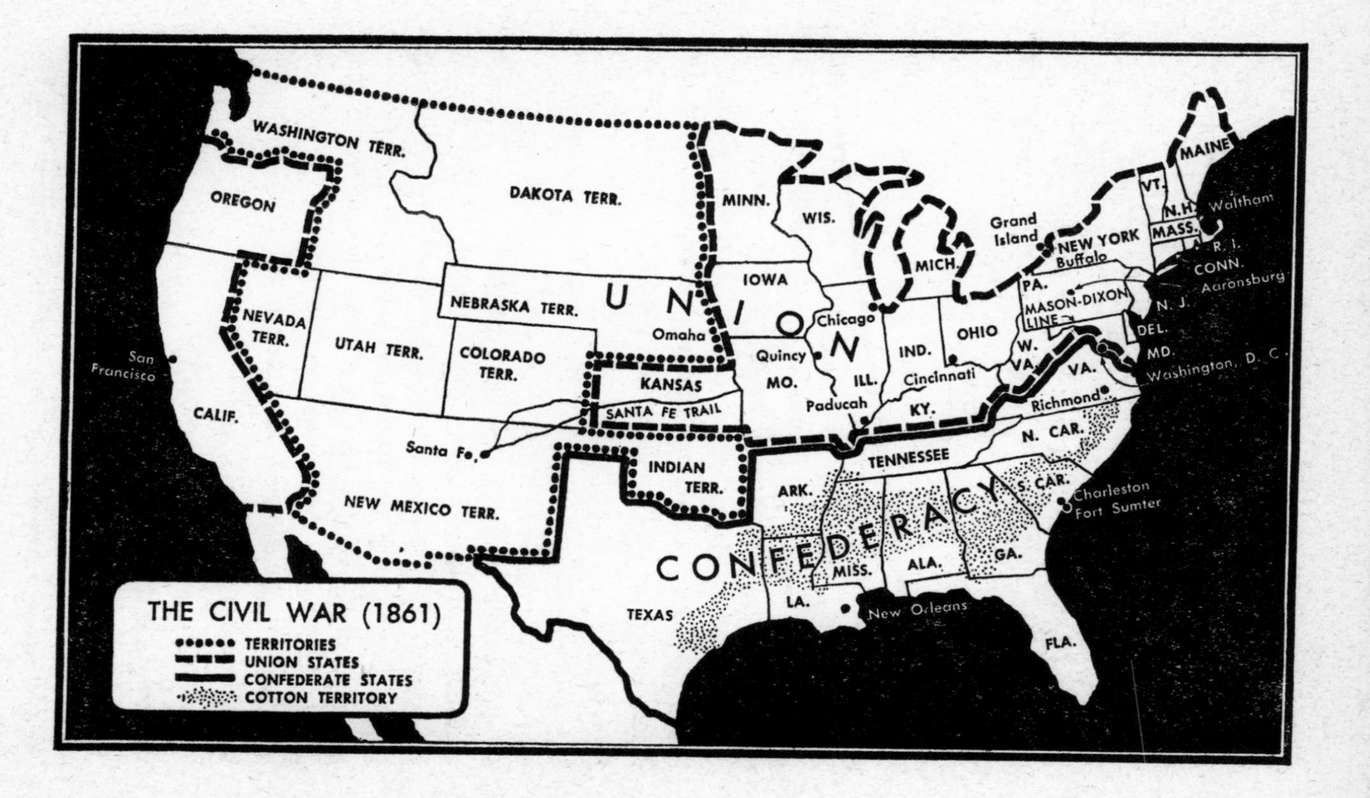
THE CIVIL WAR (1861)
TERRITORIES
UNION STATES
CONFEDERATE STATES
COTTON TERRITORY
UNION
CONFEDERACY
WASHINGTON TERR.
OREGON
DAKOTA TERR.
MINN.
WIS.
MICH.
Grand Island
NEW YORK
Buffalo
MAINE
VT.
N.H.
MASS.
Waltham
R. I.
CONN.
Aaronsburg
N. J.
DEL.
MD.
Washington, D. C.
PA.
MASON-DIXON LINE
OHIO
W. VA.
VA.
Richmond
IOWA
Chicago
IND.
Cincinnati
ILL.
Quincy
MO.
Paducah
KY.
NEBRASKA TERR.
Omaha
NEVADA TERR.
UTAH TERR.
COLORADO TERR.
KANSAS
SANTA FE TRAIL
San Francisco
CALIF.
Santa Fe
NEW MEXICO TERR.
INDIAN TERR.
TENNESSEE
N. CAR.
S. CAR.
Charleston
Fort Sumter
ARK.
MISS.
ALA.
GA.
LA.
New Orleans
TEXAS
FLA.

Many had openly said that it would have to be abolished. In 1740, the trustees of the colony of Georgia prohibited the use of slaves, bringing a crisis to the settement and causing many colonists to leave their homes.

All this was changed, however, when machines like the power loom and the spinning jenny were brought into the factories of England. England was now able to produce much more cotton goods, and she sought more raw cotton from the States.

In 1793, when Eli Whitney invented the cotton gin, a machine which separated the cotton seeds from the fibres, the planters at last had a more rapid way of providing the raw cotton. However, the cotton gin was like a hungry beast. More and more cotton had to be planted and picked in order to satisfy this new, improved means of production.

At this point, slaves became most important to the cotton industry and to the economy of the planters. The slaves provided the necessary "hands" to do the work in the fields at very little cost. More and more the entire industry of King Cotton was based on slavery and on the three million slaves of the South.

The wealth that cotton brought to the planters was so great that they were committed to the system of slavery which made it possible. They would no sooner give up slavery than they would give up using the cotton gin. Gradually, they even began to justify slavery. John C. Calhoun, the famous statesman and spokesman for the South, once went so far as to say that slaves were necessary because "there cannot be a durable republic without slavery."

Why did the Abolitionist movement arise in the North?

The Northerners did not grow cotton, and the need for slaves in their economy was not vital. Because they felt no pressure for slavery, they were able to examine it objectively. They saw it as the terrible evil it really was. As a result, many Northerners banded together to form the Abolitionist movement to uproot slavery.

What are Jewish ethics concerning slavery?

Jewish teaching had always been opposed to slavery on moral and spiritual grounds. Even in the time of the Bible, when the peoples of the world all kept slaves and defeated nations became the property of the conquerors, the prophets cried out against it. Although such teaching was contrary to the general way of life in those days, the Torah taught that masters must be considerate of their slaves. If a slave received bodily injury at his master's hands, he was to go free automatically. The Torah also forbade returning a fugitive slave to his master. The Bible frowned upon slavery, but since slavery existed, it taught kindness and consideration for the servant and slave.

By the 19th century, slavery was no longer a part of the world's way of life. The great Gaonim and rabbis of the Talmud expressly forbade it. Jewish history and experience of hurt and persecution at the hands of others had burned the ideas of equality and freedom into the minds and hearts of the Jews. Even among Jewish plantation owners in the South, where slavery was a natural part of society, it was not held in esteem. Most Jewish plantation owners, imbued with the spirit of the Torah, were as kind and considerate of their slaves as they were of their own families. But this was not the solution. Slavery had to be abolished.

Who were some of the Jewish Abolitionists?

Many prominent Jewish leaders stood at the head of the Jewish antislavery movement. David Einhorn, a Reform rabbi in Baltimore, was almost mobbed by secessionists because of his outspoken attacks on slavery. He was finally forced to flee to Philadelphia for safety.

Einhorn, in fighting for abolition, presented a new idea to the American community. He said that Negro slavery represented a threat to the rights of Jews and other minorities as well, because when one minority is deprived of its liberty, the respect for law and civil rights is destroyed. Other minorities are soon menaced in the same way. Jews and Catholics might be just as affected as Negroes.

Other outspoken opponents of slavery were Sabato Morais, the minister of Mikveh Israel in Philadelphia; Bernhard Felsenthal, the rabbi of a congregation in Chicago; and Rabbi Samuel M. Isaacs, of New York.

Rabbi Morris J. Raphall, of New York City, achieved temporary fame when he seemed to have preached a sermon in favor of slavery. A hue and cry was raised that Raphall had said that the Bible was not against slavery. Actually, Raphall distinguished between the attitude of the Bible and the system of the South "which reduces a slave to a thing." It is not likely that Raphall had any proslavery leanings, since his own son and son-in-law fought in the Union forces. He himself was later received by President Lincoln.

What part did Jews play in the Civil War?

When the first shot of the Civil War was fired at Fort Sumter in South Carolina in 1861, all doubts that might have existed on either side were silenced. The Jews of the South threw themselves into the battle on the side of the Confederacy. Although they were opposed to slavery, they were loyal to the states they lived in. Northern Jews fought valiantly in the Union cause.

Rabbi Maximilian Michelbacher, a rabbi in Richmond, Virginia, composed a prayer for Jewish soldiers in the Confederate Army. The prayer urged them to battle heroically against the foe who threatened "to desecrate our soil and to murder our people." Similar sentiments were circulated among Jews in the Union ranks.

Who was called the "brains of the Confederacy"?

Among the Southern statesmen, there were two prominent Jews. One was David Levy Yulee, the first Jew to serve as a Senator in the United States Congress. Yulee came from Florida, and was appointed to the Senate when Florida was admitted as a state in the Union.

The other prominent Southern Jew was Judah P. Benjamin, a senator from Louisiana. When the Confederacy came into being, Yulee and Benjamin both left Washington to serve in the Southern cause.

Benjamin knew very little of his faith, and apparently ignored any connections with the Jewish community. Both he and Yulee had married outside of their faith. But their Northern enemies insisted on referring to their Jewish origin and made many insulting remarks about them.

Little as Benjamin knew about his religion, he was nevertheless quick to defend it. It is said of him that even before the Civil War, when he was once called "that Jew from Louisiana" in a heated Senate debate, he responded, quick as a flash:

"It is true that I am a Jew, and when my ancestors were receiving the Ten Commandments at the hands of God at Mount Sinai, the ancestors of my opponent were herding swine in the forests of Great Britain."

A similar reply is attributed to Disraeli, who was also born a Jew and who rose to become Prime Minister of England. In later years, Benjamin and Disraeli were fast friends.

Judah Benjamin had been a highly successful lawyer in Louisiana, serving in the state legislature before he came to Washington. In the Senate, he was known for his keen wit and brilliant mind. With the outbreak of the Civil War, he turned his genius to the Confederate cause.

Jefferson Davis, the President of the Confederacy, appointed Benjamin to his cabinet as Attorney General. Later he was elevated to Secretary of War and finally to Secretary of State. Because of his diplomacy and statesmanship, Judah Benjamin almost won British and French recognition of the Confederacy, which might have brought them military help as well. So much was Benjamin relied upon for advice and strategy, that he was called the "brains of the Confederacy."

What happened to Benjamin and Yulee after the war?

When Gen. Robert E. Lee finally surrendered at Appomatox in 1865, Benjamin was forced to flee the country. By a series of hair-raising escapes, he finally reached England. There he became one of the most brilliant and outstanding members of the bar. He was honored by two Prime Ministers, Disraeli and Gladstone, and by the Lord Chief Justice as well.

David Yulee was less fortunate. His efforts on behalf of the Confederacy caused his arrest. After the war, he languished for a year in prison. After that, no more was heard of him.

How many Jews took part in the war?

No reliable figures exist as to the number of Jews who served in the Civil War. The Board of Delegates attempted to assemble all the facts about Jewish participation in the war, but lacked the organization to complete the work.

It is estimated that there were from ten to twelve thousand Jews in the Confederate Army. Among them there were 9 generals, 18 colonels and many, many officers of lower rank.

There were more Jews in the Confederate Army than the Northern because those who were in the South were native-born and had deep roots there. But, similarly, many Jews served in the Union forces and achieved high rank in them.

Why did anti-Semitism break out after the Civil War?

The suffering of the country as a result of civil war was intense. In many families, Jewish and non-Jewish, there was bereavement. There were instances in which two, three, and even five brothers from one family enlisted in one or the other of the armies. It was enough anguish when one member of the family was killed. To lose more was to suffer indescribable pain.

In addition, the country, particularly the South where the battles had occurred, was a shambles. Poverty, filth, and disease were widespread. In their distress and pain, Northerners and Southerners alike turned to find someone whom they could blame for their troubles. They looked for a scapegoat. Many of them chose the Jew.

Northern journalists used Judah Benjamin's Jewish origin as an excuse to attack all Jews. They accused the Jews of secretly having smuggled supplies and weapons to the South. Not only was this accusation false, it was the direct opposite of the truth. The Jewish banking house of Seligman and Company, of New York, had raised the huge amount of $200,000,000 in loans on behalf of the Union. Joseph and Jesse Seligman, the heads of the firm, were warm friends of President Lincoln and General Grant.

Another financier, Auguste Belmont, who had represented the United States as Chargé d'Affaires to Holland, raised and equipped an entire regiment for the Union Army. He also used his influence in European circles on behalf of the government.

But in the heat of prejudice, all this was forgotten.

The South, too, turned upon Judah Benjamin and censured him for not properly supplying a military base which had fallen to the Union. He was accused of protecting the "foreign Jews" and helping them to gain a monopoly of commerce in the South! Such was the extent of their hate-mongering!

In one town in Georgia, a resolution was adopted to banish all Jews. In the same state, in Talbatton, the home of the famous Strauss family, Jews were found guilty of "evil and unpatriotic conduct."

What was Order No. 11?

And so it went. Both North and South overlooked the sacrifices and loyalties of their Jewish citizens. Eager to find excuses for their own errors, hurt by the fire of war, they let their prejudices control their minds and hearts.

The most serious attack on Jews, however, came not from newspapers and politicians, but from a government proclamation known as Order No. 11.

The order was issued on December 17, 1862, in the heat of war, by General U. S. Grant, while he was in command of the Department of Tennessee. In effect, it condemned the Jews "as a class" of "violating every regulation of trade established by the Treasury Department...." Grant ordered his post commanders to expel all Jews from the Department of Tennessee, which was a territorial designation for parts of Tennessee, Kentucky, and Mississippi.

The order struck like a bolt of lightning against the entire Jewish population of the United States. It struck directly at all Jewish traders and businessmen who lived under Grant's jurisdiction. But worse than that, it seemed to confirm the false charges that Jews were smugglers and traitors. It also singled out the Jews "as a class." This meant that both good and bad Jews were equally to be punished regardless of the merits of the individual case. If there were any single Jews who were guilty of these charges, the fair and just position to take was to expel those who were indeed violating the law. In addition, it should have applied to Christian and Jew alike. Instead, Grant condemned a whole people. According to his order, if you were a Jew, you were automatically marked as a smuggler.

What was Grant's personal attitude toward the Jews?

With the announcement of this order, there rose before the eyes of the Jewish people the haunting fears of persecutions and mass expulsions such as they had known in Europe. Was the same thing going to happen in America?

Grant, when he later became President of the United States, appeared to have had no hatred towards the Jews. In 1870, he vigorously intervened to protect Jewish rights in Rumania. He appointed a Jew as the American Consul General in Bucharest. After his election to the presidency, he explained that the nefarious order was not of his doing. It had been issued by one of his subordinates on a blank form which Grant had unknowingly signed. It was not purposely meant to defame the Jews.

Some historians maintain that the order was issued as a result of pressure by other traders to remove their successful Jewish competitors. In other words, it was an economic move more than an anti-religious move. But when the order was issued, Grant was condemned as an anti-Semite who wanted to hurt the Jews.

How did Cesar Kaskel rise to the emergency?

In Paducah, Kentucky, part of the territory in which the order applied, a quiet, retiring Jew named Cesar Kaskel responded to the emergency with great energy and wisdom. He recognized the fact that the order was not representative of free American thinking, that it must have come from a handful of selfish, conniving men.

Kaskel's first move was to send a telegram to President

Abraham Lincoln, informing him of the facts. Then he sent out a message to prominent liberal newspapers, and to influential Jews everywhere, asking them for their unqualified aid.

After that, Kaskel left for Washington, for an audience with the President. He had with him many documents and letters proving the patriotic role that Jews had played in the sad war.

On January 3, three weeks after the order was announced, President Lincoln received Kaskel. On learning the facts, he immediately instructed General Henry W. Halleck, Commander-in-Chief of the Union Army, to cancel the order. The very next day, the order was revoked.

The issue raised by Order No. 11 had created a furor in American life. In the election campaign of 1868, when Grant was a candidate for President, the subject was again raised. The story of Order No. 11, to this day, remains what *The New York Times* called "one of the deepest sensations of the war."

When were Jews allowed to become chaplains in the Army?

Throughout all the agonizing years of the Civil War, throughout the bloodshed, bitterness, and destruction, one figure stood out strong, courageous, and calm. He was Abraham Lincoln, President of the United States.

Lincoln's sense of justice drove him to continue the war which he hated so much, in order to end slavery and preserve the Union. His great wisdom led him to realize that the war had to be won, not only to abolish slavery but in order to unite the country, for as he said, "a house divided cannot stand." Gentle and kind, just and fair, Lincoln was revered and loved by the Jews. This was not only because he countermanded the infamous Order No. 11 but also because he was the symbol of righteousness and goodness.

Almost as soon as the Civil War had broken out, Congress passed a law providing for chaplains to be attached to the Union Army. The law required that these chaplains be regularly ordained ministers "of some Christian denomination." Naturally, this wording made it impossible for a rabbi to be chaplain.

A young rabbi from New York, Arnold Fischel, met with the President to inform him of the anxiety that Jews felt about this exclusion. The Board of Delegates also prepared documents to be circulated in Congress, explaining the unfairness of this limiting law.

Two days after Fischel met with the President, Lincoln wrote him to say that he would make every effort to have the law broadened to include ordained ministers of *any* religious denomination. Because of the President's efforts, the law was so amended. The first Jewish chaplains were able to take to the field with their men, in the bloody battles of the Civil War.

Since that time, Jewish chaplains have served regularly and with distinction in the armed forces of the United States.

Why did Jews compare Lincoln to Moses?

Jews had a great deal of respect for Lincoln because he had courageously assumed the role of the Great Emancipator. They were reminded of the great Moses, who had led the Jews forth from the slavery of Egypt. Since Jews had suffered so much by the oppression of other peoples, they felt, even more strongly than the rest of the nation, appreciation for the man who was opposed to all oppression.

Lincoln had many Jewish friends. One of his "most valued friends" was Abraham Jonas, of Quincy, Illinois. Abraham Jonas was the brother of Joseph Jonas, whom we mentioned as the first Jewish settler in Cincinnati. He served four years in the Kentucky legislature, and was one of Lincoln's staunchest supporters. Jonas' four sons fought for the Confederacy. When one of them was captured by the Northern forces, Lincoln showed a great kindness for his old friend. The older Jonas was dying at the time. A letter exists in Lincoln's own hand which reads:

> Allow Charles H. Jonas, now a prisoner of war at Johnson's Island, a parole of three weeks to visit his dying father, Abraham Jonas at Quincy, Illinois.

How did Lincoln's death affect the Jews?

Because the Jews loved Lincoln so deeply, they were profoundly shocked by the news of his sudden death. It was on April 15, 1865, when the Festival of Freedom, the holiday of Passover, was being celebrated, that the sad tidings of Lincoln's assassination came. The Festival, for the Jews everywhere, was turned to mourning. The altars of the synagogues were draped in black, and memorial prayers were offered for his soul.

When Lincoln's body was prepared for burial, he lay in state at the Chicago court house. Above him was a canopy inscribed with King David's lament on the death of King Saul: "The beauty of Israel is slain upon the high places."

The Jews mourned Lincoln because they had lost a spokesman for freedom and a leader in establishing the equality of man. These two blessings–freedom and equality–Lincoln had helped bestow upon the entire country.

His support, as well as the victory of the Union, had guaranteed that America would continue to be the land of the free and the home of equal rights. Now the Jewish people in America would be more free to build the largest Jewish community in history, to bring Torah to a new peak of glory.

Things to Remember

1. How did economics play a part in the fight over slavery?
2. Who was Judah Benjamin? What was his importance?
3. What was Order No. 11?
4. Who was Cesar Kaskel? Why is he remembered today?
5. How did Lincoln help Jews to become chaplains during the Civil War?

Things to Think About

1. Do you think it's proper for economic interests to influence a man when there's a question of right or wrong involved? Explain your answer in relation to slavery in the South.
2. Your text says that anti-Semitism occurred after the Civil War because the people needed a "scapegoat." What does this mean? Do you agree or disagree? Give reasons for your answer.
3. Do you think Lincoln was ahead of his time? Would he be able to accomplish more if he were living today? Back up your answer with facts.

UNIT TWO:

THE DEVELOPING AMERICAN JEWISH COMMUNITY

The American government in its early days had not yet granted equal citizenship rights to all minorities. Nevertheless, it was strongly devoted to the principle of religious freedom. Article VI, clause 3, of the Constitution states that "no religious test shall ever be required as a qualification to any office or public trust under the United States." The Founding Fathers, by including this clause, affirmed the right of each American to be a full citizen regardless of what his religion was. There was to be no state religion here as there was in Spain, where the Catholic Church virtually controlled the state, or as in England, where the Protestant Church of England was the "established" church. This does not mean that the government opposed religion. It means that the Federal government recognized all religions, but neither favored nor was controlled by any particular one.

More specific guarantees of personal liberties were added to the Constitution in 1791, in the first ten amendments which we know as the Bill of Rights. Article I of the amendments further guaranteed religious liberty for all Americans, and the complete separation of religion from government, of church from state. The Federal government, in adding this amendment, was giving the individual states an additional push toward creating a free religious environment for their citizens. Such religious freedom did not exist in Europe where the gov-

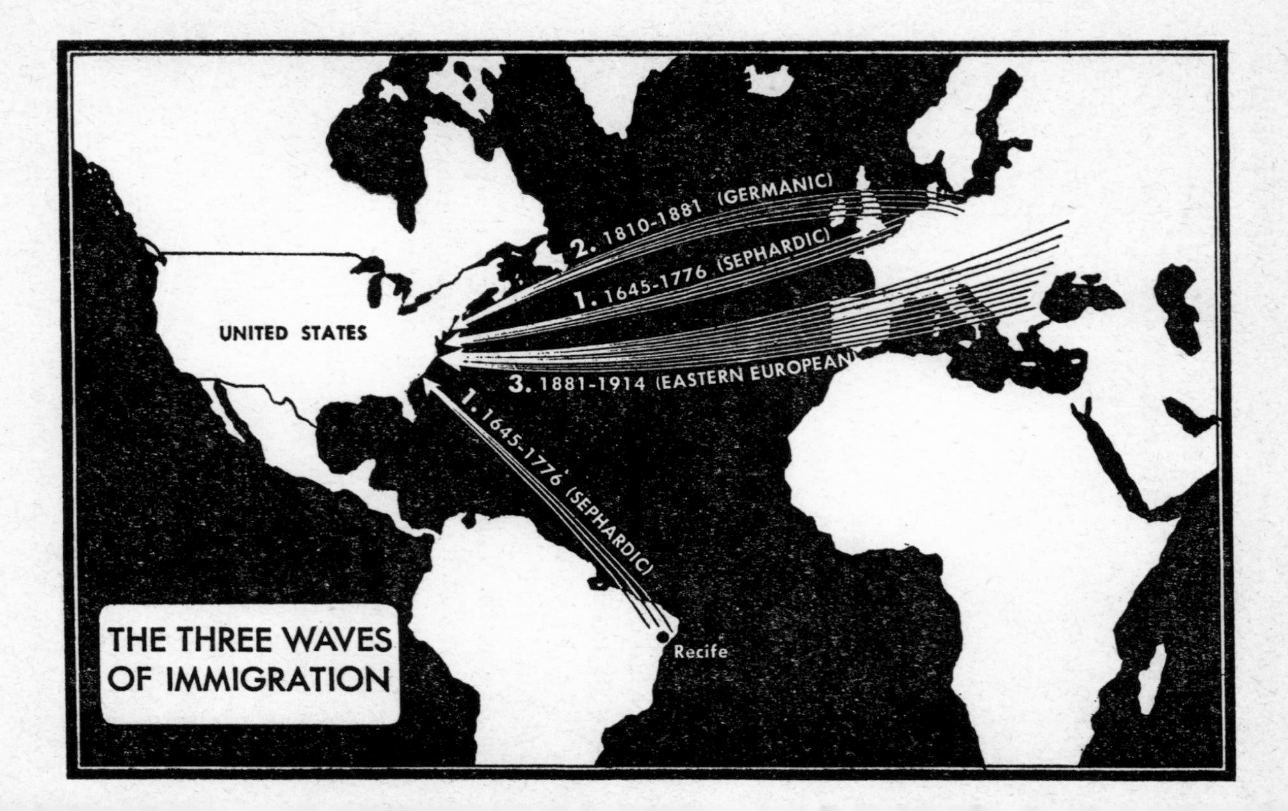
2. 1810-1881 (GERMANIC)
1. 1645-1776 (SEPHARDIC)
3. 1881-1914 (EASTERN EUROPEAN)
1. 1645-1776 (SEPHARDIC)
UNITED STATES
Recife
THE THREE WAVES
OF IMMIGRATION

ernments recognized only certain religions and persecuted others. For Jews, this factor of American freedom was most important, for their most distinguishing characteristic was their religion. One was not a Jew because he lived in the land of the Jews, or had a specific type of Jewish literature, or wore the uniform of a Jewish army. He was a Jew because he practiced the Jewish religion. His history was largely the story of his religious life in the Holy Land, and before and after that, in alien countries. The culture, the history, the literature, and the practices of the Jew were almost entirely an expression of his religion. Therefore, how his religion was treated or mistreated was of utmost concern to the Jew's welfare.

In this unit, you will learn how in the free religious climate of America, Jews responded in different ways. Some, given freedom, turned away from their ancient faith and adopted other forms of belief. Others remained loyal to Torah. Through it all, through the striving and the yearning to find security, you will see a new American Jewish life evolving, and you will better understand yourself and those about you.

CHAPTER SEVEN

REFORM JUDAISM

The ideals of America were deeply rooted in the pursuit of freedom. Roger Williams founded Rhode Island in order that "all men may walk as their consciences persuade them, every one in the name of his God." William Penn established a colony in Pennsylvania where anyone who believed in the existence of God was welcome. Many of the early colonists had come to the New World specifically for the purpose of escaping religious or political persecutions. For them, America was a symbol of hope.

The great joy the Jews felt in being allowed to enjoy the climate of religious freedom was expressed in a letter which the congregation of Newport wrote to George Washington on August 17, 1790.

> Deprived as we hitherto have been of the invaluable rights of free citizens, we now (with a deep sense of gratitude to the Almighty Disposer of all events) behold a Government...which to bigotry gives no sanction, to persecution no assistance, but generously affording to all liberty of conscience and immunities of citizenship...for all the

blessings of civil and religious liberty which we enjoy under an equal and benign administration we desire to send up our thanks to the Ancient of Days.

Because America guaranteed freedom, new settlers coming from different parts of the world, with various cultures and religions, were able to maintain the traditions of their old countries. They spoke the language of the old country, attended whatever house of worship they desired. America became like a great symphony in which there were many instruments, each of a different shape and quality and giving forth different musical sounds. But they were all united in one great theme, the one political faith which was loyalty to the United States and belief in its future.

How did Reform Judaism come to America?

In the United States, Jews did not have to hide or change their religion in order to be free. But in Europe, where they were oppressed, there were some Jews who believed that they should change their religion to make it as much like that of the Christians as possible. They thought that they were persecuted because they had a different religion. Remove many of the differences between their religion and that of the Christians, they thought, and they would be given the same rights that their neighbors enjoyed. We saw this in Volume 3, when we studied the rise of Reform Judaism in the beginning of the 19th century in Germany. We saw how German Reform denied the laws of kosher food, rejected the importance of the Sabbath, gave up the hope of rebuilding the land of Israel, and repudiated most of the mitzvoth. In some synagogues, men and women were seated together, men prayed with bare heads, some days of the Festivals were even abolished, and many other religious innovations were instituted.

In America, however, Jews were free enough. They did

not need to imitate the religion of their non-Jewish neighbors or deny their Judaism in order to maintain their citizenship. For this reason, the Judaism of the Sephardim in America remained unchanged for them and for their families. It was the same Orthodoxy that was practiced in their old country, and by the Jews of Poland and Russia. It differed in that there were no great yeshivoth in the United States, as in East Europe. As a result, the American Sephardim did not have the same intensive knowledge of Talmud. But the belief in God, in the Torah, and in the mitzvoth was the same.

In the Second Wave of Immigration, when great numbers of Jews came from the Germanic lands, the religious picture of the Jewish community began to change. In the first place, some of the immigrants who came after 1840 had already been influenced by Reform in Europe. In addition, those who came immediately after the unsuccessful revolutions of 1848 were not religious at all. They were primarily socialists and atheists who were part of the revolutionary groups. Neither of these accepted Orthodoxy as the Sephardim did.

Another group of Jews who forsook Orthodoxy did so because out of great loneliness they had married Christian women or Indian squaws. In the undeveloped wilderness of America, they had struck out boldly, but had found no Jewish women to give them companionship. Tragically, their children were raised as non-Jews and grew up without any Jewish knowledge or loyalties at all.

There were also a large number of German immigrants who had become peddlers and traders. Had they made their homes where there were Orthodox settlements, these Jews might have retained their true religious devotion. Settled, however, in the hinterlands and frontier areas, where there were no other Jewish families, they found it increasingly hard to practice Judaism. Sometimes these hardy pioneers were the only Jews within a radius of several hundred miles. They were caught in a web of circumstances which did not allow them to fulfill their religious requirements. There was no kosher meat to be had. There was no teacher to educate the children in the ways of Torah. It was difficult–in fact, almost impossible–to observe the Shabbat and the Yomin Tovim. There was no way of buying tefillin, a siddur, or a mezuzah. There were no rabbis to give spiritual guidance and leadership. Sometimes, Jews who were far from the center of the Jewish population did not even have Jewish calendars, and so they never even knew when to observe the holidays.

These Jews found it impossible to observe Judaism. They *felt* that they were Jews, but they no longer acted like Jews. In time they began to think that it was enough to do just what they were doing and still be "good" Jews. Their children, growing up in this environment and knowing no better, took it for granted that their form of Judaism was the true form of Judaism, or at least as valid as Orthdoxy. In this way, thousands of Jews and the generations that followed them lost contact with the true faith of Israel. Their form of religious practice did not come out of the conviction that they were right but rather out of convenience and ignorance. These Jews did not say that the Jewish religion had to be changed because they did not believe in the mitzvoth. On the contrary, many would have wanted to observe the mitzvoth had they only been able to. What they said in effect was, "We will consider ourselves as Jews even if we do not fulfill all the religious requirements that our fathers did."

By coincidence, their way of life was very similar to that which Reform Jews had preached in Germany. Both neglected most of the mitzvoth. As time passed and Reform was brought to America by the Reform rabbis who came from Germany, these settlers naturally identified themselves with Reform and became part of the movement.

How did Reform in America differ from Reform in Germany?

The beginnings of the Reform movement in America were altogether different from its beginnings in Europe. In Germany it began when Reform Jews consciously rejected the mitzvoth in order to be like their neighbors. In America it began because the Jews were so much like their neighbors and so much intermingled with them that they were unable to keep the mitzvoth. In Germany, Reform came into being because of the lack of Jewish rights; in America, it developed for the very opposite reason, because Jews had freedom and equality.

In what way is the Reform movement not of American Jewish creation?

The Jewish pioneers who were lax in their religious observances had no idea of founding a new division among Jews. They would have weakened and lessened their fulfillment of the mitzvoth, but they would have remained part of the Orthodox community. As long as they knew that they were not living up to requirements of the Torah, there was hope that they might return. In time, as religious schools, synagogues, and rabbis appeared on the scene, they or their descendants would have been brought closer to the traditional Jewish way of life. However, when Reform rabbis, coming from Germany, began to teach Reform belief, these Jews saw a religious way of life which seemed like theirs and which justified all their religious omissions and sanctioned their violations. This they could join without feeling any sense of sin or guilt. It made their lives easier and their religious requirements fewer. In the end they became identified with Reform, giving strength and impetus to a movement that was not their own, that was not an American Jewish creation.

What was the first Reform synagogue?

The first organized Reform effort took place in the largest and richest congregation of the United States, Congregation Beth Elohim of Charleston, South Carolina.

Congregation Beth Elohim, the second synagogue in the United States, had been built by Sephardic Jews in 1749, but by 1820 a large number of German Jews had already joined its membership.

In 1824, several of the members asked that some of the prayers be shortened, that a few of them should be read in English, and that there should be a sermon in English.

By modern standards these were not radical demands, although they did represent a departure from the usual nature of the services. There is no Orthodox objection to delivering a sermon in any language. Nor is there any great objection to certain prayers being read in English, where there is no specific prohibition in Jewish law.

The request for shortening some of the prayers, however, did present a question of tampering with the entire prayer service. It raised certain "halachic," or legal, questions that needed deep consultations among great scholars.

The request for these changes in themselves did not imply an attack on the mitzvoth or on the teachings of the Talmud or the Torah. They were more in the nature of a desire to improve the form of worship than to become identified with Reform thinking as it had been initiated in Germany.

The trustees of Congregation Beth Elohim, however, rejected the petition, and in a short time, the Congregation was about equally divided on the subject of changes. Bitterness and anger reigned until those who were against the change withdrew and formed a new and strictly Orthodox congregation. Beth Elohim, meanwhile, under successive Reform leaders, drifted from its original traditional position, and finally became established as a Reform congregation.

Why did Reform attract followers in other cities?

The pattern of Beth Elohim was repeated in other cities where often some desire for a simple change, not involving the denial of the revealed Torah or of the mitzvoth, ended in the formation of a new congregation. European Reform rabbis who came later then directed these congregations into a new and different way of life.

Often these congregations were more attracted by the new rabbi's English sermon and orderly services than by his radical religious beliefs. The early American congregations were not looking for religious reforms. They were seeking more dignity in the synagogue during the worship period and better understanding of the Hebrew services. Unfortunately, there were no Orthodox rabbis in America at this time who could speak English and so could provide the needs of congregations.

To what ideas was Isaac Mayer Wise dedicated?

The most important Reform rabbi of these early years was Isaac Mayer Wise, who came to America from Bohemia in 1846. He settled in Albany, New York, as the minister of Congregation Beth El, but his determination to make drastic Reform changes brought him into constant conflict with his congregation and he was finally forced to leave. In 1850, he became the rabbi of Anshei Emeth, a new Reform congregation that he established in Albany.

Wise was energetic, enthusiastic, and hard-working. He was a zealot of the Reform movement, and devoted his entire life to seeing that it took root in America. Towards this end, he decided on three major projects. In order to perpetuate the Reform movement, he wanted to create a union of all the Re-

form congregations. He saw, too, the need for founding a rabbinical college where English-speaking rabbis, trained in America, would be prepared for leadership. Finally, he was determined to establish an Anglo-Jewish newspaper which would reach all the Jews of America and discuss their common problems.

Wise traveled west, and in 1854, he settled in Cincinnati. This "Queen City of the West" held the third or fourth largest Jewish community in the nation, and furthermore most of its Jewish people were of German origin. There Wise began his work. He was a highly talented man, an excellent speaker, and a prolific writer. All these qualities were in his favor in reaching the goals he set for himself.

How did Wise institute mixed seating?

Wise's religious ideas were sometimes more practical adjustments to circumstances than the results of theological convictions. For example, a historian of the Reform movement in America describes how Wise introduced mixed seating of men and women in American Reform temples. Reform in Europe had still maintained the separate seating of men and women.

But when Isaac Mayer Wise was barred from his old synagogue in Albany, he was forced to use a Baptist church for his dissenting Reform congregation. The church naturally had no arrangement for separate seating for men and women as the synagogue did. But Wise found the mixed seating of the church so satisfactory that he decided to maintain this seating pattern in the future.

How was a national Reform organization financed?

When Wise came on the American scene, the German-Jewish congregations were still very poor. But time as well as circumstances were with him. The little institutions for charity, the self-help societies, and the small synagogues were growing up. The immigrants were slowly becoming more well-to-do and able to support large national organizations. This new-found wealth helped Wise's plans for a union of congregations and a rabbinical school.

What was the "American Israelite"?

Wise established an Anglo-Jewish newspaper called the *American Israelite.* He also founded a German-Jewish newspaper, and wrote articles for both. Through these publications, he was able to reach thousands of German Jews, and to bring them his message of Reform Judaism.

What are the UAHC and the HUC?

In 1871, under Wise's leadership, a Union of American Hebrew Congregations was formed. As one of its functions, the Union absorbed the work of the Board of Delegates of American Israelites, which had been formed earlier to protect Jewish rights in the United States. In addition to assuming this responsibility, the Union of American Hebrew Congregations united Reform congregations all over America, giving them added strength and dignity.

Four years later, the Hebrew Union College was founded in Cincinnati, and in 1883 the first four graduates were ordained. Today the Hebrew Union College is merged with the Jewish Institute of Religion in New York City. Hundreds of graduates of the two schools are serving as rabbis and teachers in the American Reform movement.

Both the Union of American Hebrew Congregations and the Hebrew Union College are more commonly referred to by the initials of their names, UAHC and HUC. The Union today is still a strong, articulate voice for Reform Judaism.

Wise had set himself three great goals. His dynamic personality and hard work had brought about their successful achievement.

What was the Pittsburgh Platform?

Although Wise seemed a drastic reformer to many Jews in America, he was considered a moderate by other Reform leaders of that day. They wanted to clarify the Reform position and thereby emphasize the difference between Reform and Orthodoxy.

In 1885, a conference of Reform rabbis met in Pittsburgh and adopted a set of principles known as the Pittsburgh Platform. In effect, the Platform echoed the teachings of European Reform. The validity of the Torah and Talmudic teaching was denied; the Bible was called "primitive," and the mitzvoth declared outworn and meaningless. A major declaration of the Platform also rejected the belief that Jews were a nation and that they should view Palestine as the Jewish homeland. Thereby Reform cut all ties with the Holy Land and the religious experiences of the Jews as a nation. As we look at the conclusions of the Conference we see that the Reform rabbis devoted more of their efforts to releasing Jews from religious obligations than to emphasizing the important principles of Judaism. As one of the historians of that period wrote, the Pittsburgh Platform did not teach Reform Jews "what to believe and what to do, but only what not to believe and not to do."

The Pittsburgh Conference also adopted a resolution permitting the transfer of religious services from Saturday to Sunday. This was a sad and tragic move, for it showed the lack of respect that Reform leaders had for the Bible and for Jewish tradition. It also showed the lengths to which Reform would go in imitating the Christians. Fortunately, most Jews refused to accept this suggestion. Even the Reformers could not forget the centuries of tradition. Many considered the suggestion to change the Jewish Sabbath blasphemous.

While the Pittsburgh Platform marked a sad turn of events on the American Jewish scene, it served to distinguish more clearly between Reform and other Jews. The rabbis who created the platform showed the direction Reform was taking. There was to be no vague division between Reform and Orthodoxy. Reform had washed its hands completely of Torah, the mitzvoth, the Sabbath, and Jewish national aspirations.

By 1889, the three arms of the Reform movement had been established. There was a union of congregations, a seminary for rabbis, and a union of rabbis who would define Reform ritual and religious policy.

Reform Rabbinical conferences have met regularly since 1889 when the Central Conference of American Rabbis was formed. This Conference is known, too, by its initials, CCAR. The Reform position on many of the principles adopted in 1885 has changed. Reform attitudes towards Israel, for example have changed drastically. Some of the greatest leaders of the American Zionist movement have come from among Reform rabbis and laymen.

The organizational three-armed pattern initiated by Isaac Mayer Wise was later followed by Conservative and Orthodox Jews as well. It helped each movement within Judaism express its principles and communicate them to its adherents.

Things to Remember

1. What does Article VI, clause 3, of our Constitution say?
2. In what way was Reform in America different from Reform in Germany?
3. What four groups of Jews were attracted to Reform?
4. What were Isaac Mayer Wise's major achievements?
5. What is the Pittsburgh Platform?

Things to Think About

1. If you had been a Jewish trapper isolated in the Northwest area, how would you have tried to remain Orthodox? What would you have done?
2. Do you think Isaac Mayer Wise made an important contribution to American Jewish life? Document your answer with facts.
3. Why did the position of the Pittsburgh Platform on the Jewish homeland collapse? Why do you think even Reform Jews could not accept it?

CHAPTER EIGHT

THE RISE OF CONSERVATIVE JUDAISM

The early Reform rabbis tended to convert the synagogues which they served. Isaac Mayer Wise was actually discharged from his first congregation in Albany because he tried to change the congregation from its Orthodox beliefs, and ridiculed publicly the mitzvoth that its members observed. When he came to Cincinnati, Wise again served an Orthodox congregation, where within months he instituted different and shortened prayers, and installed an organ to be used in the service. In a short time, the entire character of the synagogue was changed.

Why was Orthodoxy weakened in the early 19th century?

During the more than half century of Reform growth, Orthodoxy continued in its steady, historic manner. Unlike the Reformers, Orthodox Jews did not force their opinions on other Jews, nor did they go out militantly to convert them. They disagreed with Reform vehemently, but never sent rabbis into congregations to change their way of belief. Thus, even though the great majority of American Jews were Orthodox and true to their faith, Orthodoxy itself did not flourish. This was true for a number of other reasons as well.

The major difficulty was that there were no good religious schools to teach Jewish children their faith. Orthodoxy can succeed only where there is a deep knowledge of Jewish religion and culture. When Jews are ignorant of their faith they drift away into nontraditional ways of life. That is why Jews throughout the centuries, and certainly in our own times, put so much effort into the intensive study of Torah, Talmud, and rabbinic writings.

Unfortunately, in the first half of the 19th century, there were no educational facilities. The men and women who had left their homes to settle in the new land were too busy earning a living, and adjusting to a new way of life. They were unable to make provisions for themselves or for their children to receive a sound Jewish education. True, some synagogues established Hebrew schools, but from the records available we know that very little was accomplished. This was a serious threat to Orthodoxy, because it permitted ignorance of the Torah.

Still another problem was created by the limited Jewish immigration to the United States at this time. There were not enough Jewish men and women in America, nor did enough immigrants come, to provide a choice of husbands and wives within the Jewish community. And so, many Jews were driven to intermarriage with non-Jews. This hurt Orthodoxy particularly, because almost all Jews in America until the middle of the 19th century were Orthodox. Intermarriage also accounted for the gradual elimination of the Sephardic Jewish community which had been a strong Orthodox element.

Finally, even where there were Orthodox Jews and Orthodox congregations, there were no Orthodox leaders. There were no qualified rabbis who had received "simcha" at the hands of great European teachers and Talmudic scholars. In the city of Cincinnati, for example, there were 4000 Jews and only one rabbi. That rabbi was Reform and he was, of course, Isaac Mayer Wise.

Reform, therefore, moved rapidly because there was a vacuum in American Jewish religious life. Had there been Orthodox rabbis spread over the United States, the development of Reform might have taken a different turn entirely. It was only with the coming of large numbers of Jews from East Europe, after 1880, that the balance began to assert itself, and Orthodoxy too began to gain strength rapidly.

How did Isaac Leeser become prominent?

The spiritual heads of the Sephardic congregations, called ministers, did their utmost to maintain the traditional way of life. Where there was no minister, the hazzan who led the prayers served as teacher of the school and the religious head of the congregation. Neither the ministers nor the hazzanim were ordained rabbis.

One of these great religious leaders of the Sephardic congregations was Isaac Leeser. Leeser was 18 years of age when he came to America in 1824, just about the time when the Reform effort began in Charleston.

When Leeser first came, he worked as a clerk for his uncle

in Richmond, Virginia. The young man was very industrious, studying and reading, assisting the local clergymen in every way possible, and daily improving his use of the English language. He wanted to become as thoroughly American as possible.

Only four years later, Leeser wrote a series of articles in the *Richmond Whig*, defending the Jews against charges which had appeared in another publication. Leeser's articles included a full explanation of the Jewish faith and religion in perfect and learned English. His defense of Judaism received much favorable comment and won him national prominence.

Why did Leeser feel the need for American-trained rabbis?

Even though he was not an ordained rabbi, the prominence which Leeser achieved brought him an invitation to become minister of the famous Sephardic congregation, Mikveh Israel, in Philadelphia. He was only 23 at the time, and the position was an important and leading one.

For the next 39 years, from the pulpit of Mikveh Israel, Leeser defended Orthodoxy and taught its principles. Leeser, in his work for Orthodoxy, preceded Isaac Mayer Wise in his work for Reform, and Wise may have been inspired in his own goals by the work of Isaac Leeser.

One of the major lacks that Leeser felt was that of English-speaking rabbis to serve the Orthodox communities. He himself had mastered the use of English in a very short time. But few other leaders realized the importance of the new language in getting their ideas across to the people. They often felt that Spanish, or German, or whatever their native tongue was, could do just as well.

Leeser knew differently. He wanted to have a steady flow of American-trained rabbis, who would speak the English language and understand the needs of the people. It would be impossible to serve the requirements of the American Jews and attract them to the synagogues otherwise!

Of what lasting value was Maimonides College?

Diligently, Leeser labored to establish a school for rabbis. Through his efforts, in 1867, Maimonides College was established in Philadelphia. Unfortunately, the Jewish community was not sufficiently united to support it. There was no union of Orthodox congregations like the UAHC to place its weight behind the school. After several years, Maimonides College was forced to close its doors.

Even though the college itself failed, the idea of such a school was now well launched. The American Jewish community began to see its merits. The HUC in Cincinnati later succeeded because of this experience. And from Leeser's suggestion, other rabbinical seminaries came into being.

Why did Leeser join with non-Orthodox rabbis?

Leeser had long since realized the importance of a united Jewish community. He was especially anxious to see all the American Jews united in common purpose and goals. As a result, he was in the forefront of all action on behalf of such an organization.

In 1855, he even joined with non-Orthodox rabbis in a conference called for this express purpose. Leeser hoped that the Reform Jews too might join in a common battle for the sake of preserving Judaism. He was so persuasive that Isaac Mayer Wise and his colleagues adopted a resolution which admitted that the Talmud was "legal and obligatory." This was actually against Reform belief, which denied the validity of the Talmud.

However, this resolution was under constant fire from the radical Reform wing. When Leeser saw that Wise and his colleagues persisted in their Reform views, he withdrew from the conference.

What was the "Occident"?

Isaac Mayer Wise had learned another lesson from Leeser, and this was the importance of the written word. In 1843, Leeser founded the *Occident and American Jewish Advocate*, the first Jewish periodical of any importance in America. Isaac Mayer Wise's *Israelite*, which was in circulation 11 years later, followed in the path of the *Occident*. For 25 years, until the day of Leeser's death, the *Occident* was published monthly. As you can see, for a large part of this time, the *Occident* was the only Anglo-Jewish periodical in the United States.

The *Occident* reflected the American Jewish life of that generation. Although many non-Orthodox articles appeared in its columns, the *Occident* became the spokesman for Orthodoxy in America.

What were some of Leeser's other contributions?

Leeser also recognized that the Jews of his time had largely forgotten the Hebrew language. He was distressed that the only available English translations of the Bible were of Christian origin and had many references to Christianity. He set to work, determined to translate the Bible from Hebrew into English, so that Jews might have an English version of the Bible in the Orthodox tradition. This was the first English translation of the Bible that a Jew had ever made.

Leeser also threw himself into the work of improving Jewish religious education and understanding. He organized the first Jewish congregational Sunday schools, in which he had the enthusiastic support and assistance of Rebecca Gratz. He introduced the use of the English sermon and greater decorum during religious services. Both these changes had been requested by the dissidents in Charleston, and could have been accomplished by them within the framework of Orthodoxy.

He also wrote new textbooks in English, and translated others from the German language. In direct opposition to the extreme Reform rabbis, who favored the use of the German language, he insisted on English as the language of instruction in the schools.

Leeser was the major force in founding the Hebrew Education Society in Philadelphia for the purpose of establishing schools which taught secular as well as religious subjects. In this sense, he was the first organizer of the Jewish "parochial" school, or all-day school.

The tireless Philadelphia rabbi was also a founder of the Jewish Publication Society, whose purpose it was to print and distribute books of interest to Jews. The JPS, as it is known, is still active today, performing noteworthy services to the American Jewish public.

There was no area of American Jewish life which Leeser's unbounding energy did not touch. The formation of the Board of Delegates of American Israelites, and the Jewish Hospital of Philadelphia, were also largely due to his efforts.

Leeser's education, background, and scholarly training were not in the tradition of the later East European rabbis. But his devotion to traditional Judaism was unlimited. It might be said that it was owing to Isaac Leeser's work that the Eastern seaboard remained Orthodox, and devoted to the Torah and to the mitzvoth.

When Isaac Leeser died in 1868, having devoted almost 40 years to the service of his people, his name was known everywhere. With the exception of San Francisco and other far-flung towns, he had been in every city in America. He taught the Jewish community that there could be a beautiful joining of Americanism and Orthodoxy. In the sense that he militantly fought for this ideal, we can call Isaac Leeser an American Jewish missionary.

Who was Samuel Meyer Isaacs?

Another prominent minister was Samuel Meyer Isaacs, of New York City. Isaacs, an English Jew, like Leeser, served the Ashkenazic congregations B'nai Jeshurun and Shaarey Tefillah for almost 40 years. The minister of Shearith Israel, the Sephardic congregation, was Jacques Judah Lyons. He too was a staunch defender of Orthodoxy.

Isaacs was the editor of the *Jewish Messenger*. He used his periodical, as Leeser used the *Occident*, to defend Orthodoxy, attack anti-Semitism, and battle Reform.

He helped Leeser in establishing Maimonides College, and was also one of the initiators of the Board of Delegates. One of the largest hospitals in New York City, Mount Sinai Hospital, was founded with the help of Samuel Meyer Isaacs. Recognizing the need for Jewish charity and philanthropy, Isaacs, too, was instrumental in organizing the United Hebrew Charities in New York.

Like Leeser, the New York rabbi delivered his sermons in English, reaching the people in their new language. Under his leadership, the Ashkenazic congregation of New York City grew and thrived.

What was Rabbi Ash's contribution?

Another rabbi, who although he took no part in national deliberations, nevertheless made great strides for Orthodoxy, was Rabbi Abraham Joseph Ash. He had the distinction of serving the first synagogue of Russian-Jewish immigrants in America.

The congregation which Rabbi Ash served was known as Beth Hamidrash. It was founded in 1852 by Russian Jewish immigrants who came to escape conscription in the Russian army. The congregation grew so large that several other congregations were formed as offshoots from it. In 1885, it took over a large Methodist church on the East Side of New York, and became known as the Beth Midrash haGadol, the best-known Ashkenazic congregation in America.

Rabbi Ash forcefully spoke against Reform. He pointed out its lacks and inconsistencies. He explained how Reform denied the very basis of Torah, its divine origin. His personality and leadership were an important factor in making Beth Midrash haGadol the outstanding synagogue it was.

When Rabbi Ash died in 1887, the mass migration from East Europe which we shall soon learn about was already well under way. By that time there were many more Orthodox synagogues in New York and in other cities. But until that time, his lone voice was strengthening and reassuring.

How did the lines between Reform and others become clearly defined?

Leeser, Isaacs, Lyons, and others, like Morris J. Raphall, also of New York, had tried to stem the tide of Reform. They hoped that they would be able to continue to work with the Reform rabbis in some common aspects of Judaism.

However, Reform was moving towards an inevitable split with the rest of Jewry. The first open clash which reached national proportions took place in 1883, when the first class was graduated from the Hebrew Union College. A sumptuous banquet, to which many prominent Orthodox Jews had been invited, was served in honor of the graduates. Imagine the chagrin and amazement of the guests when they discovered that trefah, non-kosher fishes and meats, were being served! When they saw that a trefah dinner could be served by a rabbinical school to rabbis, they realized that Reform had thrown off all its ties with traditional Judaism, and that the two groups could no longer work together.

The split widened when the Reform rabbinate formulated the Pittsburgh Platform at a convention in that city in

1885. All Orthodox Jews were shocked by the proclamations of the Platform which denied the truth and the validity of the Torah, and repudiated the mitzvoth. They were aghast at the idea of desecrating the Sabbath. In their love of Zion they could hardly understand a Platform that repudiated the national homeland. A great reaction set in to counteract the principles of Reform. The gulf, now, was too wide to be bridged.

Who was Sabato Morais?

The East European Jews, who were newly arrived, were hardly in a position to contribute to any movement to frustrate Reform. The Sephardic ministers, however, who represented the leading traditional Jews of that era, who were already settled and well established in the country, were in a much better position to do so.

Leading the movement was Sabato Morais, Leeser's successor to the pulpit of Mikveh Israel, and one of his co-workers in Maimonides College. Morais was an Italian Jew, who had studied in England and emigrated to America in 1851. His stay in England had helped him master the English language, which he spoke beautifully.

Morais' hope to combat Reform was rooted in the idea of a rabbinical school like the one he had supported in Leeser's day. If there were well-trained Orthodox rabbis, they could preach the beauties of Orthodoxy and strengthen the people against Reform. This, he knew, was the only hope for the continuity of Orthodox Jewish life.

Fortunately for him, the community now had greater means and was already educated to the plan and prepared for the idea. Morais diligently set about enlisting assistance and financial pledges. In 1887, he opened the doors of the Jewish Theological Seminary of America in New York City. Morais was its president until the day that he died.

How did the JTS start a new Jewish philosophy?

When Morais died—and his energetic personality with him—a new group of supporters took over the Seminary. They were mainly composed of German Jews, who did not have the same intense loyalty to Jewish tradition that the Sephardic founders of the school had possessed. In 1902, they called Solomon Schechter from England to become its president.

Schechter was a well-known scholar, who had made some remarkable literary discoveries among manuscripts that he found in Egypt. He was a maskil, for he had studied in Vienna, where he had dipped deeply into the secular sciences. As a member of the faculty of Cambridge University, Schechter had won universal Jewish respect.

The new president assembled a faculty of Jewish scholars to help him in the work ahead. He had new ideas to implement, new ways for American Jews to follow. These ideas were neither Reform nor Orthodox. They were given the name "Conservative."

The Jewish Theological Seminary, to this day, is the center of the Conservative movement. In recognition of the great work that Solomon Schechter did in building its reputation, the Seminary is often referred to as Schecter's Seminary.

What is Conservative Judaism?

Conservative Judaism evolved from the time of Solomon Schechter. It appealed to those Jews who felt that Reform had made too sharp a break with the age-old traditions of Jewish life. It said that one could not disregard completely the teachings of the Torah, nor deny the value of Talmudic instruction. On the other hand, however, it did not accept the teachings of the Torah and the Talmudic sages as the last word in Jewish law.

Conservative Judaism said that religion had to change with the requirements of the times. Those teachings of Judaism which did not come into conflict with modern life should be retained. Others could be amended or discarded.

In this way, Conservative Jews kept the idea of a Jewish homeland and a return to Zion. They maintained the holiness of Hebrew as a sacred language, and they studied the Bible and the Talmud. But they did these things to a much lesser degree and with lesser intensity than did the Orthodox Jews.

Once, however, Conservatives had permitted the sanctity of the entire Torah to be challenged, all parts of the Torah lost their strength and influence. As time went on, Conservatives continued to make more and more changes. Many of the Conservative rabbis today encourage mixed seating and the use of the organ played on Sabbath in the synagogues, and even permit driving to services in an automobile on the Sabbath. The laws of kashruth have been weakened. The prayers have been shortened and changed. Many mitzvoth are disregarded, and the general attitude towards the holiness of the Torah and the teachings of the rabbis has been undermined.

The great reverence and respect that was given to the tanaim and amoraim and the great Talmudic scholars throughout the ages has been lessened. Students at the JTS, as the Jewish Theological Seminary is known, study considerably less Talmud and Codes than students in Orthodox seminaries.

Sabato Morais and the early graduates of the JTS would be profoundly amazed by the transformation that has taken place in their school.

How did the Orthodox view the Conservative?

Orthodoxy claimed that the teachings of the Bible could not be broken down into little pieces to permit individual Jews to select the mitzvoth that they preferred to observe and to discard the others. This, they said, would lead to a complete breakdown and destruction of the entire web of Jewish life. The Lord did not give one mitzvah to be observed in the 17th century, and to be discarded in the 18th. All of God's Torah was one at all times, with equal value and holiness.

What are the three arms of Conservative Judaism?

The Conservative movement has made great headway on the American scene. The United Synagogues of America is the body in which all their congregations are joined. Their Rabbinical Assembly is similar to the Reform CCAR. At Assembly conventions, questions of Jewish law and practice are discussed and decided upon. The JTS, of course, is the seminary where rabbis are trained to serve Conservative congregations.

In addition, the Seminary has a Cantorial Institute for training cantors, a Teacher's Institute, for preparing Hebrew teachers, and the Seminary College of Jewish Studies, for advanced study in Hebrew and Hebrew subjects.

Things to Remember

1. Why was Orthodoxy weakened in the first half of the 19th century?
2. Mention three accomplishments of Isaac Leeser. Why are they important?
3. Why is Sabato Morais important?
4. How does Conservative Judaism differ from Reform? From Orthodoxy?

Things to Think About

1. What do you think is the basic difference between Reform, Orthodox, and Conservative Jews?

2. Do you think that only those who keep the traditional way of life guarantee the survival of Judaism? Give facts to substantiate your answer.
3. Isaac Mayer Wise, Isaac Leeser, and Solomon Schechter each made a contribution to American-Jewish life. Were their contributions important or unimportant? Give reasons for your answer.

CHAPTER NINE

THE THIRD WAVE OF IMMIGRATION

The immigration of Jews in the colonial period had brought the Sephardim, the Spanish and Portuguese Jews who had fled the Inquisitions of Spain and Portugal, to America. They had come by way of South America, Holland, England, and the West Indies.

The Second Wave of Immigration began after 1810 and brought a preponderance of German Jews to colonial shores.

During the period between 1881 and 1914, the Third Wave of Immigration to America, composed of East European Ashkenazic Jews, sailed to the land of the free. Each wave also marked the end of the preceding wave. By 1880, for example, the Jews in the Germanic lands had long achieved the political and religious freedoms that they sought. And so, with the removal of the cause which had driven them earlier to America, their immigration was almost at a standstill. The East European immigrant, therefore, had almost a monopoly in molding the future of the community to which he came.

What caused a mass immigration from East Europe in 1881?

The year 1881 takes its place beside the year 1492 as a date unmatched in evil, hatred, and bigotry. In the year 1492 Jews were cruelly expelled from Spain, in Western Europe. In 1881, another type of persecution, equally cruel, was started against the Jews in Imperial Russia, in Eastern Europe.

This cruel persecution brought the Jews to America in large numbers, and caused a phenomenal growth in the Jewish community of the United States.

What were the May Laws?

In Volume 3, we studied the beginning of that period of savagery under the czars in Russia. Government and church joined in coordinated, directed "pogroms" against the Jews. In these pogroms thousands of Jewish men, women, and children were mercilessly maimed, butchered, and slain.

After the pogroms had run their course and the "blood bath" was over, a "cold pogrom" was instituted by the Russians. This was like our recent "cold war," in which no battles were fought, but hatred and opposition persisted. The "cold pogrom" was a continuation of the Russian animosity towards the Jews. It was spelled out in laws issued in May, 1882, and therefore called the "May Laws."

Under these laws, Jewish traders and businessmen were discriminated against. Only a small number of Jewish children were permitted to attend schools. Worst of all, the Jews were forced to live in restricted areas called "Pales of Settlement." Jews who went forth outside of the Pale were given terrible punishment. In effect, the Pale of Settlement was the Russian version of a medieval ghetto.

What was the political reason for the May Laws?

The author of these oppressive measures against the Jews was Czar Alexander III. Alexander III succeeded his father, Alexander II, who had been assassinated. The assassination was the result of discontent among the Russian people with the poverty, disease, and lack of freedom that were their lot.

Alexander III did not intend to improve the lot of his people. By singling out the Jews for punishment through the May Laws, he tried to make it appear that the Jews were guilty of the troubles that had befallen Russia. Anxious to divert the anger of the Russians from his throne, Alexander III made the Jews his scapegoat, and encouraged his peasants to take their revenge on them.

What was the position of the Orthodox Church?

The Orthodox Church of Russia also urged the adoption of the May Laws. The czar's chief adviser, who was an officer of the Church, had helped plan the persecution. He announced publicly that as a result of the persecution, he hoped that a third of the Jews of Russia would accept baptism, a third would starve to death, and a third would emigrate!

With the support of the czar and the Church, the misery of the May Laws and the cold pogrom were intensified. Actual pogroms regularly replaced the cold pogrom, with bloody outbreaks still taking place well after the beginning of the 20th century. Jewish life in Russia and other East European countries, especially in Poland and Rumania, grew worse and worse.

While there were occasional Jews who permitted themselves to be baptized, the Church was most successful in its pious wish that Jews starve to death. Many Jews died of starvation, of lack of shelter or of clothing. But the great majority of Russian Jews decided to emigrate, to leave the land which was so harsh and cruel to them. They became convinced that they could never find peace or happiness in Russia.

What two magnets drew the East European Jews?

The persecutions gave new impetus to the hope of a return to the Holy Land. By settling in Palestine, Russian Jews knew that they would not only fulfill the age-old dream of rebuilding Zion, but would also provide a haven of refuge for themselves and their tormented brothers. Organizations like the "Chovevei Zion," the Lovers of Zion, raised money to help settle immigrants in Palestine. The association of Bilu, a name composed of the first letters of the Hebrew phrase, "Bet Yaakov L'chu V'Nelcha," House of Jacob, Let Us Go Forward, was composed of young idealists who, with their families, determinedly moved to Palestine. The first pioneers of modern Israel came to cultivate the new land as a result of the ideals of the Zionist philosophy and the vicious May Laws.

The overwhelming majority of the great outpouring of Russian Jews, however, found its way to the shores of the famed "land of the free."

Between 1881 and 1924, when United States immigration laws limited the number of people who could enter our shores, two million Jews came to America from the bloody countries of East Europe. They came from Russia itself, from the Russian-dominated part of Poland, from Austria-Hungary, especially the province of Galicia, and from Rumania.

Many more might have arrived in America had not the World War of 1914 temporarily halted most passenger traffic across the Atlantic. After the war, there was a great deal of anti-immigration agitation in America. In 1921, the Johnson Act, followed by further restrictions in 1924, almost completely shut down Jewish immigration.

Who was Emma Lazarus?

It was true that the immigrants in the Third Wave came to America because their hopes and homes in Europe had been destroyed. But they wanted to stay and remain here for another reason. America was the "Goldenne M'dina"—the Golden Land where freedom was guaranteed to all its inhabitants. Letters from relatives in the New Land had always excited and thrilled them. But, poverty-stricken as they were, they had never hoped to see it. With the hot breath of the pogroms upon them, however, they picked up their pitiful belongings and finally realized their dream.

The symbol of America as a haven for the distressed and the unhappy had been best expressed in a poem written by a young Jewish poetess, Emma Lazarus. Emma Lazarus, in her short life of 38 years, has left an unforgettable impression not only on Jews but on all Americans.

She was of Sephardic ancestry, and until the time of the persecution of the Russian Jews, chose the usual themes for her poetry—themes of love and death and nature. But when she saw the many thousands of Jews beginning to arrive in the Land of Promise, when she saw their weary, broken spirits, she was filled with a sense of anger at the society that permitted such inhumanity. Her heart was filled with compassion for her people, and with identification with their eternal suffering. Although Emma Lazarus had never been taught much about Judaism, she now decided to learn all about her faith. She threw herself into the study of Hebrew, Jewish history, and religion.

When a gift from the people of France, the Statue of Liberty, was anchored in New York harbor, Emma Lazarus' inspired sonnet "The New Colossus" was cast in bronze and placed at its base. Every American, and certainly every American Jew should be familiar with its immortal words. In it, Emma Lazarus pictured America as the "Mother of Exiles." To the tired immigrant who landed in the port of New York, the familiar figure, with the torch held high, beckoned warmly and encouragingly. And the words of Emma Lazarus' poem poured forth of themselves and reached each new arrival's heart.

> ...Give me your tired, your poor,
> Your huddled masses yearning to breathe free,
> The wretched refuse of your teeming shore,
> Send these, the homeless, tempest-tossed, to me.
> I lift my lamp beside the golden door!

Emma Lazarus had been a personal friend of Ralph Waldo Emerson and other noted men. But her genius was not fulfilled until she received her inspiration from her own people. "The New Colossus" is the expression of America's attitude towards the "wretched" people of the world. It is loved by all Americans.

What was the ICA?

Most of the new immigrants were completely destitute. With little more than the necessary ship's ticket, a family would take off for America. The faith that they had in the ability of America to provide for them was of an almost religious fervor.

This faith was fulfilled in the way older Jewish settlers received the new immigrants. Way stations in principal cities were created to help the immigrants on their way, to give them food and a little bit of money, and to make their voyage easier.

In France, the great Jewish philanthropist, Baron Maurice de Hirsch, gave 50 million francs to create a Jewish Colonization Association. The ICA, as it was known, established hundreds of offices throughout Russia, in order to promote emigration from Russia and colonization in the Western Hemisphere.

Why did Jews fail at agriculture?

When the immigrants reached the United States, they were helped by the many benevolent associations already in existence. Besides ICA, Baron de Hirsch had founded the Industrial Removal Office. In America, these two organizations tried to encourage the new arrivals to leave the concentrations of the big cities, and to move to the West and South. In this program, the Alliance Universelle Israelite and other groups joined in as well.

With their prodding, some Jews did attempt to form agricultural colonies and farms. Different colonies were started in Louisiana, South Dakota, Colorado, Oregon, Kansas, Michigan, Virginia, Connecticut, and New Jersey. With the exception of Woodbine, in New Jersey, all these experiments failed. The Jew had too long been denied the right to occupy land. In Europe, he had never been given the opportunity to own land, to till the soil, and work the crops. He had been driven into trade for a livelihood. For years, his talents had been developed in other occupations. He had lost the knack of making the land produce for him. It was only many years later, in the State of Israel, that Jews took up successfully the challenge of agricultural development.

To this very day, there are fewer than 100,000 Jews in the United States who have remained in agriculture.

How did HIAS develop?

There were many organizations that helped look after the needs of the immigrants by providing them with temporary shelter, with food and clothing. These organizations were in the main founded and supported by well-to-do German-Ashkenazic Jews who had preceded the Third Wave of Immigration. Personally, they often looked down with contempt upon the East Europeans. Since the latter were new in the land, or "green," they were called "greenhorns," and they were considered uncouth and uncultured strangers by their benefactors. Even though the German Ashkenazic Jews supported the assistance program, they kept themselves socially aloof.

Forty years earlier, they themselves had received the same treatment from the Sephardic Jews. Now, having become "Americanized," they did the same to the East European Jews.

During this time, too, the National Council of Jewish Women was organized to help single girls who entered America to adjust to their new life. Later a new and greater organization to help the immigrants was formed. It was called the Hebrew Sheltering and Immigrant Aid Society and became known by its initials, HIAS.

What is the function of the HIAS?

The HIAS is operating to this very day, helping new immigrants in every possible way. Just as it did for the East European Jews of the Third Wave of Immigration, HIAS still finds temporary living quarters for new arrivals. It gives help and advice in locating friends and relatives. It gives food and clothing, and instruction to prepare the immigrant for a trade.

It does everything possible to make the entry of Jewish immigrants at the various United States ports, comfortable, easy, and happy.

How did "Landsleit" help the new immigrants?

Destitute as they were when they landed on these shores, only a small percentage of the immigrants had to turn to communal organizations for help. Most of them, almost immediately, were able to turn to the friends, relatives, or "Landsleit" that they had.

Landsleit were people who came from the same village, town, or city in the "old country." Even if they were unknown to each other, the new arrival was always free to call upon his "landsman" (the singular of "landsleit") for help.

The landsman took the newly arrived immigrant into his home, fed him, lent him some old clothes, and helped him to find a job. As more and more immigrants settled in the country, there was a greater number of relatives and landsleit to care for those who came later.

In time, the landsleit organized the same type of self-help and mutual-aid societies as the German Jewish immigrants had done earlier. Thus, the landsleit of Petrikov organized in one "landsmanschaft;" the landsleit of Kurow organized in another landsmanschaft. These landsmanschaften often developed into congregations and fraternal and social organizations. More often than not, they remained as relief organizations for the help of Jews who were still left in Europe.

The "greenhorn" was helped by two other factors. The first was that the United States was in the midst of a great industrial expansion. Jobs, even though they paid very little, were not too hard to find. Secondly, the new immigrant, because of his joy at being a resident of the United States, adjusted very quickly to the new society. He worked hard, sought to improve himself, got along on very little, and was willing to do anything to succeed.

What were the sweatshops?

The five-day work week and the eight-hour day were unheard of in those times. Men worked as many days as they could and as many hours as they could. There were countless little factories, dimly lit and crowded together, where the East European immigrant got a job. In such sweatshops, as these factories were called, the immigrant sometimes worked as many as 16 hours each day–twice as long as laborers on the same jobs do today.

There were no unions to safeguard the rights of the workers, and the lack of sanitation and safety precautions in the sweatshops was frightening. Tuberculosis and other diseases resulted from the lack of sleep and nourishment. Fires which frequently broke out in the shops took the lives of many workers, because there were no fire escapes and the dark, crowded sweatshops were death traps. In one fire, 146 workers were killed because the doors had been locked to prevent them from leaving their sewing machines and "wasting time"!

For all this work, the laborers received a mere pittance, their salaries ranging between $3 and $10 a week. Sometimes, they even were expected to furnish their own sewing machines!

How did ghettos develop?

Because the immigrants naturally turned towards each other and their fellow Jews who preceded them, they tended to live in the same neighborhoods. These soon became "ghetto" areas with dirty, uncared-for tenement houses which had no heat, no hot water, and only the most primitive of toilet facilities.

The wages and conditions of labor remained so poor because there was a steady reserve of manpower made up of new immigrants, who arrived almost every day and who were willing to work under any conditions.

The ghettos also remained because as some Jews improved themselves and moved out into better neighborhoods, their landsleit stepped in to take their place.

In Europe, the ghettos had actually been forms of restriction and imprisonment forced upon them by the government. In America, the ghettos were formed voluntarily for friendship and out of loneliness. As the need disappeared, the ghettos disappeared.

What has happened to tenements and ghettos today?

In the 19th century and the early 20th, working conditions were bad for Jew and non-Jew alike. As the workers began to organize themselves to protect their rights, these conditions improved. With improving working conditions, Jew and non-Jew alike sought to improve their living quarters. They left the tenements and the ghettos as soon as they were able. In addition, as immigration slowed down because of anti-immigration laws passed by Congress, there were few newcomers to move into the ghettos.

Today, the ghettos have been deserted for more prosperous neighborhoods. Those areas in the big cities where Jews had once lived in such large numbers, with few exceptions, no longer have Jewish population majorities. The same is true of the "needle trades," as the trades that manufacture wearing apparel are called. At one time, the majority of the employers and workers were Jews. Today, only a small proportion of the employees in the needle trades are Jewish.

What were some contributions of the East European Jews?

The life of the East European Jewish immigrants was one of constant rushing and bustling. They wanted to keep their jobs to make ends meet. They had to learn the language and try to acquire the rudiments of an education. They wanted to help new arrivals. Above all, they wanted to improve their lot and make it possible for their children to become successful Americans.

Despite all these pressures and tensions, the immigrants produced a rich and handsome contribution to American life.

From the teeming background of East European Jewish life, there rose organizers of labor, and welfare workers, masters of finance and industry, great physicians and scientists, lawyers and statesmen. There were liberal idealists, who led the Socialist movement, and there were religious idealists, who led the Zionist movement. There were athletes and entertainers, poets and dramatists. From the heart of the East European immigrants, there rose up famous Jewish judges and teachers, scholars and religious leaders.

All would play a part in molding America. Devoted to the ideals of freedom and democracy, and imbued with the spirit of God and of Torah, they would make an invaluable contribution to American Jewish life.

Things to Remember

1. What were the three waves of immigration? Approximately when did they occur, and what were the native countries of the Jews that made up each wave?
2. What causes brought the East European Jew to America?
3. Why is Emma Lazarus remembered?

4. What societies helped East European Jews to get settled in the new land?
5. What are three important contributions that East European Jewry made in America?

Things to Think About

1. How does Emma Lazarus' "New Colossus" sum up the spirit of America?
2. What advantages would there be to living in a ghetto, assuming physical conditions were comfortable? Would you prefer it? Give reasons for your answer, with facts from the life of East European Jews.
3. Do you think that Czar Alexander III actually did the American-Jewish community a favor? Explain.

CHAPTER TEN

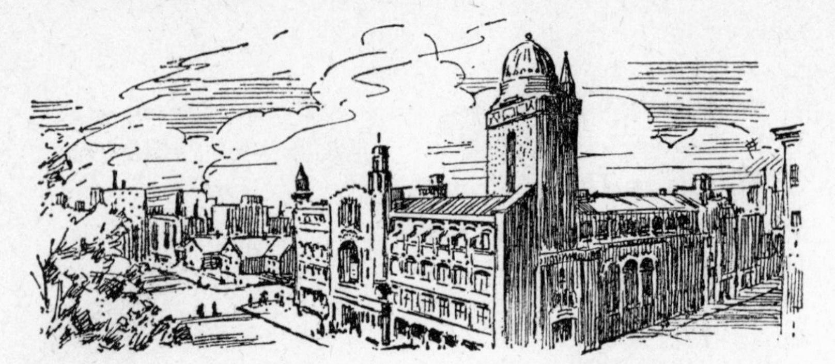

THE ADVANCE OF ORTHODOXY

The greatest and most important disappointment that faced the Jews who made up the Third Wave of Immigration to the United States was the absence of a rich religious life.

It is true that many Jews who arrived after 1881 had already weakened their religious ties. Some had fallen under the spell of Socialism which promised a better life for everyone through economic and political changes. Others had become charmed by the Haskalah, which taught that the Jewish future lay in a rebirth of Hebrew language and literature. Still others thought that Zionism, returning to the Holy Land and colonizing it, was the answer to the Jewish problem. Although their original ideas all stemmed from the Torah, in many ways, these three types of Jews had become indifferent to the faith of Israel and the belief in God.

What type of Jew was the average East European? Fortunately the vast majority of the East European Jews who came to this country were pious and God-fearing people. Their European homes had carefully guarded the Sabbath and the Holy Days. They and their fathers had always been devoted to study and to Torah.

There was hardly a Jew who came from East Europe who did not know the Bible, who did not "davven" daily, and who did not observe kashruth and the Sabbath. A large number of the new immigrants were highly qualified students of the Talmud and the Codes.

What religious conditions did the new immigrants find?

In bustling cities like New York, Boston, Philadelphia, Chicago, Baltimore, or Rochester, the East European immigrant was shocked by what he found. There were few Orthodox synagogues, and there were no religious schools for the instruction of his children. Despite the efforts of a spiritual leader like Leeser, Orthodoxy had barely held its own. Reform Judaism, which the East European immigrants did not even consider as being Jewish, seemed to dominate the American scene.

In the entire city of New York, where the largest population of Jews was concentrated and where the vast number of immigrants came, there was only one Hebrew school at the beginning of the 1880s. Had there been twenty more Hebrew schools, it would not have been sufficient! It is estimated that 50,000 of the almost 250,000 Jews in the United States, in 1880, were East Europeans. By 1890, there were almost four times as many of these new immigrants. Certainly one Hebrew school could not satisfy their needs!

Despite the problems of adjusting to a new land and to a new language, despite their meager incomes, the immigrants slowly, with the same determination that had led them to the new land, began to work at solving their religious problems.

What was the "cheder"?

Synagogues began to multiply. The landsmanschaften formed synagogues which met in rented rooms, in basements, and in stores. As they grew to larger proportions, some of these landsmanschaften built beautiful buildings for their synagogues.

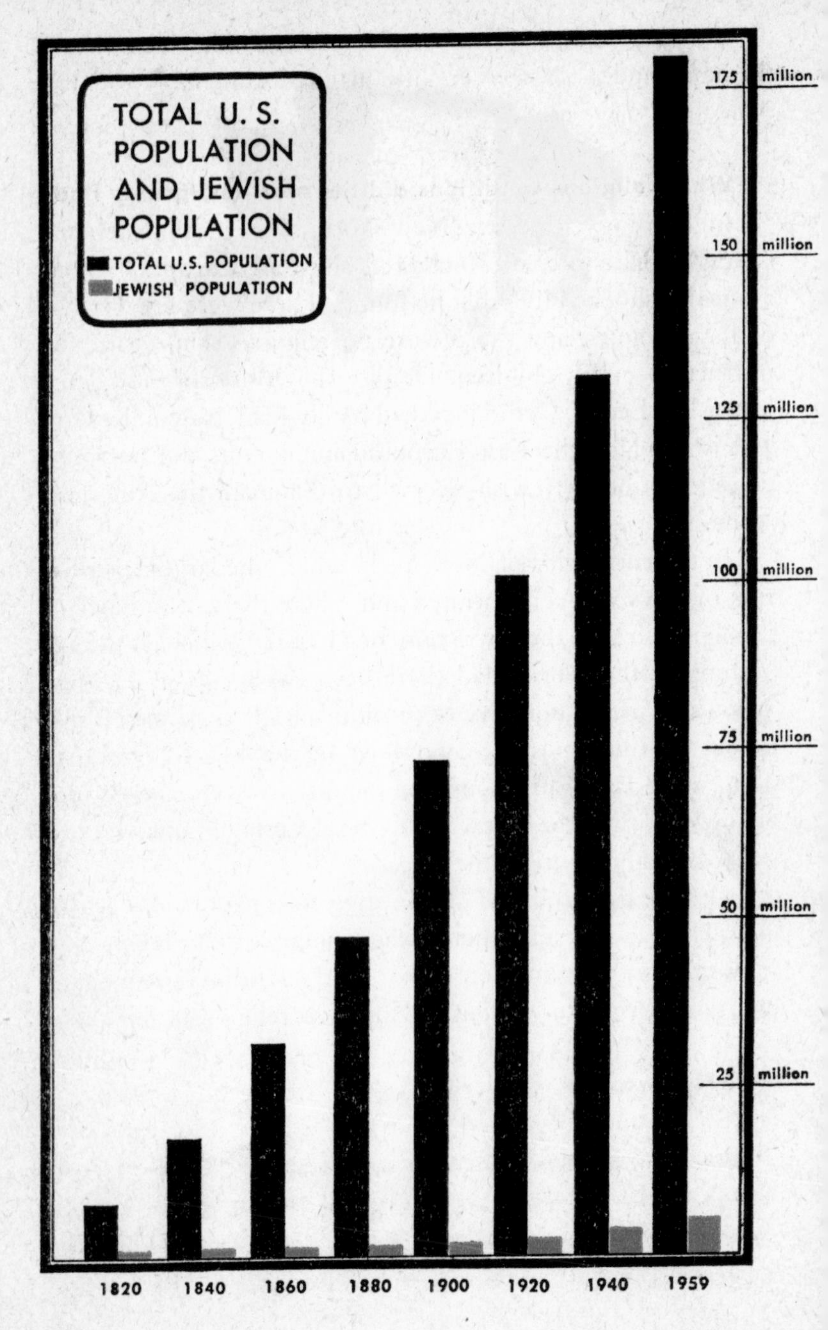
TOTAL U. S. POPULATION AND JEWISH POPULATION
TOTAL U.S. POPULATION
JEWISH POPULATION
175 million
150 million
125 million
100 million
75 million
50 million
25 million
1820
1840
1860
1880
1900
1920
1940
1959

Professional teachers and learned people among the immigrants themselves began to give private instruction to the children. Some used their own homes for this purpose. Others rented space in vacant stores or apartments. They placed a sign in the window announcing the establishment of the school, and parents brought children to them, to be taught the Torah and the mitzvoth.

Such a school was known as a "cheder," or one-room school. The same methods of teaching were used here as had been used in Europe. Pupils, sitting at long tables, were taught to "davven," to read the Siddur and to follow the prayers in the synagogue. They also learned the Bible, the Chumosh, by translating it into Yiddish, just as they had in the old country.

How did the Talmud Torah develop?

As the need for schools multiplied, people who were not always qualified to teach, but who had no other trade at hand, also opened such schools or gave private lessons. The new immigrants saw that this was not satisfactory. There was no proper supervision, and very often the teachers were so inadequate that the pupils did not learn anything.

They therefore decided to sponsor schools through their synagogues or other community organizations. This new type of school was called the Talmud Torah.

The Talmud Torah had regularly scheduled classes, and supervision by the rabbis of the synagogues to which they were attached or by the members of a Board of Education. Unlike the cheder or the private teacher, the new schools also accepted poor students whose parents could not afford to pay tuition. They were able to do this because of the community support that they received. In this way, no Jewish child was deprived of an education.

As new, more modern, synagogues were built, classrooms and sometimes entire wings were set aside for use by the Talmud Torah. Because it was a more successful form of education, the Talmud Torah replaced the cheder completely. Today, the Talmud Torah is the most popular form of supplementary Jewish education.

What were the yeshivoth of Europe?

The greatest contribution that East European Jews made in the field of Jewish education was the introduction of yeshiva education to American soil. The yeshiva type of school grew into a great movement and became the most important factor in the growth and preservation of Judaism in America.

In Europe the yeshiva was the name given to a special type of advanced religious school. There, an intensive study of Talmud was the major course of study and its students were at least in their middle and late teens. A yeshiva was not found in every village or town. Students who showed promise in their local communities were sent off to a yeshiva, much as boys and girls go to out-of-town colleges today.

In the European yeshivoth, there were 10, 12, and sometimes 15 hours of study each day. These hours were spent on the Talmud, the Commentaries, the *Shulchan Aruch*, and the later Codes and Responsa. As many as 10 years could be devoted to study in one yeshiva, after which the student emerged as a mature man and a great scholar. When his period of study was finished, the student, if he so desired, would present himself before a board of rabbis and be tested for the purpose of himself becoming a rabbi. He would then be ordained and take up a pulpit in a community.

What was the first yeshiva in America?

The East European immigrants were men of imagination. They realized that the cheder, the private tutor, and even the Talmud Torah, were all inadequate to convey a true knowledge of Judaism. They also realized that it was most important to provide a secular education for their children as well, because a Jew in America had to have both religious and general instruction. In order to make this possible, they organized a new type of school which included both forms of learning. It was a full-day school, in which the morning and early afternoon were devoted to religious studies. The rest of the day until 7 P.M. was given over to the study of reading English, writing, arithmetic, history, and other subjects. Because they had high hopes for the achievement of this type of school, they named it a yeshiva, after the European academies which were the center of Jewish learning. However, the American yeshiva was different from the European yeshiva in that elementary school children were included in the program and in that secular, as well as religious, studies were taught.

The first of the yeshivoth in America was founded in 1886. It was aptly called "Etz Chaim," a Tree of Life, because the Torah "is a tree of life to all those who grasp it." It carried over the tradition of the European yeshiva and blended it with the American educational heritage.

One of the great admirers and supporters of the Yeshiva Etz Chaim was Rabbi Jacob Joseph, a great European scholar and teacher, who was the Chief Rabbi of the Orthodox congregations of New York at that time. When he passed away, the second elementary yeshiva in New York City was named in his memory, the Rabbi Jacob Joseph School.

Etz Chaim was absorbed in Yeshiva University, as we will soon see, but the Rabbi Jacob Joseph School is still continuing its teaching of Torah and Talmud under its original name. Today, there are more than 180 elementary yeshivoth, or day schools, all over the United States, all teaching Judaism and the American way of life.

What step forward was made by Rabbi Moses Matlin?

The Etz Chaim Yeshiva adequately served the needs of elementary school children, but there were older boys, coming from Europe daily, who needed further instruction. They were too far advanced in their studies to attend Etz Chaim, and there was no other institution which provided for their needs. It was obvious that a more advanced school was necessary.

Ten years after the founding of Etz Chaim, the solution was found. A kind-hearted and scholarly rabbi, named Moses Matlin, had gathered a handful of such young men to his home to give them advanced teaching in Talmud. He had been moved to do this because of the pressing needs of his own son, who was included in this class. The students met daily in the modest apartment of Rabbi Matlin, on the third floor of an old tenement building on the East Side of New York.

How did the Rabbi Isaac Elchanan Theological Seminary develop?

The group soon grew too large for Rabbi Matlin to accommodate in his tiny apartment. The class, therefore, began to hold its sessions in a synagogue building. In 1896, it was officially incorporated into a school.

The school was named after the sainted and revered Rabbi Isaac Elchanan Spektor of Kovno, Lithuania. Rabbi Isaac Elchanan had just died the year before, and he was acknowledged as one of the greatest Talmudic scholars of his generation. It was hoped that the students of the school bearing the name of this distinguished rabbi would likewise achieve greater scholarship.

The new seminary differed from the European yeshivoth not only in the program of study, which included some general subjects, but also in purpose. One of its major aims was to prepare students for the rabbinate. The founders of the seminary knew that the immigrant living in the new land required not the European rabbi, but a modern rabbi who could speak the language of the younger generation.

In 1908, the first three students of the Rabbi Isaac Elchanan Theological Seminary were ordained by great and distinguished rabbis.

How did Dr. Bernard Revel further develop the new seminary?

For some years, the Yeshiva Etz Chaim and the Rabbi Isaac Elchanan Theological Seminary remained as separate schools, growing slowly. In 1915, they merged to become one school, under the leadership of one of the most profound Talmudic scholars and thinkers in the Orthodox movement. His name was Bernard Revel.

Dr. Revel had been ordained in Europe where he had as a youth achieved the reputation of being an "Ilui," a genius. In America, he studied in various schools and achieved his doctorate. When he was less than 30 years of age, he was called upon to assume the direction of the Seminary.

Dr. Revel approached his duties as president with great energy and understanding. Having studied in American universities, he knew what kind of staff was required to make a good general studies department. He recruited outstanding scholars and introduced many new courses for the students.

Under his inspiration, too, the first Yeshiva High School, known as the Talmudical Academy, was established. Later he incorporated a Teacher's Institute into the academic program, to train teachers for the many Hebrew Schools and Talmud Torahs. By this time, the elementary department was allowed to lapse. Dr. Revel felt that elementary yeshivoth would continue to grow all over America. It was the higher school that he was interested in.

How did Yeshiva College come into being?

By the middle of the 1920s, RIETS as the Rabbi Isaac Elchanan Theological Seminary was known, was producing scholarly rabbis, well-educated laymen, and excellent Hebrew teachers. As soon as they were graduated, these men went out to render service to American Orthodox Jews everywhere.

But Dr. Revel had another great dream. He was saddened by the fact that many promising students, who did not care to continue their studies as rabbis, would leave the yeshiva after completing their high school studies. This meant that many bright young men who might have continued their religious education left the yeshiva in order to attend college in other places.

Dr. Revel was determined to create a college of the finest caliber of instruction and standards. He wanted his students to receive their secular education under the wings of the yeshiva, where great rabbis and the spirit of Torah could always influence them.

In addition, those students who were indeed continuing their religious studies, leading to the rabbinate, would have a college under the same roof, where they could study secular subjects as well.

For years Dr. Revel cajoled, urged, influenced, and finally

even browbeat Orthodox Jews in New York and across the country to hear his dream. Finally, in 1928, it was fulfilled. The Rabbi Isaac Elchanan Theological Seminary moved from the East Side of New York City to an elegant building in upper Manhattan. In conjunction with its rabbinical and teaching program, it now had a college as well. The college to this day is known as Yeshiva College. It was the first college under Jewish auspices in the Western Hemisphere, and it came into being because of the efforts of Orthodox Jews.

What were Dr. Revel's achievements?

Dr. Revel's great labor on behalf of the college and the new building had sapped his strength. The financial obligations brought about by the new structure were enormous. The challenge to make the College successful and to keep the high level of scholarship in every department was almost superhuman.

When financial pressures were great, Dr. Revel refused to accept any salary for his services. One day in 1940, while he was delivering a Talmudic discourse to an advanced class of rabbinical students, Dr. Revel was blinded by a stroke. He was rushed away to receive medical treatment, but it was too late. In the quarter of a century that he had been at the helm of RIETS, the great man had burned himself out on behalf of his people. He died at the early age of 55.

Dr. Revel had literally driven himself to his death, but he had achieved the fulfillment of a great dream. Under his administration as president of RIETS, the first Jewish high school and the first Jewish college privileged to award the degree of Bachelor of Arts and Bachelor of Sciences had been founded. Hundreds of rabbis had been ordained at his hand, in the highest tradition of rabbinical scholarship. Many qualified teachers had gone forth to teach the sons and grandsons of the East European immigrants. Dr. Bernard Revel's name was revered by all.

What was the function of the Union of Orthodox Jewish Congregations?

With the founding of RIETS, East European Jews had accomplished one major step in creating the instruments for a healthy, flourishing community. They now needed a synagogue union and a rabbinical organization as well.

In 1888, an effort had been made to create a federation of Orthodox congregations in New York City. Rabbi Jacob Joseph of Vilna was brought from Europe to serve as its spiritual head. Unfortunately, the experiment, which might have been a pattern for a national synagogue body, failed.

Ten years later, however, a more successful attempt was made. With the help of H. Pereira Mendes, minister of the Spanish-Portugese synagogue in New York, the Union of Orthodox Jewish Congregations was formed.

The Union is an active and dynamic force to this day. It speaks for Orthodoxy on the national scene, representing the wishes of Orthodox Jews to the President and to the legislators in Washington. It helped pass a law in New York State prohibiting the sale of non-kosher food as kosher. Similar laws have been passed in other states. Because of this law, Jewish housekeepers can buy with confidence any item that is labeled kosher.

The Union also supervises the production of many food products and products that come in contact with food. An item which has the U-O insignia is an item which is strictly kosher and which is closely supervised. U-O is watched for by Orthodox housewives as their guarantee of kashruth.

Most important of all, the Union has brought together well over seven hundred Orthodox congregations, uniting them in a common body under their banner, and helping each other reach their common goals. The Union is commonly known by its initials, UOJC.

What are the Orthodox rabbinical bodies?

In 1902, an Orthodox rabbinic organization was also formed. This body was called the Union of Orthodox Rabbis, or Agudas haRabonim. Originally, it consisted of European-ordained rabbis, and to this day, most of its members have that same distinction.

The Agudas haRabonim was devoted to intensifying religious observance in the United States. For many years they were staunch supporters of RIETS. But as the graduates of the yeshiva multiplied, many differences between the European and American rabbis became apparent.

The American rabbis had college and often graduate school training. They spoke English fluently, they understood the needs of the American community much better, and they were able to participate in many more synagogue activities than were the European rabbis. Because of this, they also held pulpits in the richer and more influential congregations.

In 1924, another Orthodox rabbinical group, called the Rabbinical Council of America, or RCA, was formed. It originally consisted only of graduates of RIETS, but it now includes other Orthodox rabbis as well. The RCA is the rabbinical authority of the UOJC. It represents the widest segment of American Orthodox rabbis.

Who were some outstanding Orthodox rabbis of the early 20th century?

There were many outstanding Orthodox rabbis during this time. Among them was Rabbi Bernard L. Levinthal, of Philadelphia, who had befriended Dr. Revel and until his death was a member of the Rabbinic Ordination Committee of RIETS. Others were Rabbi Aaron M. Ashinsky, of Pittsburgh; Rabbi Eliezer Silver, of Cincinnati, who has long stood at the head of the Agudas haRabonim; and Rabbi Jacob Konvitz, of Newark,

New Jersey. In New York, there was Rabbi Jacob Vidrevitz, the onetime Rabbi of Moscow, Rabbi Moses Z. Margolies, and Rabbi Israel Rosenberg. Rabbi Margolies had been a president of RIETS before it merged with Etz Chaim, and Rabbi Rosenberg had acted as president of the Agudas haRabonim and vice-president of RIETS.

In the formative years since its beginning in the United States, the East European community had done nobly. It had developed its own seminary, synagogue union, and rabbinical organization. It had created an unheard-of institution, the first Jewish college on American soil. And it would do unheard-of things in the future.

Orthodoxy was well on the way to establishing a strong and well-organized movement to counteract the growth of Reform and to root Torah living deep in American soil!

Things to Remember

1. What are the differences between the cheder, the Talmud Torah, and the day school?
2. How did RIETS come into being? In what way were Rabbis Matlin and Revel responsible for its development?
3. Why is Dr. Bernard Revel remembered today?
4. What are the three arms of Orthodoxy in the United States?

Things to Think About

1. Do you think a Talmud Torah education can be as good as a yeshiva or day school education? Give reasons for your answer.
2. Do you think Dr. Revel's dream to establish a Yeshiva College was a good one? Whether you agree or disagree, substantiate your answer with facts.
3. Why is the U-O symbol so important to American Jewish housewives today? Explain your answer.

CHAPTER ELEVEN

ORGANIZATIONS AND CONTRIBUTIONS

The East European Jews had long been suppressed by social, financial, and religious restrictions. Now in the atmosphere of freedom their life began to expand in many directions at once. We have seen how they began to create a religious, social, and fraternal atmosphere for themselves and their children. In addition they tried to achieve financial security.

Most of the immigrants found employment in industries where the skills they had developed in Europe could be used. The clothing industry that required sewing machine operators, cutters, finishers, and those of similar skills absorbed most Jewish immigrants. They also found their way into other industries as semiskilled workers, slowly perfecting themselves until they were skilled workers.

Why did Jews help found the labor movement?

In Europe, Jewish employees had already learned about the labor movements that united the workers to protect their rights and interests. In the American sweatshops, the need for guaranteeing the workers' rights was even greater. With the same energy that they had studied Talmud, Jewish workers studied labor needs and conditions; and with the same devotion that they had given to their faith, they struck out for the rights of working people. In the very sweatshops in which they worked, the East European Jews developed the Jewish labor movement.

Although many of the Jewish men and women who worked for the labor movement were not religious, their very support of the workingmen stemmed from their Biblical inheritance. The prophets had taught them the principles of social justice, that the rich should not exploit the poor and helpless and squeeze as much as they could out of them. Their zeal for equality, for humane working conditions, and for the rights of the impoverished and downtrodden came from the Holy Torah.

Through the formation of the labor unions, the Jewish immigrants dedicated themselves to wipe out the sweatshops, earn for the worker a decent wage and decent working conditions, and shorten his working day. Many great unions, as we shall see, came into being as a result of the agitation of East European Jews who were inspired by the Biblical teachings which had been implanted in them.

What were some "Jewish" unions?

As early as 1888, the United Hebrew Trades was organized. This was not a union made up of workers in one particular type of trade. It cut across different industries, uniting all Jewish workers regardless of the trades in which they were employed or the work that they did. Thus, for example, bakers, actors, musicians, printers, waiters, teamsters, and needle-trade workers were joined together in improving their working conditions and shortening their working day.

Another labor organization, not specifically Jewish but led by a Jew, was the American Federation of Labor, which was founded in 1886. Then known as the AFL, and now part of the AFL-CIO, the Federation was founded by a Jewish immigrant from London, a cigarmaker named Samuel Gompers. Under Samuel Gompers, who with the exception of one year, was its president until his death in 1924, the AFL became a giant of the American labor movement.

In 1900, the International Ladies Garment Workers Union, the ILGWU, was founded for workers in the women's apparel industry. The Amalgamated Clothing Workers of America was formed in 1914, in the men's apparel industry.

These two great unions were predominantly made up of Jews. They were responsible for clearing out the sweatshops and improving the sanitary conditions in the factories. They worked out wage agreements and generally bettered the conditions of the workmen in their industries.

Who were some leading Jewish labor leaders?

Among the outstanding Jewish labor leaders, in addition to Samuel Gompers, were Joseph Barondess, Sidney Hillman, and David Dubinsky.

Sidney Hillman was the head of the Textile Organizing Committee of the CIO. During World War II, he served as adviser to President Franklin D. Roosevelt in matters affecting war production. He left thousands of dollars to the Amalgamated Clothing Workers Union after his death to create the Sidney Hillman Foundation. This foundation today promotes better industrial and race relations and world peace.

David Dubinsky served as president of the International Ladies Garment Workers Union. Although Dubinsky had very little formal education, he had a real understanding of the importance of education. To this day, he has promoted the use of union funds to help educate his union members.

Who were the Jewish Socialists?

The Jewish Socialists believed that eventually, through government changes, the workingman would be the main force in the political and economic life of the government. They hoped that a Socialist state would develop where there would be no private ownership of property, but where the government would own everything, and would control all production and business for the good and welfare of all the people. In this system, since there would be no private owners seeking profit at the expense of the workers, the laborer would find security and happiness.

One of the great influences on the Jewish labor movement was Abraham Cahan, journalist and novelist, who was editor of the *Jewish Daily Forward*. For half a century, Cahan was editor of the paper, and during that time, his voice was raised on behalf of Jewish socialism and labor.

Another important Jewish Socialist leader was Meyer London. In 1914, London was the second Socialist Congressman elected to the House of Representatives. The first Socialist congressman was also a Jew, Victor Berger, an Austrian immigrant who was elected to the House in Milwaukee in 1910.

There were many other Socialist workers who dominated the Jewish labor movement in the early days. Daniel de Leon, a Sephardic Jew from Chicago, headed the Socialist Labor Party. Morris Hillquit, another important figure in American socialism was the Socialist candidate for Mayor of New York City in 1917. Even though he was defeated, Hillquit polled a large number of votes.

What was the purpose of the "Arbeiter Ring"?

In order to continue their contact with the immigrants even outside the sweatshops and factories, the Socialists founded a fraternal order called the "Arbeiter Ring," the Workmen's Circle. The Circle provided cemetery benefits, recreational, and social activities, and educational projects. These included a web of afternoon schools for children of the members. Since the Socialists were not religious, their schools taught Yiddish and Yiddish literature. These subjects took the place of Hebrew and Torah.

The schools created by the Arbeiter Ring today have diminished in size. While in the old days, these schools were opposed to a Jewish homeland in Palestine, today they are pro-Israel. Their antireligious nature has also diminished. Even their staunch support of Yiddish has faltered, for many branches are now English-speaking.

Why was Yiddish called the "mama lashon"?

Yiddish was the language of the Jewish labor movement because it was the language of the Jewish immigrant. Actually, Yiddish was made up of a mixture of languages. Its vocabulary consisted of 70 per cent German, 20 per cent Hebrew and Aramaic, and 10 per cent Slavonic words. Because it was a corruption and mixture of languages, Yiddish was called "jargon."

But it was more than a language. A remarkable literature in Yiddish and a deep attachment to it had grown up. It was the language of instruction in the cheder and the yeshiva. It was the language of the mother's lullaby. It was the language of the everyday businessman, as well as the spiritual language of the rabbi. It was the language of the fable and story. It was the stream in which Jewish culture passed from generation to generation. For this reason Yiddish was known as the "mama lashon," the mother tongue, the one with which the immigrants were most at home.

In American surroundings, Yiddish became even more important. That, and the study of Torah for the religious Jews, were the only legacy and heritage that the immigrants brought from Europe. The language and its peculiar phrases brought fond memories and warm moments to hearts that were often lonesome and melancholy. The Socialists recognized this deep attachment. They revered Yiddish and considered it almost a holy language, and for them its culture and literature replaced the Bible.

What newspapers did the early immigrants read?

The East European was an avid reader, always anxious to hear what was happening in his community and in the world. Many newspapers brought the outside world to his ghetto door. The *Jewish Daily Forward* we have already mentioned. There were also the *Jewish Daily News* and the *Jewish Gazette.* Later the *Jewish Morning Journal* and then the *Day* appeared. For a while, too, there was a Communist daily called the *Freiheit*, or *Freedom.*

These and several other newspapers represented all shades of political, religious, and Zionist thinking. Each reader could select the newspaper that suited him best. In addition to the newspapers, there were countless periodicals, weeklies, and monthlies. Most of them were published in New York City. But Chicago also had such publications. All the larger cities received these newspapers and publications through the mail. These Yiddish newspapers were an important factor in keeping alive Jewish knowledge and culture in particular, as well as furthering the general education of the Jew.

With the decline in the use of Yiddish only two daily newspapers remain, the *Jewish Daily Forward* and the merged *Jewish Day–Morning Journal.*

Why did immigrants enjoy the Yiddish theater?

The Yiddish theater had been founded in Rumania by Abraham Goldfadden in 1877. When the East European came to America, he brought the idea of the Yiddish theater with him. Its center was in New York, where there was a large population to support it.

The plays which the Yiddish theater presented were often translations from the Russian or from the great English dramatist, Shakespeare. Goldfadden's own operettas were presented. There were original plays as well. Jacob Gordin, an outstand-

ing Yiddish playwright, had 70 original and translated plays to his credit.

At a time when there were no movies, radio, or television, the theater was the only form of entertainment for the immigrants. It offered relaxation and a pleasant evening for those who worked so bitterly all day. There, in their own language, the East European immigrants heard, and saw recreated, heroes of the past and heroes of the present. The problems of everyday life in America were portrayed before their eyes. Sometimes the theater offered them an opportunity to laugh at themselves and at the struggles they were going through. But always the theater was a way of escape for the immigrants, freeing them for a while from the constant battle for survival. Alas, today, because there are fewer Jews who speak "mama lashon," the Yiddish theater is almost entirely gone.

What place did the Hebrew language take?

Hebrew among the religious Jews was left for correspondence between rabbis and the very cultured and literate members of their congregations. Responsa, answers on Jewish questions of law, were written in Hebrew. Hebrew as distinguished from Yiddish, the mother tongue, was the Lashon haKodesh, the Holy Tongue, and the immigrant was reluctant to use it in his daily experiences.

The use of Hebrew for daily communication and for literary work became popular with the Maskilim in Europe and spread to the United States as well.

The first Hebrew weekly appeared in 1871 in New York City. Up until the 20th century, its appearances were irregular, and its subscription lists small. But as soon as Zionism grew and took hold of the great public, as soon as interest in the national homeland was reawakened, the Hebrew language too was rejuvenated.

Today Hebrew is to a large extent replacing Yiddish and is being used widely in yeshivoth and Talmud Torahs as a living language. It is also taught in many public high schools and colleges. Among many others, a periodical published in America called *Hadoar* is one of the leading Hebrew weeklies of the world.

What was the purpose of the YMHA?

One movement that began as far back as the middle of the 19th century was the Young Men's Hebrew Association. The first Association was formed in Baltimore by German Jews in 1854. In 1880, there were 50 such associations in different cities of America. By 1902, the first Young Women's Hebrew Association was established.

The YMHA and YWHA were modeled after the Protestant Young Men's Christian Association. Their purpose was to provide social and recreational facilities for young Jewish people. Unfortunately, there was no Jewish content in the program of the "Y." During World War I, there developed the Jewish Community Center movement, which placed more emphasis on educational programming. In many instances today, the Y's and the JCC's have merged.

What was the Kishinev pogrom?

Some of the most important Jewish organizations came into being not to meet the economic and social needs of Jewish immigrants in America, but to protect the Jewish people from unwarranted attacks both abroad and in the United States. In 1903, a wild mob rioted through the Jewish section of the city of Kishinev in the province of Bessarabia in Russia. As a result of their burning and looting, more than 2000 Jewish families were left without home or possessions. More than 600 were injured, and 50 were killed.

This cold-blooded crime was made worse by the fact that it was planned and directed by the government and the Church. Army officers and students for the priesthood led the pogrom. As in the earlier pogroms, the Russian police stood by watching so that no Jew should protect himself.

From time to time, there were additional attacks against Jews in various parts of the world. As early as 1859, in reaction to the Mortara affair, the Board of Delegates of American Israelites had been organized to protect Jewish rights. But when the Board was absorbed in the UAHC, no organization existed to combat this terrible anti-Semitism.

What was the American Jewish Committee?

As a result of the Kishinev massacre, 60 of the ablest Jews of the United States met together. Feeling the need of a spokesman for the Jews whenever such bloody violations of justice occurred, they formed the American Jewish Commitee. At its head stood Judge Mayer Sulzberger, of Philadelphia. Louis Marshall, a brilliant lawyer and community leader of New York, succeeded him. Later, Dr. Cyrus Adler, of the Jewish Theological Seminary, was its President.

These prominent individuals, and others who served with them, like Julius Rosenwald, the famed Chicago philanthropist, were not elected by the Jews at large and their great influence did not come because they represented the masses of Jews. But because they each were so individually important their opinion was heard and respected. The Committee's purpose to fight restrictions against the Jews was fulfilled by these important individuals.

How was the American Jewish Congress formed?

The masses, however, were not completely satisfied by the Committee, especially since the large numbers of Russian Jews were not recognized in its make-up.

In 1916, American Jewry wanted an organization which represented them more democratically. The large Jewish community also wanted an organization which was openly pro-Zionist, in favor of a national Jewish homeland. They were afraid that the American Jewish Committee would not be pro-Zionist. They, therefore, formed a new and more popular organization called the American Jewish Congress. Over 300,000 Jews voted for this Congress which was convened in 1919.

Both these organizations represented American Jewry at the Peace Conference following World War I. The American Jewish Congress continues as a spokesman for a large number of American Jews until this very day. The greatest leader of the Congress was that ardent Zionist and unusual personality, Dr. Stephen Wise, a Reform rabbi. Dr. Wise was its president until 1930.

Why was the Kehillah formed?

Soon after the American Jewish Committee was formed, an article by the Police Commissioner of New York, Theodore Bingham, on the subject of crime in the city, aroused the Jewish community. The report, which appeared in 1908, stated that the "Russians," the name by which he called the Jews, had committed 50 per cent of the city's crimes, even though these "Russians" were only 25 per cent of the population.

The American Jewish Committee forced an admission from Bingham that there was no truth to support his accusation. Later investigation proved that only 7 per cent of the criminals were "Russians." And of this small percentage many were merely guilty of peddling, or trading on Sunday, which were indeed minor infractions.

But the excitement that had been caused by Bingham's slur on the morality of the immigrants did not die down. In 1909, the Jews of New York formed a local body to unite the thousands of different landsmanschaften, congregations, schools, and other associations to which the million and a half Jews of the city belonged. The organization created a vast Jewish community organization, which was given the name "Kehillah," after the old European self-governing Jewish committee.

Just as the American Jewish Committee, and later, the American Jewish Congress, were to operate on the broad national and international levels, the Kehillah was to be represent the Jews of New York "with respect to all local matters of Jewish interest." As such, it became the New York branch of the American Jewish Committee.

Why did the Kehillah fail?

The Kehillah concerned itself with many religious questions, with improving Jewish education and with making up-to-date studies of the Jewish population and needs. It helped to care for the underprivileged and the crippled. It even arbitrated between employer and employee.

A Board of Rabbis was appointed to regulate Jewish marriage, divorce, and matters of kashruth. In addition, the Board of Rabbis supervised the rites of milah, circumcision, throughout New York.

The Kehillah was accepted as the spokesman for the Jews of New York. It acted in matters of Sunday observance laws and other legislation that affected Jews.

At the head of this great superbody, stood a fiery orator and dreamer, Rabbi Judah L. Magnes, a brother-in-law of the famous Louis Marshall. Unfortunately, the Jews of New York, their organizations and their points of view, were too many to be held together by one organization. There was no common meeting ground for Orthodox, Reform, and Conservatives; for Socialists, agnostics and Zionists; for employers and employees and their numerous social agencies.

The Kehillah lasted for almost 13 years, and then quietly fell into disuse. Dr. Magnes later became Rabbi of Temple Emanu-El, the leading Reform congregation in New York, and after that was named the first President of the Hebrew University in Israel.

What was the work of the Bureau of Jewish Education?

One important aspect of the Kehillah left its mark on the city of New York, and that was the Bureau of Jewish Education, headed by Dr. Samson Benderly. Dr. Benderly was a native of Palestine, who had been a Baltimore physician before coming to New York. His Bureau attempted to set high standards and to provide good textbooks and qualified teachers for the Talmud Torahs. He also sought to give more importance to the study of Hebrew and Hebrew literature in the Talmud Torahs.

Benderly dreamed of organizing a Hebrew High School for graduates of Talmud Torahs, for he saw that they needed more training in order to learn of their Jewish background. In later years, he formed the Marshallia, a Hebrew high school named after Marshall, for just such a purpose. The Marshallia and another high school organized along the same lines, known as the Herzliah School, still exist today.

Benderly was an able and energetic man, but he was hampered a great deal. He was considered not religious enough by Orthodox Jews, and too Zionistic by the radicals. He succeeded, however, in giving dignity to the profession of Jewish education. He inspired some excellent men to enter the field of Jewish education as principals, or as heads of bureaus of education in other cities.

The Bureau of Jewish Education was absorbed by the Jewish Education Committee in 1939. The JEC, as it is called, is now the central agency for Jewish education in New York City.

What is the work of Federation?

In 1874, the United Hebrew Charities was formed. It was an excellent idea, for it organized the charitable giving of the Jews of New York City. By giving one donation to the United Hebrew Charities, many needs and charities would be helped. The city of Boston followed the lead set by New York, and the idea soon spread to other cities and communities. When it was formed, the Kehillah absorbed the functions of the United Hebrew Charities.

When the Kehillah deteriorated, a new organization called the Federation of Jewish Charities and Philanthropies came into being on an independent basis. Federation, as it is known, has had many favorable results, for it unites all the fund raising, and then efficiently and fairly distributes the funds to its member agencies. Today, there are such federations or welfare funds in almost every city in the United States. Once a year these federations conduct a campaign among all the Jews of the community. Then the governing board of the federation allocates the funds. In New York, for example, there are 117 hospitals, nursing homes, camps for underprivileged children, orphan institutions, and others who receive more than $25 million dollars yearly from the Federation. The New York Federation also supports the Jewish Education Committee.

When the tragedy of two world wars engulfed the world, the American Jewish community was already well defined. There were synagogues, educational institutions, social and welfare organizations, and Jewish defense committees.

The wars were to bring additional changes in the American Jewish scene. The two most important were the emergence of the long-hoped-for Jewish homeland, and an upsurge of devotion to Judaism which created more synagogues and a great number of new yeshivoth all over America.

American Jews were to see the emergence of the golden thread of Torah in their lives once again.

Things to Remember

1. How were Jews active in labor organizations?
2. Why is Yiddish still known as the "mama lashon"?
3. Why was the American Jewish Committee formed? What is its purpose?
4. Why was the American Jewish Congress formed? What is its purpose?
5. What are some of the remaining benefits of the Kehillah?
6. What does Federation do?

Things to Think About

1. Do you think that American Jews are missing something by their lack of knowledge of Yiddish? Give reasons for your answer.
2. Do you think a Kehillah is a good idea? Would we have success with it today? Discuss this fully in class.
3. Do you think an untrue accusation could be made today by a police commissioner against any minority group? What would you do if you read such an accusation? If you wouldn't do anything, how would you feel about it? Discuss fully.

UNIT THREE:

THE WORLD AT WAR

We are getting closer and closer to the present time, to "Now." Let us look backward to see what had been happening in Europe since the time of Abraham Lincoln.

While America was becoming more unified and devoted as a nation to its new way of life, democracy, European countries too were becoming more unified. Some time after the death of Napoleon, France became a republic, a form of government which she maintains to this day. The German states, together with Prussia, united to make a strong, powerful nation called Germany, which was ruled by an emperor known as the Kaiser.

Italy, too, had been only a collection of small states. The king of one of these Italian states, King Victor Emanuel of Sardinia, helped by his Prime Minister, Cavour, and a popular hero named Garibaldi, united all the Italian states into one country.

As Europe was becoming better organized, new inventions were perfected, and these came to revolutionize the world. It seems hard to imagine that before 1800 there were no telephones, telegraphs, steamboats, steam railroads, electric lights, automobiles, radios, airplanes, motion pictures, or television. All these things have been developed in the last 150 years.

Canada
United States
Belgium
England
France
Germany
Turkey
Russia
Japan
South Africa
Australia
New Zealand
THE BALKANS
AUSTRIA-HUNGARY
BOSNIA
Sarajevo
RUMANIA
MONTENEGRO
BULGARIA
Constantinople
ITALY
ALBANIA
Gallipoli
GREECE
TURKEY
OTTOMAN EMPIRE
WORLD WAR I
ALLIES *Italy left Central Powers and joined Allies in 1915.*
CENTRAL POWERS
NEUTRAL COUNTRIES

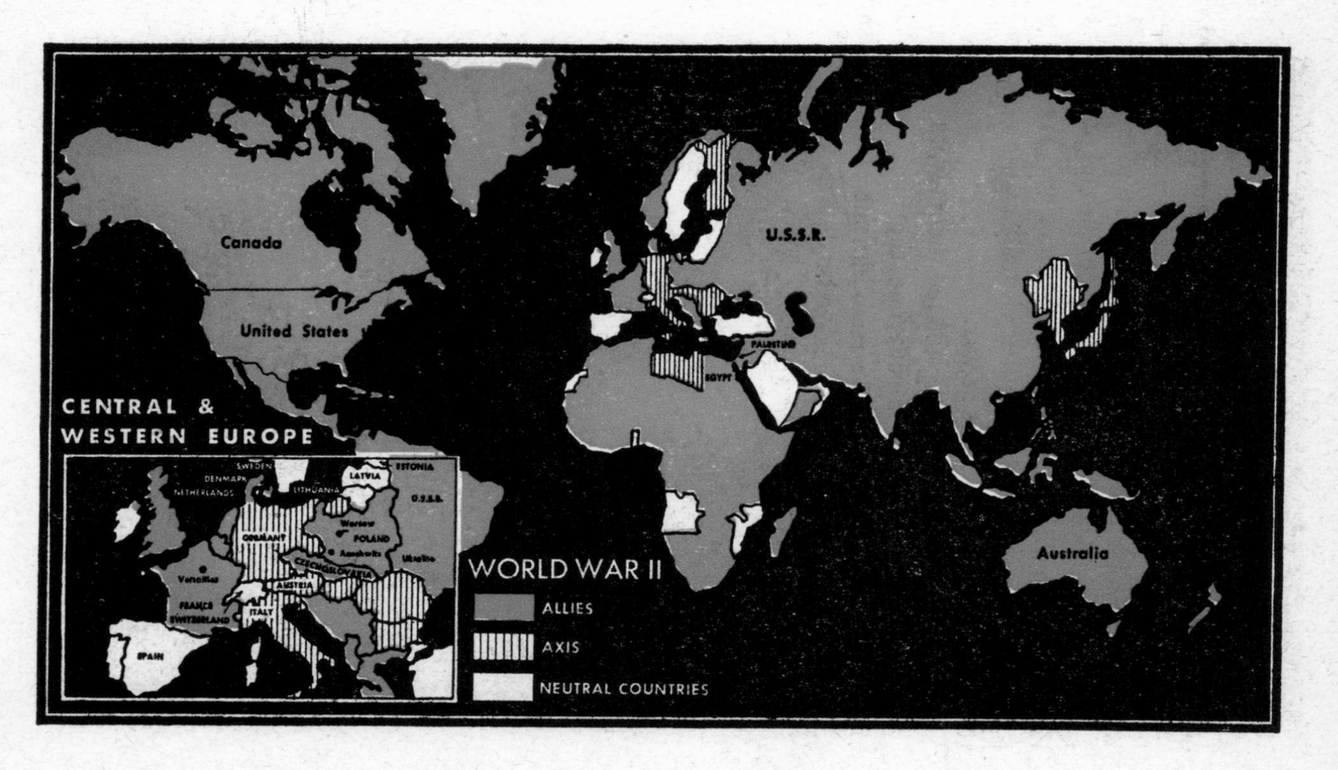
Canada
United States
U.S.S.R.
PALESTINE
EGYPT
Australia
CENTRAL &
WESTERN EUROPE
SWEDEN
DENMARK
NETHERLANDS
LITHUANIA
LATVIA
ESTONIA
U.S.S.R.
GERMANY
Warsaw
POLAND
Auschwitz
Ukraine
CZECHOSLOVAKIA
Versailles
AUSTRIA
FRANCE
SWITZERLAND
ITALY
SPAIN
WORLD WAR II
ALLIES
AXIS
NEUTRAL COUNTRIES

Watt's steam engine, Fulton's steamboat, Morse's telegraph, Marconi's radio, and of course, Thomas Edison's electric lights completely changed peoples' ways of living, all over the world.

You would think that all the improvements and inventions would help people to live better with each other, to understand each other's problems better. Instead, from the end of the 19th century on, the world teetered on the brink of war. War finally broke out, in a conflict so great that virtually *all* the world, for the first time in history, was at war.

Through this war, the Jews suffered the most, as you will soon see. But through their suffering, the most wonderful dream of all—the dream of the establishment of the Jewish national homeland—came to be realized.

CHAPTER TWELVE

WORLD WAR I

There was a small country in Europe called Serbia, now part of Yugoslavia. It bordered on the larger country of Austria-Hungary. There was constant strife between Serbia and Austria-Hungary because of the way that Serbian people who lived in Austria-Hungary were treated. When Prince Ferdinand of Austria was shot by a zealous Serbian patriot, Austria declared war on Serbia.

This declaration of war was made on July 28, 1914—and the fighting spread as quickly as fire on a dry plain. Russia, as might have been expected, took the side of Serbia because most of the Serbian people were Slavs, like the Russians, and because Russia had long been a rival of the Austrian Empire. Germany took the side of its old ally, Austria. France was an ally of Russia, and so the Germans, expecting that France would soon enter the war, and not wanting to be caught between France on one side and Russia on the other, marched their armies through Belgium in order to strike at France. Soon England entered the war on the side of France, Belgium, Russia, and Serbia—the group known as the Allies. Then Bulgaria, Turkey, and Italy entered the bloody fray on the side of the Central Powers—Germany and Austria-Hungary. All Europe, the British dominions in all parts of the world, and later the United States, were involved in the war. Because virtually the whole world was caught up in the fire it was called the World War. Later historians renamed it The First World War, or World War I.

Why did America enter the war?

In 1917, almost three years after the war had begun, the United States entered the combat. It did so because German submarines were sinking American ships on the high seas and drowning American citizens. The people of America were also outraged by the cruelties of the Germans against those they conquered. Finally, therefore, the United States entered the war on the side of the Allies against the Central Powers. Italy, originally one of the Central Powers, did an about-face in the middle of the war and joined the Allies.

In a short time, America had sent two million soldiers across the ocean. Under General Pershing, they fought nobly and bravely. On November 11, 1918, an Armistice was finally declared. For many years, November 11 was celebrated as Armistice Day, the time when fighting stopped on both sides. Today, Armistice Day has been changed to Veterans' Day, when America honors the soldiers who fought in all its wars.

The war was over, but suffering, pain, and grief were not. The people who suffered most were the Jews.

What was the Russian Revolution?

During World War I, millions of soldiers were killed and wounded. Billions of dollars were spent for armaments and instruments of death. American soldiers believed they were fighting a "war to end all wars" and to make the "world safe for democracy."

But even while these slogans appeared in every newspaper in America, Russia underwent a Revolution that was destined to change the political face of the world, breed new wars, and make the world *unsafe* for democracy. In 1917, the Russian people, decisively defeated by the Germans, rose up to kill the czar and the ruling nobles of his court, and set up a new type of government. The new government was soon taken over by the most extreme group of revolutionaries, called Bolsheviks. The new Bolshevik rulers, intent upon establishing Soviet Communism throughout all Russia, made a separate peace with the Germans and withdrew from the war.

During the seesawing battles that took place in the czar's territory until the collapse of the Russian armies in 1917, the Jews suffered terribly. Three-quarters of the Jews of the world lived in that part of the continent where the battles raged furiously—in Russia, Poland, Rumania, and Austria. Between the Russian and the German and Austrian occupation and counter-occupation, they were exposed to more than their share of atrocities.

Both the Russians and the Germans confiscated property and possessions, food and clothes. Since the Jews lived in areas that changed hands frequently, each side accused the Jews of espionage, treason, smuggling, and of welcoming the other side. Whole Jewish communities were sent by the Russians to Siberia, in boxcars or on foot. Thousands died on the way.

How did the Jews help the Allies?

From the start, the sympathies of most Jews, like those of most Americans, had been in favor of the Allies, although there certainly was no great Jewish love for the Russians. When the czar was toppled in the Russian Revolution, and when three weeks later Congress declared war, the Jews of the United States were the strongest supporters of the American decision.

The Jews suffered more than their share of casualties and contributed more than their proportionate share of soldiers. During the course of the war, a million and a half Jews were actually under arms on both sides, in addition to the many who did nursing, welfare, and volunteer work.

Approximately a quarter of a million Jews served in the American armed forces. Among them were 100 colonels, 500 majors, and thousands of lower-ranking officers. Two Jews were generals in the Army. One, Milton I. Foreman, was also the first National Commander of the American Legion.

The ranking Jewish officer in the Navy was Rear Admiral Joseph Strauss. Brigadier General Charles H. Lauchheimer was the ranking Jewish officer in the Marines. Jewish military men received a large number of citations, medals, and commendations. Three were awarded the highest honor of all, the Congressional Medal of Honor.

One of these three, Benjamin Kaufman, with one hand smashed by a bullet, single-handedly silenced a German machine-gun nest and took its crew prisoner. In 1941, Kaufman became National Commander of the Jewish War Veterans of the United States.

Sergeant William Sawelson, lying in his shelter, heard a wounded man cry for water. Leaving his shelter, he crawled

through heavy machine-gun fire to give the wounded man some water. He had returned to his shell hole to obtain more water and was on his way back to the wounded man when he was killed. Sawelson received the Congressional Medal of honor posthumously.

In the Russian army, where they were not allowed to hold officers' rank, almost 700,000 Jews served.

There were also many Jewish generals and other high-ranking officers in the French, Belgian, and British armies. In the British Commonwealth forces, the ranking Jewish officer was Sir John Monash, a lieutenant general and commander of the entire Australian Expeditionary Force in France.

Were there Jews in the armies of the Central Powers?

We have excellent records of Jewish service in the German army because anti-Semitic members of the German Parliament charged that Jews were not doing their duty in the war effort. The Prussian Minister of War had a survey made, and discovered to his chagrin that there were 100,000 Jews in the army. This was a much higher percentage of war service than was found in any other population group.

In the Austro-Hungarian armies there were more than 300,000 Jews including, again, high-ranking officers and generals.

Of the 100,000 Jews who fought in the German army, 28,000 were killed; and a similar proportion lost their lives in the other armies. This means that more than one-fourth of the Jews in the armies never returned to their homes!

How did Zionism contribute to the Allies' victory?

Almost at the outset of the war, battles broke out in the Palestine area. The Suez Canal in Egypt was a vital strategic waterway and became a major target which both sides wanted. Palestine itself, which was a Turkish possession, was anxiously desired by the British because of the important position it held as the gateway to the Middle East. There, the military blockade, which interrupted the flow of exports and incoming foodstuffs, caused the Jews to suffer terribly. At the same time, the Turks plagued the Jewish settlers with the charges that they were plotting to set up an independent Zionist government and that they were loyal to the Allies.

When the English campaign against the Turks in Palestine began, Jews saw the opportunity to make a specific contribution to the war effort, in their own name and identity as Jews, and not merely as citizens of one country or another. They presented a plan to the British to form a Jewish Legion to participate in the battle of Palestine.

Foremost in urging the plan were two great Zionists, Trumpeldor and Jabotinsky.

What was the Zion Mule Corps?

A large number of Jews had been exiled from Palestine by the Turks because they were citizens of an enemy power, Russia. Many of these exiles found refuge in Egypt. Among them was Joseph Trumpeldor, a great Zionist leader. Trumpeldor had lost his right arm in the Russo-Japanese War of 1904. His heroism was so great that the Russians had made a rare exception in his case. They promoted him to the rank of captain, even though Jews were not allowed to be officers in the Russian army.

Trumpeldor and Vladimir Jabotinsky, another gifted Zionist, brilliant writer, and bold soldier, presented the idea of the Jewish Legion to the British.

The British were not too anxious to help the Zionist cause, for they saw that a Jewish legion might eventually fight for a Jewish Zionist state. They rejected the offer, much as they needed help. Instead, the British permitted the Jews to organize a supply corps to carry necessary equipment to British soldiers engaged in the Battle of Gallipoli. The Zionists reluctantly accepted this proposition because, while it did not permit them to serve as active soldiers, at least they were helping. About six hundred men made up what was called the Zion Mule Corps.

The language of conversation and command in the Corps was Hebrew, and their flag was the blue-and-white flag with the Mogen David, the Star of David. During its short period of service, one-tenth of the Corps sustained casualties. Their commander praised the Zionist force as courageous, intelligent, and brave.

However, in the spring of 1916, the campaign was given up, Gallipoli lost, and the Zion Mule Corps disbanded.

What was the Jewish Brigade?

Jabotinsky and Trumpeldor were not content to remain inactive. They began to agitate again for the formation of a Jewish force. Over great opposition, even by some English Jews, the British War Office finally authorized the formation of a Jewish Brigade. Jabotinsky had been recruiting volunteers among the Russian Jews in England and America. Two other great Zionist leaders, whom we will meet again later, were active in the enlistment drive in the United States. They were David ben Gurion and Yitzchak ben Zvi.

Two battalions, numbering about five thousand volunteers, were soon formed to join another battalion of Palestinian Jews. They were all placed under the command of Gen. Edmund Allenby in Palestine. Jabotinsky himself was a lieutenant in one of the battalions.

The Jewish Brigade defeated the Turks at a crucial spot near the Jordan River, opening up the way for a great British victory. This victory ended in the final rout of the Turkish and German forces in Palestine, and led to the Turkish surrender.

The war was over before another Jewish battalion training

in Canada could be brought into active service. But the Jewish people, through the Jewish Brigade, had made a specific contribution to the Allies' military victory.

Their war service and the experience they received in handling arms were to be of great value to the Jews of Palestine in the important years ahead.

What were the three major relief organizations?

The Jewish soldiers who served in the war, in every Allied country, were given the privilege of bearing arms and defending themselves, or at least dying for a cause to which they were pledged. The civilian population was less fortunate.

All people in the way of moving armies were brutally dealt with, but the Jews suffered the worst. They were killed, maimed, beaten, and starved in Russia, in Poland, in Germany, and in Austria. Even in Palestine, the blockade was causing them untold hardships. Henry Morgenthau, the American Ambassador to Turkey, alerted American Jews to the desperate needs of the 85,000 Jews in the Holy Land who were dying of starvation and the lack of even the most elementary necessities.

In Europe, the situation of the Jews seemed hopeless. Before the war, immigration to the United States had offered them a measure of relief. With the coming of the war, that avenue of escape was cut off. And so the Jews suffered miserably, bound by the cruelty of both sides, and caught by the cross fire of both armies, Russian and German.

The appeals for help that kept coming from the war zones became greater and more piteous with each day that the conflict lasted. The first group to respond was the East European Orthodox Jewish community in America. More than any other Jewish group, these immigrants knew what hunger, torture, and persecution meant. Many of them still felt the memory of the Cossack's whip on their own backs. They still heard the fiendish cry of the Russian and Polish peasants as they attacked a Jewish community.

Three months after the war broke out in Europe, the Central Committee for the Relief of Jewish War Sufferers was organized. At its head stood Leon Kamaiky, publisher of the Orthodox *Jewish Daily News*. Among its leaders were the prominent Orthodox rabbis of New York.

A short time later, the American Jewish Committee formed the American Jewish Relief Committee, with Louis Marshall as its chairman.

The Socialist Jews organized the People's Relief Committee the following year.

These three organizations started to raise money with great vigor and personal sacrifice on the part of the contributors.

What was the Joint Distribution Committee?

Distributing the large sums of money to needy areas was a difficult matter. It was necessary to have one united agency to deal with the foreign governments, in order to eliminate duplication, prevent omission, and present a united front to the world.

In November, 1914, one month after the Central Committee had begun its work, the American Jewish Joint Distribution Committee came into being. By 1915 it had taken over the task of fund-raising as well, so that the other three organizations were no longer necessary.

Who were some Jews active in the JDC?

Responding with its usual generosity, the Jewish community contributed amounts that had never seemed possible. At a single appeal one evening in New York, almost $1 million was given in cash and in jewels contributed by warm-hearted women. Chicago and Philadelphia each raised half a million. Julius Rosenwald alone offered $1 million towards the $10 million goal set in 1917. So it was throughout the country and throughout Canada as well.

The most outstanding Jews of the United States volunteered to serve the needs of the JDC. Its first chairman was Felix Warburg. He was assisted by the renowned philanthropist Jacob H. Schiff, the leading member of the American Jewish Committee, and by Jonah B. Wise, son of the founder of Reform Judaism in America.

In addition, a well-known Orthodox layman, Harry Fischel, one of the strong supporters of RIETS, served on the Committee. With him were prominent Orthodox rabbis—Rabbi Meyer Berlin, Rabbi M. Z. Margolies, and Rabbi Leo Jung.

Rabbi Aaron Teitelbaum and Dr. Judah Magnes were among those who made many trips overseas on behalf of the JDC.

What was the work of the JDC after the war?

The JDC was highly successful in its wartime work of relief. But its function did not end with the cessation of hostilities. After the war, the Committee had to find homes for thousands of refugees and to help the Jews reestablish themselves economically. It provided medical aid to the sick, and even founded schools. It extended loans, taught new trades, encouraged cooperatives and farm settlements, and did all that was necessary to rehabilitate the victims of war.

The JDC has remained to this day one of the outstanding achievements of the American Jewish community. It was the first organization that united every Jew of every shade of religious, social, and cultural background. How powerful is the threat of disaster!

What was the work of the Jewish Welfare Board?

Large numbers of Jewish servicemen enlisted in World War I, and there was need to provide for their welfare. In 1917, only a few days after the country entered the war, the National Jewish Welfare Board was formed.

At home and abroad, at all military installations, the Jewish Welfare Board provided for the religious, personal, and recreational needs of the Jewish servicemen. It held religious services for them no matter where they were stationed. It gave them an extra bit of happiness when a Jewish holiday came around. It gave them a place where they could meet other Jewish servicemen and relax in a pleasant atmosphere. The Board also became the official body to certify chaplains for service in the different branches of America's defense forces. The JWB joined other religious groups to make up the USO, the United Service Organization for National Defense.

After the war, the JWB assumed other important duties. The Division of Religious Activities has carried on the military work for the Board through World War II, the Korean War, and at peacetime installations as well.

What did the Jews contribute on the home front?

The man behind the gun cannot be victorious unless there is another man behind him to furnish the necessary war materials, foodstuffs, uniforms, medical supplies, and machinery.

Jews on the home front during World War I made as vital a contribution as the men in the field. The most important single agency in the United States at that time was the War Industries Board. It was given the task of improving and expanding industrial production for the war effort.

At the head of the War Industries Board was Bernard Baruch, a well-known financier, who since has become adviser to Presidents, and the "elder statesman" of America. Among the six other members of the Board, were the powerful president of the American Federation of Labor, Samuel Gompers, and Julius Rosenwald, head of Sears, Roebuck and Company, the largest mail-order house in the world.

Another Jew, Professor Felix Frankfurter, of Harvard University, later Supreme Court Justice, was called upon to act as special assistant to the Secretary of War.

In 1918, Eugene Meyer, Jr., became manager of the War Finance Corporation, which helped finance the business organizations that produced vital war materials.

A leading advertising executive, Albert Lasker, was appointed by President Harding right after the war to be chairman of the U.S. Shipping Board, which reorganized the American merchant fleet.

The Jewish people, like other Americans, had put all their efforts into winning the war. When World War I ended, people everywhere hoped and prayed that there would be no further wars. They still believed that it had been "the war to end wars."

But 20 years later, another and even more horrible war broke out.

Things to Remember

1. What was the immediate cause of World War I?
2. How did Jabotinsky and Trumpeldor help the war effort?
3. How was the Joint Distribution Committee developed? What is its work?
4. How was the National Jewish Welfare Board developed? What is its work?
5. The following men contributed to the United States war effort. Tell in what capacity. Baruch, Frankfurter, Meyer, Lasker.

Things to Think About

1. It has occasionally been said that American Jews have too many organizations. Do you agree or disagree with this statement? Explain why.
2. Jabotinsky and Trumpeldor were most anxious to have a Jewish Brigade during the war. Do you think this was a good idea? Why? Why not?

3. Your text says that the JDC, because it united all Jews, was one of the outstanding accomplishments of the American Jewish community. Why was the JDC able to succeed where others failed? Why is it an important accomplishment to unite the Jews?

CHAPTER THIRTEEN

THE DREAM OF A JEWISH HOMELAND

World War I and the years leading up to it had brought frightful disaster upon the Jewish communities of Europe. Yet, out of the heartbreak following the May Laws in Russia had come fresh hope for the Jewish people. It was the new-old dream of establishing a Jewish homeland—a land which would welcome Jews from all over the world and allow them to live in freedom, dignity, and independence. The war and its tragedies resulted in bringing the dream nearer to reality.

Who were some of the early Zionists?

The Russian pogroms and persecutions helped the dream of Palestine become real. The Haskalah and the rebirth of the Hebrew language, which we studied about last year, helped the Zionist dream express itself. Many of the early Maskilim, as they revived the ancient Hebrew language, began to think of returning to their own land, where Hebrew would become the national language.

In 1881, Dr. Leo Pinsker, a Russian physician, wrote a book

called *Auto-Emancipation.* "Auto" means "self," and the book urged that Jews should free themselves by seeking the establishment of a Jewish state.

Before him, a German, Moses Hess, in his book *Rome and Jerusalem* had urged similar action.

In England, even a Christian writer, the famous "George Eliot," had come to the same realization. In her book, *Daniel Deronda*, George Eliot had expressed the need for a home for the Jewish people.

And in America, even as early as 1825, Mordecai Manuel Noah was agitating for a Jewish state, where Jews could live in peace.

Many thousands of Jews had been waiting for a miracle to take place, for God to bring them into the Promised Land. But rabbis like Shmuel Mohliver and Zvi Hirsch Kalischer did not believe that Orthodox Jews should just sit back and wait for a miracle to happen. They began to write books and pamphlets and traveled from hamlet to hamlet and town to town urging Jews to settle in the Holy Land.

How did the Dreyfus affair help Zionism?

But it was not until the coming of Theodor Herzl that Zionism was launched in an organized and purposeful manner.

Herzl was a Jewish Viennese newspaper man who had been sent to Paris by his editors to report the trial of another Jew, Capt. Alfred Dreyfus. Dreyfus, a captain in the French army, had been accused of treason. In 1895, the year of this trial, he was adjudged guilty and sent to prison.

Impartial observers at the trial were convinced that Dreyfus was innocent. Herzl, like the others, felt that this was an act of anti-Semitism rather than an act of justice. He watched the after-effects of the trial, the heated and frenzied mobs who marched through the cities of France shouting "Death to the

Jews." He saw that, regardless of whether Dreyfus was innocent or guilty, the people were condemning all Jews for the alleged misdeed of one of their kind. Here it was doubly frightening, for it was obvious that Dreyfus was not even guilty in the first place.

Herzl pondered the problem. Dreyfus, like himself, was completely removed from the Jewish religion and from his fellow Jews. And yet Dreyfus could not escape the hatred and viciousness of anti-Semitism. Herzl came to the conclusion that it really did not matter whether you were a Jew in Russia or in France. It did not matter whether you wore a beard and were steeped in Torah, or whether you were in Army uniform and were as nonobservant as a Christian. In the eyes of the anti-Semite, you were always a Jew, to be hounded and persecuted.

The howling of the French mobs for Dreyfus' blood, echoed and reechoed in Herzl's brain. He who had never been observant, who had never even identified himself with Jewish causes, who knew nothing about Judaism, now began to think only of the Jews. He could not rest.

In a small, slender volume which he called *The Jewish State*, Herzl wrote that the only solution to the Jewish problem was the establishment of such a state. Unacquainted with Jewish history, Herzl thought that his was a new idea. He did not know that Hess, Pinsker, Mohliver, Kalischer, and others had written so much about it. He did not know about the "Chovevei Zion," the Lovers of Zion, which through its many branches throughout Russia, had already helped settle small groups of immigrants in Palestine.

What was political Zionism?

Nevertheless, Herzl made an unusual impression. The early Zionists had aimed their writings at the Jews, and hardly thought the non-Jews would help them. In addition, they had never thought in terms of a free, independent Jewish state. Herzl went one step further.

Through his newspaper work, Herzl had experience in dealing with diplomats and statesmen. He know that Zionism could become a reality only through political recognition and with the help of the governments of the world. Zionism now took on an important adjective. It became "political" Zionism —because it was aimed at the establishment of a political Jewish state, with the aid and consent of the nations of the world. And the work was directed not only towards organizing the Jews but towards influencing world governments and public opinion as well.

Why did some oppose Herzl?

Herzl's energy and enthusiasm on behalf of the new Jewish state were not shared by all Jews.

The Jews of Western Europe were afraid that action for a Jewish state might raise doubts as to their own loyalty to the countries in which they lived. They were afraid that it would raise the question of "dual allegiance."

The leaders of Reform Jewry objected, because this was a challenge to their principles as expressed in the Pittsburgh Platform, in which they denied a return to the Jewish homeland. They showed their opposition in a tragic way. Herzl had finally succeeded in persuading the Zionists of the world to meet together in an international conference. The first world meeting of the Zionist movement was scheduled to be held in Munich, Germany. But the Rabbinical Association of Germany, a group of Reform rabbis, vigorously protested against the meeting and against holding it in Germany. Because of this, they have gone down in history under the name of the "Protest Rabbis." In this protest, they were seconded by a unanimous resolution of the CCAR, the American Reform rabbinate, as well.

Many Orthodox Jews also objected to Herzl. Even though rabbis like Rabbi Zvi Hirsch Kalischer and Rabbi Shmuel Mohliver had been urging the movement upon them, some Orthodox Jews still held back. They believed that the Holy Land would be given to the Jews only with the coming of the Messiah.

Even some of the Chovevei Zion, the settlers of Palestine, were reluctant to support Herzl. They were afraid that his emphasis on political Zionism, on establishing a state, would interfere with their plans for setting up colonies in Palestine in the meantime.

What differences did the Congresses face?

Despite opposition, Herzl's ideas continued to attract followers. His determination and personal magnetism electrified the world and won thousands of Jews to the cause. The international conference was rescheduled, and in 1897 the first meeting of world Zionists was held in Basle, Switzerland. This meeting was called the First Zionist Congress. For six years, the Congress continued to meet annually. After that, its meetings were called every two years.

More than two hundred representatives came from Europe, Palestine, and America to attend the historic meeting. It was an exciting moment for all Jewry. Looking back on that occasion, Herzl said, "It was at Basle that I created the Jewish State."

However, not even all Zionists had the same point of view. At the first and later congresses, several different factions were to be seen.

The representatives of Western Europe were deeply concerned with establishing a Jewish homeland. But they were willing to accept such a homeland in any part of the world that would be given to them. They were called Territorialists.

The East European Jews would hear of no other location for the homeland than in Palestine. They knew that Palestine was the Holy Land, the Promised Land, which was interwoven into the very life, ideas, culture, and history of the Jewish people. A large number of the East European delegation were members of a religious group called the "Mizrachi." Under the leadership of Rabbi Yitzchok Yaacov Reines, they also agitated for a homeland in Palestine but insisted that the new state should observe all the religious laws of the Torah and the Talmud.

There were also Socialist Zionists, called the "Poalei Zion," who saw in the creation of the homeland a chance to test their ideas of Socialist living.

Another group followed the ideals of Ahad Ha'Am. Ahad Ha'Am, which means in Hebrew "One of the People," was the pen name for Asher Ginzberg, a profound thinker of the early Zionist movement. He preached that the Jews were not ready for a state with all the political, military, and economic requirements of such an organization. What they needed first was to build up their cultural and spiritual strength, to build up the national character of the Jew. This did not require a state, Ahad ha'Am argued. This required a spiritual center which would be like a university for all the people. Palestine should be such a spiritual center, and from it would go forth new inspiration to all Jews. After that, it would be natural to establish a Jewish state.

In effect, Ahad Ha'Am said, every Jew could live in two countries. One would be the country in which he resides and which controls his political and economic life. The other, Palestine, should control his spiritual and national life. Eventually, these two concepts could merge and become one in the Jewish state.

What did the Zionist Congress accomplish?

As the Congresses continued to meet regularly, most of the problems were ironed out. The Territorialists, headed by the great English author Israel Zangwill, were defeated, and Ahad ha'Am's followers were absorbed by the others. The major question was resolved when the Congress adopted a platform which stated that Zionism was pledged to the creation of a Jewish homeland, to be established only in Palestine. This is called the Basle Platform.

The Congresses then organized a Colonial Bank to finance the work of the proposed new nation and state. Through a proposal of Hermann Schapira, the Jewish National Fund was established. The purpose of the fund was to buy land in Palestine, to help settle immigrants, and to help drain marshes and swamps.

Now that machinery had been organized to keep the movement alive, Herzl began to engage in diplomatic negotiations to acquire the land for the homeland.

In quick succession, Herzl met with the German Kaiser and his Secretary of State, the Turkish Sultan, the English Foreign Minister, King Victor Emanuel of Italy, Pope Pius X, and ranking ministers of the czar. Unfortunately, none of these men gave any positive promise of help.

Why does Herzl have a "place of honor" in history?

Wherever Herzl went, he was greeted by Zionists as if he had been the Messiah. In his audiences with royalty and government officials, he was given the deepest and highest respect. But these audiences were frustrating, for they brought no fruit, nor did they achieve the desired goals.

Between preparation for the Congresses, the international travels and intrigues, the search for funds and the soliciation of support, and the countless worries for the success of his movement, Herzl's strength was soon sapped. On July 3, 1904, at the age of 44, Theodor Herzl died of a heart attack.

Max Nordau, one of his dear friends and supporters, eulogized Herzl as one of the greatest Jews of all time. Herzl had,

Nordau said, "set a broken people upright, had given it hope, and had shown it its path. Although he had not seen the attainment of his goal, the nobility of his dream and the purity of his aim assured him a place of honor in history."

How did Zionism continue?

By the time Herzl died, the Zionist movement was no longer merely a wishful hope in the hearts of some Jews. It was definitely established as a world-wide organization with adherents in every country. In the United States, the Federation of American Zionists had been organized in 1898. By 1918, it had changed its name to the Zionist Organization of America, and brought a great deal of support for the work of the Congresses.

Herzl was succeeded by great and dedicated Zionists like David Wolffsohn, Max Nordau, Menachem Ussishkin, Max Mandelstamm, Arthur Ruppin, and others.

Colonization went on in Palestine. By the outbreak of World War I, there were 43 colonies in the Holy Land. Instruction in agriculture was being given to the settlers. Schools and medical facilities were provided.

Who was Eliezer ben Yehuda?

One man dedicated his life to seeing that Hebrew should become the language of the new state. His name was Eliezer ben Yehuda. Through his fanatic devotion to the idea of Hebrew as a living language, Hebrew was rejuvenated. He established the "Va-ad haLashon," the Academy of the Hebrew Language, and composed a "Milon," a dictionary tracing the sources of the Hebrew language and creating many new Hebrew words for the situations that were arising daily in Palestine. Slowly, the settlers in Palestine begin to speak Hebrew, to drop the jargon of the Diaspora and to accept the language of the new state.

Plans were also being made to build a Hebrew University, to develop the Hebrew language and culture. The Jewish community in Palestine was preparing itself to become a cultural center as Ahad Ha'Am had urged, even as it was becoming a center of actual Jewish living.

World War II held up the progress of Jewish colonization in Palestine, but the diplomatic work begun by Herzl continued.

What was the contribution of Chaim Weizmann?

Among the outstanding leaders of Zionist thought was Dr. Chaim Weizmann. Weizmann had been born in Russia, but left that country to follow his interest in the study of chemistry. Although he was a brilliant and imaginative chemist and could have won fame in that field alone, Weizmann chose to dedicate his entire life to Zionism. Having seen the pitiful unhappiness of Jewish life in Russia, and convinced that a Jewish homeland was the only hope for Jewish survival, Weizmann began to eat, sleep, and drink Zionism. He became active in the Zionist Congresses, and soon stood out as the successor to Herzl as the symbol of Zionism.

In Zionist circles, Weizmann was the chief defender of "political" Zionism as against those who were in favor of practical Zionism. Political Zionism, as we have seen, held that it was not enough to colonize Palestine. Its followers felt that Zionists should exert all their efforts to get political assurances from the great powers that they would recognize a Jewish homeland and give it status. Without such assurances even the establishment of many colonies would mean nothing.

The "practical" Zionists had no patience with political negotiations. They placed all their emphasis on setting up colonies. Later, they said, when the land was fully colonized, the Jewish home would have to be recognized by the world.

Weizmann proved that political Zionism was the proper

approach to the Zionist problem. During the war, he was Professor of Chemistry at the University of Manchester in England. In this capacity, Weizmann conducted experiments which resulted in an important discovery that proved vital to the British war effort. He discovered an inexpensive and simple process of manufacturing acetone, an essential ingredient in the manufacture of explosives.

This great discovery was one of the most important contributions to the Allied cause. It brought Weizmann into close contact with the members of the British Cabinet. When Weizmann was offered a government distinction for his discovery, he refused it and asked for a gift to his people instead. This gift was the recognition of a Jewish homeland in Palestine! Out of gratitude to Weizmann, the British were ready to listen with sympathy to his request. The British had another reason for considering Weizmann's plan. America had not yet entered the war, and they felt that if they could rally world-wide Jewish opinion to their side, they might bolster favorable sentiment for the Allies in America and gain still another ally.

While Chaim Weizmann was emerging as the greatest Zionist personality in Europe and the world, another great Zionist was emerging in America.

What was the work of Louis Brandeis?

Despite the opposition of the Reform rabbinate, American Zionism was growing. Dr. Harry Friedenwald of Baltimore, Louis Lipsky of New York, and Shemaryahu Levin, a European, stood at the helm of the movement. Poalei Zion and Mizrachi began to flourish. Under the inspiration of Henrietta Szold, a national women's Zionist organization was formed. It was called "Hadassah."

When the Kishinev pogroms took place, even more Jews were converted to Zionism, because they realized that only a Jewish homeland could give the Jew peace and security. In 1914, American Zionism acquired its most distinguished leader in the person of Louis D. Brandeis.

Louis Brandeis was born in Louisville, Kentucky, of parents who were "Forty-eighters." A keen mind and deep understanding caused Brandeis to become most successful in his chosen profession of law. In his early forties, he was already recognized as one of the greatest legal minds in the country, and was well known all over the United States as the "People's Attorney."

For a long time, Brandeis was so far from Judaism that he was not even considered to be a Jew. His Jewishness was first aroused when he served as mediator in a garment industry strike and became acquainted with Jews in the needle trades. Soon he was attracted to Zionism. Even though he was the first Jew to be appointed a Justice of the United States Supreme Court, he continued as one of the leading and most active personalities in the American Zionist movement.

Brandeis, great American that he was, did not feel that his Zionist interest caused any lessening or weakening of his loyalty to the United States. Mordecai Manual Noah had disproved the nasty charge of "dual allegiance." Brandeis faced it openly and denied it.

In his famous work, *The Jewish Problem—How to Solve It*, he wrote that there was no conflict between Americanism and Zionism. And who was to know better than a Justice of the Supreme Court? This is what Brandeis said: "It became clear to me that to be good Americans, we must be better Jews. And to be better Jews, we must become Zionists."

What was the Balfour Declaration?

The personal influence of Dr. Weizmann and Justice Brandeis, and the growing strength of Zionism everywhere, had finally caused England to permit Jabotinsky and Trumpeldor to organize the Jewish Brigade in June, 1917.

But this hardly satisfied the political Zionists. They wanted nothing less than a promise that England would recognize a Jewish state. Many world figures supported the Zionist hopes. President Woodrow Wilson, too, gave his strong and enthusiastic support.

Finally, on November 2, 1917, Britain issued the Balfour Declaration. It was named after the British Foreign Minister, Lord Arthur Balfour, who composed and issued the document. It was actually a letter written to Lord Lionel Rothschild, president of the English Zionist Federation, and gave the Jews the promise they had sought.

The significant part of the three-paragraph note read as follows:

> His Majesty's Government views with favor the establisment in Palestine of a national Jewish home for the Jewish people, and will use their best endeavors to facilitate the achievement of this object. . . .

Before issuing the document, England had consulted with czarist Russia, Japan, the French and Italian governments, and thus had the approval and support of all its allies. President Wilson also repeated his support of the Balfour Declaration in

a letter to Dr. Stephen Wise. Later, Wilson confirmed his position to a delegation of the American Jewish Congress, saying that he was persuaded that "the Allied Nations, with the fullest concurrence of our own government and people, are agreed that in Palestine there should be laid the foundation of a Jewish commonwealth."

Both Houses of Congress unanimously adopted a resolution in favor of "the establishment in Palestine of a national home for the Jewish people."

At the same time that the Balfour Declaration was made, the Central Powers made a similar offer. The Turkish Grand Vizier announced that his government was planning to permit local independent self-government for the Jews in Palestine. This was with the full consent of their German allies.

It has been the feeling among some historians that Britain did not issue the Balfour Declaration because of its favorable interest in the Jews, but because it was aware of the Turkish and German proposal, and tried to be the first with an offer to the Jews. Later, it became known that the British had made a contradictory promise to the Arabs in Palestine at the very same time that the Balfour Declaration was issued. Their actions towards the Jewish colonists in Palestine, in the years between the wars, has also demonstrated that they never meant to fulfill their glowing promise of 1917.

Why was there a Jewish delegation to Versailles?

With the end of World War I and the victory of the Allies, the Balfour Declaration became a subject of intense Zionist activity, even though, now that the war was over, the British showed less enthusiasm for the plan.

In 1919, a Jewish delegation came to the Peace Conference in Versailles to persuade the great powers to help fulfill Britain's promise. This delegation was made up of the leading Jews of America. It represented the Zionist groups, the American Jewish Committee, and the American Jewish Congress. It joined with Jewish representatives from other countries to plead the cause of a Jewish state. It was the first time in modern history that Jews represented themselves in their own right before a world assembly of nations.

Among these delegrates was Louis Marshall, head of the American Jewish Committee and regarded by many as the unofficial Jewish ambassador to the rest of the world. There were also Judge Julian Mack, President of the American Jewish Congress, Rabbi Stephen Wise, Rabbi B. L. Levinthal, Dr. Cyrus Adler, and others. In France, they joined Dr. Weizmann and Dr. Nahum Sokolow, a great Zionist and Weizmann's personal friend.

The task of the delegation was twofold, to secure the guarantee of Jewish citizenship and civil rights in Russia, Poland, Rumania, and the Balkan countries, and to seek the fulfillment of the Balfour Declaration.

The fight for Jewish civil rights in Europe will be discussed later.

How did the British go back on the Balfour Declaration?

The Zionist delegation to Versailles proposed that the historic right of the Jews to create a Jewish home in Palestine should be fully recognized by the world powers. They further requested that Palestine should be permitted to become an independent Jewish community. Until it could stand on its own feet, the delegates were content to have Palestine administered by England under the supervision of the League of Nations. The delegates asked, too, that a "council representing the Jews in Palestine and of the world" should be allowed to cooperate in promoting Jewish immigration and settlement.

Even while the negotiations were going on, the British occupation forces in Palestine acted as if the Balfour Declaration were only a wartime promise which was never meant to be kept. They harassed the Jewish settlers and gave them no protection against frequent Arab attacks.

In one of these attacks in 1920, in an isolated settlement in Palestine named "Tel Chai," five Jews were murdered, among them the famous war hero, Joseph Trumpeldor. A monument to Trumpeldor now stands in the place where he lost his life.

Other attacks took place in Jerusalem, where British troops gave indirect assistance to the Arab vandals. As the rioting continued, the whole world protested against the bloodshed, and even leading English newspapers called upon the government to fulfill its promise.

What was the British Mandate?

The riots had the effect of forcing positive action on the

Palestine problem. Finally, in April, 1920, England was selected by the League of Nations to administer Palestine. The administration of Palestine was called the Mandate, and England was the Mandatory Power. At the same time, the Balfour Declaration was made part of the peace treaty with Turkey. The Mandate meant that the British were to remain in Palestine only until the new state would be able to stand on its own feet and govern itself. It was also the responsibility of the Mandatory Power to help create the Jewish state. A High Commissioner for Palestine was appointed. He was Sir Herbert Samuel, an English Jew, who was believed to be friendly to Zionism.

The announcement of the Mandate was hailed with joy and enthusiasm by Jews all over the world. Now they were closer than ever to the dream of a free Jewish state. In America, huge parades and thanksgiving demonstrations were held. Everyone hoped that 1920 was to mark the beginning of a new era for Jews.

Unfortunately, millions of Jews were to be killed, and more than a quarter of a century was to pass, before the terms of the Balfour Declaration would be carried out.

Things to Remember

1. What was the importance of Theodore Herzl, Chaim Weizmann, and Louis Brandeis in the establishment of a Jewish state?
2. What was the contribution of Eliezer ben Yehuda?
3. What was the Balfour Declaration?
4. What was the English Mandate over Palestine? When was it given?

Things to Think About

1. The Territorialists at one time threatened to divide the Zionist Congress. Do you see their point of view? Give reasons for your answer. Do you agree or disagree with

them? Do you think they were doomed to failure? If so, why?

2. Do you think Chaim Weizmann was an unusual man? Do you know of a living Jew who can be compared to him? Who?
3. Politics prompted Great Britain to issue the Balfour Declaration. Can you prove or disprove this statement?

CHAPTER FOURTEEN

WORLD WAR II

The delegates representing world Jewry at the Peace Conference of Versailles, in 1919, seemed to be successful in both the goals they had set for themselves. By designating England as the Mandatory Power in Palestine, and by accepting the Balfour Declaration, the world powers had recognized the principle of a Jewish homeland. They even more readily agreed to the second request by the Jews which demanded equal rights and the guarantee of citizenship privileges for Jews in the East European countries.

This request was made because of the wretched lives that Jews were forced to lead up to and during World War I. As the territories of the defeated Central Powers were being carved up into new states, it was felt that this was the time to discuss equal rights for minorities.

Did civil rights clauses help the European Jews?

The Jewish delegation succeeded in having the Conference insert "minority rights" clauses into the Peace Treaties that were drawn up between the Allies and the Central Powers. These clauses restated the rights of all minorities to equal citizenship and privileges regardless of their religion and race.

But the guarantees were not worth the paper on which they

were written. In the Ukraine, the traditional center of Russian anti-Semitism, mobs roamed the countryside killing and looting. Beginning with the Russian Revolution, two thousand massacres were recorded in the Ukraine alone, where nearly a quarter of a million Jews were killed. Countless others died of hunger and disease. In other parts of Russia where the Bolshevik Revolution was liquidating all opposition, additional scores of thousands of Jews were killed.

The new Poland was no better than the old Poland. Only 10 days after the Armstice, the Poles had broken into the Jewish sector of Lemberg and staged a full-scale pogrom. This was followed by an epidemic of pogroms that took a terrible toll of Jewish lives and continued well after the signing of the Peace Treaties.

In Rumania, too, anti-Semitism broke out again, bringing anti-Jewish regulations and horrible treatment.

Sadly and tragically enough, during the pogroms in Russia, years after the war was over, two American Jewish representatives of the JDC were killed. They were Professor Israel Friedlander, a member of the faculty of the Jewish Theological Seminary and a brilliant thinker and writer, and Rabbi Bernard Cantor. Their mission had been to survey the needs of the Jews in Poland and Russia. As they entered the Ukraine from Poland, they were attacked by Ukranian peasants and brutally murdered.

How did America's immigration policy change?

The civil rights clauses for minorities seemed farcical in view of what was happening. In addition, the last avenue of escape that had until now been available to hard-pressed Jews, immigration to America, was slowly being shut down. During the war years, a very small number of Jews were able to escape to America. From 1919 through 1924, a larger number, amounting to 300,000 Jews, found refuge in the land of liberty.

The year 1924, however, was the last year of relatively free immigration to the United States. Anti-immigration forces had been fighting for a long time to restrict the number of newcomers. Finally, the Johnson Act, which seemed especially aimed against Jews, was passed. Under the terms of the Johnson Act, Jewish immigration was limited to about ten thousand annually. This was one-tenth of the usual number of immigrants.

The Johnson Act cut off any hope for large numbers of Jews to come to America. It left them like prisoners in the gigantic jail of East Europe.

By 1933, not only the Jews of Eastern Europe, but those of Germany, Austria, Czechoslavakia, and other European countries were looking desperately but in vain, for an open door. A scant 15 years after the passing of the Johnson Act and the close of immigration in the United States, Jews were to be massacred by the millions because there was no land to receive them. Millions had to die before even Palestine, which had been promised to the Jewish people in 1920, would be permitted to absorb the broken remnants of Israel.

In the early 1920s and 1930s, more and more of world Jewry was becoming concerned with the hopeless plight of the Jews in East Europe, and appalled by their own inability to do much to help them. The JDC was doing superhuman work wherever it was allowed to enter. But all relief efforts were like trying to fill a bottomless well.

And, then, suddenly, in the midst of the relatively secure Jewish group which was living in a country considered to be one of the most cultured in the world, disaster struck.

Who was Adolf Hitler?

Early in 1933, President von Hindenburg of Germany called upon an obscure paper hanger, who had by bluff and audacity risen to political heights, to head the new cabinet of Germany. His name was Adolf Hitler.

Hitler seized the opportunity to take complete control of Germany. He established a dictatorship with himself at its head. The new form of government was akin to communism in that it was a dictatorship in which the state held complete control over the lives of its citizens. It was called National Socialism, or Nazism, for short.

Hitler's Nazis preached the supremacy of the German race. They said that the only people who were worth anything at all were Germans. All others deserved to be exterminated or at best reduced to the status of ignorant slave labor.

Hitler established a reign of fear and hatred in Germany. The most hated of his soldiers were the so-called "storm troopers." They were cruel and inhuman, thoroughly drilled in Nazi psychology and trained to be brutal killers.

The emblem of the new German government was a black swastika. Wherever the swastika flag was to fly, death and torture would come to millions of innocent people.

What was Hitler's attitude towards the Jews?

Using the age-old tactic of finding a scapegoat and distracting the people from the real problems at hand, Hitler, like the madman he was, began to rave and rant against the Jews. He said that they were an inferior people, that they had caused Germany to lose World War I, and that they had to be annihilated.

In May, 1933, the mad Fuehrer, or Leader, as Hitler was called, ordered that there be a public burning of books written by Jews. Invaluable manuscripts, literary works, scientific studies, poetry, philosophy, and religious tomes – all were burned in this horrible desecration. Anything that any Jew had ever written or contributed to the world's culture was destroyed.

In physical terms, except in the case of manuscripts and rare volumes that could not be replaced, the book burning was only a costly destruction of property, because there were other copies of the books all over the world. But in another sense, it was a frightening attempt to erase from Germany and from the minds of Germans any reference to Jews or Judaism. It was as if Hitler were rewriting history and erasing the name and accomplishment of each Jew as it appeared in civilization's record. It was a gigantic effort to reduce the Jewish people from their eminent position in culture, science, and religion to beasts whose life and death means nothing to man.

In September, 1935, Hitler issued the infamous Nuremberg Laws—the next step in the systematic destruction of the Jews. These laws stripped all Jews of their citizenship, deprived them of the right to serve in the professions, and forced them to wear a yellow badge with the word "Jude," Jew, written on it. The Jews were compelled to do forced labor, and they were under the direct rule of the Gestapo, the Secret Police.

In two short years, Hitler and Germany had reverted to the inhuman cruelty of the Middle Ages. They were soon to go even beyond the fiendish tortures of the Inquisition, the murders of the Crusaders, and the bloody pogroms of czarist Russia.

How did the people of the world react to Nazism?

No sane person anywhere in the world could believe the monstrous stories that were coming out of Germany. Nor could they believe that the Nazis really meant to kill the Jews.

Those Christians who did believe in the Nazis' boast to destroy the Jews, were not terribly upset either. They had done nothing to help the Jews of Poland or of Russia. Why should they do more for the Jews of Germany?

What they failed to realize was that the Nazi threat against the Jews was also a threat against all other minorities and nations. The Nazis would attack any people or country that was too weak to resist. Other minorities, like the Catholics, in some countries, would be persecuted too.

In a larger sense, an attack against Jews should have been

understood as an attack against godliness and humanity, and even as an attack against the Christian spiritual culture which had its roots in Judaism. A war against Jews was really a war against all religion and against decent people all over the world.

Hitler soon proved that in addition to mass murder he was also planning to end all religious life. He even managed to have his picture hung in some of the Protestant churches of Germany, and venerated as the mystic leader of the German people. In some churches prayers were actually offered to the picture, "Adolf Hitler we believe in thee...." In effect, Hitler not only exercised the right of life and death over his subjects but also demanded to be worshiped in place of God. To this extent had madness possessed Germany and its leaders.

However, as long as only Jews were being threatened, world diplomats were content to call it an "internal" German affair, and not an international crime that called for world concern and action. Had there been more compassion for the Jews, and had the nations of the world intervened to save them, they would have checked the rise of Nazi and German militarism. The world would have been spared a second and bloodier World War.

How did World War II break out?

The Western powers, which still did not believe what was happening or did not care to be touched by German "internal affairs," soon saw that evil never remains in one narrow channel but spreads out like an epidemic in all directions.

Soon Hitler overran Austria and shrewdly then, still because they refused to act, he forced England and France into an agreement which ended in his annexing a part of Czechoslovakia to the Nazi empire. In diplomatic history, this is known as the "betrayal" of Czechoslovakia.

Almost as if to celebrate the event, on November 10, 1938,

a pogrom of colossal proportions was carried out against the Jews of Germany. By fiendish coordination of the Nazi criminals, Jews in hundreds of cities were all attacked at one time. All the synagogues were demolished. Jewish shops and homes were looted, and thousands of men, women, and children were maimed or murdered. Thousands of others had their property confiscated, and were driven to concentration camps. The concentration camps were another invention of the twisted Nazi mind. They were huge prison compounds for from 50,000 to 200,000 people, where the vilest and most evil of tortures were carried out.

Still there was no international reaction. President Franklin D. Roosevelt was the only statesman who acted to show disapproval. He recalled the American Ambassador from Berlin.

In March, 1939, Hitler marched into what was left of free Czechoslovakia. During the spring and summer, he concluded treaties with Italy and Soviet Russia, and then on September 1, 1939, German troops invaded and conquered Poland. Unfortunately for the Jewish people, there were three and a half million Jews within the borders of Poland, and a bitter fate awaited them.

With his conquest of Poland, Hitler now had more than half of Europe in his hands. The Western World, which had allowed Hitler to grow strong and to fatten on murder and wholesale brutality, could retreat no longer. The fight which they did not want to wage on behalf of the Jews, they now had to wage for their own survival. But they were now facing a stronger, more confident foe in 1939 than they would have had to face in any of the years between 1933 and 1938.

How did the Jews of America protest Germany's treatment of Jews?

In America, the news of the growing proportions of Hitler's murders was heard by the Jews with consternation and disbelief. When the truth was known, the organized Jewish bodies began to exercise all their efforts on behalf of European Jewry.

The American Jewish Congress organized demonstrations, parades, and an anti-German boycott. The American Jewish Committee and the B'nai B'rith, which had become a major American Jewish organization, urged appealing to the world on humanitarian grounds. A nonsectarian anti-Nazi League was organized to mobilize all faiths against Nazism. The Anti-Defamation League of the B'nai B'rith, which had come into being in 1913 to expose and to fight anti-Semitism, also joined the fray.

However, all the efforts of American Jewry were of no avail. By the time the British, French, and Americans began to understand the nature of Nazism, World War II had broken out. Diplomatic contact with Nazi Germany was at an end.

What is genocide?

When World War II erupted in September, 1939, the three and one half million Jews of Poland, the 200,000 Jews of Austria, the 350,000 Jews of Czechoslovakia, and the approximate 250,000 Jews of Germany, were in the grip of the madman of Europe. Soon Germany occupied Rumania with its 900,000 Jews, and Hungary with its 700,000 Jews, bringing the total number of Jews under Germany's direct domination to almost 6 million.

In June, 1940, France and the Low Countries fell. Then, breaking their treaty with Russia, the Germans swept through that country. Now the 700,000 Jews of France, Belgium, Luxembourg, the northern countries, Greece, and the 2 million Jews in the part of invaded Russia were also in the hands of the Gestapo, the murderous Nazi Secret Police who had a special division which dealt with killing Jews.

As the geographical extent of the war spread, the Germans

threatened the invasion of Egypt, and the entire Jewish population of Palestine was endangered as well. It seemed that only the Jews of the Western Hemisphere and of Australia might survive.

The years under Nazi domination became years of death for the Jews. It is almost impossible to describe the enormity of the crime that Germans committed against the Jews. Today such a crime has a special name, genocide. This means the destruction of an entire people. And this is what the Nazis had pledged themselves to do.

The Nazis set up special units of the German army whose task it was to kill Jews. Killing meant as little to them as it would to a community which had set up a police detail to shoot all stray dogs.

What were some of the concentration camps?

With systematic devotion to detail, the Germans built huge camps in Poland, Czechoslovakia, Austria, and Germany. These concentration camps were equipped with specially constructed gas chambers and crematoria. As country after country fell to the Germans, the Jews were rounded up, packed into railroad boxcars, and transported to the concentration camps. Sometimes the trip took a week or longer. The boxcars were sealed so that nobody could get out. Inside, there were no sanitary facilities and very little food. People were packed in them like sardines, and many died even before they got to the camps.

The most infamous of the camps were in Poland, and were named Auschwitz, Treblinka, and Maidenek. In Germany, there were Buchenwald, Dachau, and Bergen-Belsen. Tens of others were to be found scattered in isolated areas in different parts of Europe.

It is appalling that the German mind could have devised such factories for murder, spending millions and millions of

dollars in transportation, manpower, supplies, and time for the sole purpose of killing innocent people.

How were Jews killed in the concentration camps?

When the Jews arrived at the various camps, those who had some remaining strength were set aside to do hard labor. The others were stripped of their meager possessions, even their clothes, and thrown into gas chambers to be killed. Often the Nazis searched through the mounds of dead bodies, knocking out gold and silver fillings from the teeth of their victims. They shaved their hair, out of which they made mattresses and pillows. Then the desecrated bodies were dumped into a huge oven, called a crematorium, to be burned.

Those who were chosen for hard labor usually died within weeks of starvation and overwork. They were forced to live like animals, work like animals, and die like animals. The Germans even wanted them to forget that they ever had names. Instead, numbers were tattooed on their arms. Twice daily, before and after work, they were lined up and counted. Each time they were beaten, struck, spat on, and jeered at.

All forms of torture were employed in the concentration camps. Sometimes during the freezing winter, at an early morning line-up, the Jews were forced to strip and were sprayed with ice water. Many were frozen to death.

There are records, too, of Jews that were skinned alive so that lampshades could be made out of their skins. Others were boiled down, and soap was made out of their remains.

In certain areas, instead of sending the helpless Jews to the concentration camps, the Germans herded them together and forced them to dig a large mass grave. They then machine-gunned them to death, so that they fell into the grave they themselves had dug.

Some Jews were earmarked for medical experiments, and German scientists perpetrated the most horrible and inhuman tortures on them. All this was done without regard to sex or age.

On December 7, 1941, after Japan's sneak attack on Pearl Harbor, the United States entered the war. In May, 1945, Germany surrendered, bringing to an end the most horrifying period in the history of the world, and certainly in the history of the people of Israel.

During the reign of Nazism, almost all of European Jewry was destroyed. Six million Jewish men, women, and children had been savagely murdered. It is estimated that of the six million Jews killed, more than one million were innocent infants and babes!

What was the Christians' attitude towards the mass genocide?

While this mass murder was taking place, most of the Christians in the occupied countries of East Europe did not raise a finger to help the Jews. They not only looked on with approval, but in many instances helped the Germans in their bloody work. Even the peoples of occupied lands, who hated the Germans and should have hated all they stood for, nevertheless were quite content to go along with and even assist in the Nazi brutality toward the Jews. In Poland, for example, many a Jew who was fortunate to escape the Germans was either turned back by the Poles or killed by them. It can truly be said that the German Nazis were the foulest beasts that ever walked on the face of the earth. But the Poles, the Rumanians, and other East Europeans who helped them in their massacres, were contemptible jackals who had not even the dignity of a mad beast.

In the West European countries and in the northern countries, many Christians did show what true brotherhood meant. There were many who risked their own lives in order to save Jews, to hide them out, or to help smuggle them to safety in Switzerland, which was a neutral country during the war. The most heroic were the Dutch and the Scandinavian people. An excellent example of Dutch help is the story of the Frank family. This was an ordinary Jewish family that was kept hidden by friendly Dutch people in Amsterdam. Unfortunately, their hiding place, in which they were successfully concealed for three years, was finally discovered by the Nazis. The only one to survive the concentration camps into which they were thrown was Mr. Frank himself. The years of hiding, of fear, which the Frank family underwent are immortalized in a diary which had been kept by the youngest daughter of the family. *The Diary of Anne Frank* will remain one of the most touching documents of all literature and of Jewish history.

In Denmark, too, there was outstanding heroism and profound human kindness and compassion. During the German occupation of Denmark, the underground resistance movement, unlike that of the Poles, worked together with the police force to hide Jews or steal them away to safety in Sweden. The German head of the occupation forces threatened King Christian X and in final anger asked why the Danes should want to help Jews.

The King replied, "Tell Berlin that the King of Denmark was never more proud of his people than he is today." As a result of the Danish help, 99 per cent of Danish Jews survived the war.

Two other humanitarian countries stand out as shining beacons of decency and sympathetic action. They are Switzerland and Sweden.

Although in the shadow of its German neighbor, Switzerland fearlessly accepted and gave protection to thousands upon thousands of Jews who found their way to its borders. The Swiss government also allocated huge sums to maintain and provide for the refugees.

Sweden distinguished itself in a similar manner. Even though the Nazis stood on its border after conquering neighboring Norway, the Swedish government bravely stood up against them. Despite powerful Nazi pressure, the great King Gustav refused to turn the Jews of his country over to them, and received with open arms those who made their way to its borders. King Gustav and King Christian were among the few heads of state who lived and acted sincerely in accordance with their religious training. They will always be remembered, loved, and revered by the Jews.

The majority of the Jews of occupied Europe who survived the murderous twelve years of Nazi rule and six years of war are those who were hidden out or were helped to escape. Almost all other Jews who had fallen into the hands of Hitler were killed.

It is sad and tragic that almost the entire world sat by with folded hands while mass murders took place. If the Allied powers had not gone to war with Germany for political reasons, they might never even have condemned her for what she did to the Jews.

Nor can we ever understand how good Christians hardly raised an eyebrow when an entire people was threatened with annihilation. Those who did nothing to help the victims of murder are almost as guilty as those who performed the murder. Those who helped the murderers, like the Poles, were even more guilty, because they voluntarily joined in the crime.

What was the Resistance?

In every country that Germany overran resistance forces went underground to continue to fight and sabotage the enemy. They performed deeds of great heroism, helped prisoners to escape, upset Nazi plans, and rescued hundreds of innocent people from the Nazi clutches.

Jews, wherever they could, joined the resistance movement. Palestine itself sent parachutists into enemy countries to go on the most dangerous of missions. In many instances Jews formed their own resistance groups within the larger underground movement.

What was the Warsaw Ghetto Uprising?

One of the bravest resistance moves was made by the Jews of Poland, who had been herded into a ghetto made up of a large section of the city of Warsaw. By October, 1940, some 450,000 Jews were prisoners behind the barbed wires and brick wall of the Warsaw ghetto.

The Nazi plan was to annihilate the ghetto within three years. At first, as disease and starvation took its toll of the crowded Jews, it looked as though the Nazis would accomplish their mission even sooner.

But the spirit of the Jewish people could not be broken. They organized a government to supervise ghetto life. They created schools for their children, and even held concerts and ran art exhibitions. Poets and authors wrote accounts of what was happening, and hid them for future reference. However, by 1943, only 40,000 Jews remained in the Warsaw ghetto.

During Passover of that year, the 40,000 Jews decided to go to war against the Germans and to make a last-ditch stand against the Nazis. Armed with the crudest of weapons and homemade explosives, with sticks and stones, they fought the Nazi panzers and machine guns. The Nazis had to send thousands of soldiers, squadrons of airplane fighters and bombers, tanks and cannon to fight the heroic Jews. For more than a month they waged a house-to-house battle, blowing up each house and then using flame throwers to burn out the defenders.

Very few survived the Warsaw Ghetto Uprising. But the memory of their valor, their courage, and their hope lives on as a glorious and inspiring act of Jewish heroism.

How did the Jews fare under Communism?

In the mid-twenties of the 20th century, there were three major geographical divisions of Jews in Europe. Those in Western Europe and the northern countries, like Norway, Sweden, and Denmark, enjoyed complete freedom. The Jews of central Europe, of Poland, Rumania, and Hungary, enjoyed no freedom except the freedom to emigrate. For them, however, the country they most desired to go to, America, was closed.

The Jews of Russia, or the Union of Soviet Socialist Republics, as it was called after the Revolution of 1917, were not even free to emigrate if they wished. They were under the regime of communism. Communism meant complete control of the individual by the state—his working hours, his job, his money, his very life, belonged to the state. Communism was also dedicated to destroying religion, since religion taught the value of human life and the dignity of the human being. The Communists would not permit loyalty to any faith because it might compete with loyalty to the state.

Why is communism antagonistic to Judaism?

Communism was particularly antagonistic to Judaism, because Judaism was the prime teacher of the rights of the indi-

RUSSIA'S TERRITORIAL GAINS
AFTER WORLD WAR II

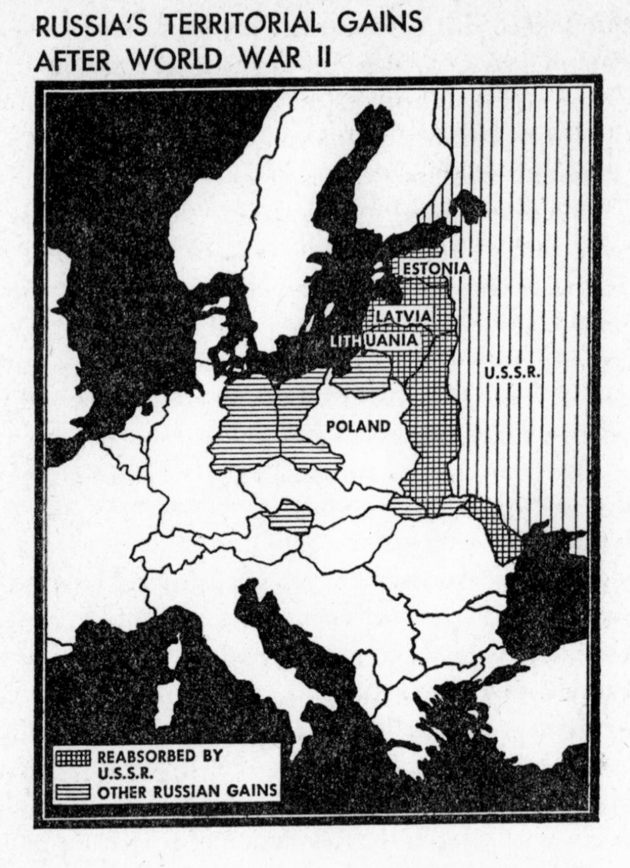

vidual. The Torah taught that all men were created equal in the image of God. Judaism, which held the dignity of the human being to be the highest and most important factor in social living, was the severest critic of the godless, soulless Communist system. The Russian leaders realized that their government could not permit the spirit of the Jewish faith to exist in their country. It would cry out forever against their inhumanity and callous disregard for human lives and human values.

In addition to their religious loyalties, Jews also felt a deep devotion to Zionism. This too was intolerable to Communists.

Zionism implied that a people had the right to seek its own national fulfillment by transplanting itself to a new land. The Russians, who ruled their people with an iron fist, refused to recognize the principle of freedom to express dissatisfaction with local circumstances and to move at will to other countries. They also forbade their citizens to show loyalty to any cause or country other than communism and Russia. For these reasons, and because of the historic anti-Semitism of Russia, the Communists persecuted the Jews.

Since the Jews were only a small minority of the Russian population, it was even easier for them than for other religious groups to be attacked. The Russian government, therefore, was able to take the greatest steps against the Jews to destroy their religious and national identification.

What is the situation of Jews behind the Iron Curtain today?

As a result, rabbis and religious leaders have been imprisoned without cause. Almost all synagogues have been closed down. Hebrew schools, the teaching of religion, Zionism, and contact with Jewish world agencies and organizations are prohibited, and even mail to and from Jews in other countries is severely censored. Jews in the Soviet Union also suffer from a lack of religious articles like tefillim, siddurim, sifrei torah, and mezuzahs. While all of this has been done to destroy Judaism, the government has, at the same time, decreed that all Jews must be identified as Jews on their identity cards, a requirement which applies to no other religious group. On the one hand, then, Jews have been deprived of all the expressions of their nationalism, and on the other hand, are forced to carry the mark "Jew" on their identification papers.

Because of this, Jews living in the Soviet Union today have almost no religious training or affiliation and almost no relationship with the outside world. The Soviet government has even accused the Joint Distribution Committee and the World Zionist Organization of preposterous crimes ranging all the way to espionage.

On the basis of these trumped-up charges, the Communists have excluded these agencies from the Soviet Union. In this way the help that Jews of Russia might receive from the JDC and the encouragement they might receive from their brethren all over the world have been taken from them. At the same time they are almost completely isolated, so that no one really knows what is happening or will happen to them.

After World War II, Communist control was extended to the central European countries as well. Poland, Rumania, Czechoslovakia, Yugoslavia, and Hungary are all behind the Iron Curtain. During 1958, the Rumanian government suddenly allowed several thousand Jews to leave for Israel. The emigration stopped as suddenly as it started. The same had happened in Poland a year before.

There is no way of predicting what will happen to the three million Jews living in Russia and their satellite countries today. In addition to the cultural and religious death which is already taking place, many fear that actual violence against Jews will follow.

What was Youth Aliyah?

One great rescue undertaking has been inscribed in the history of our people as the most imaginative and successful of all times. It was inspired by Henrietta Szold, the great founder and leader of Hadassah, and was called Youth Aliyah.

The purpose of Youth Aliyah was to save Jewish children and bring them to Palestine. Aliyah is the Hebrew word for "going up," and is the word used for immigration to Palestine.

Youth Aliyah began in 1934 when Henrietta Szold realized what lay in store for European Jewry. A unique organization was set up whereby children were removed from Germany, from occupied lands, and even smuggled out of concen-

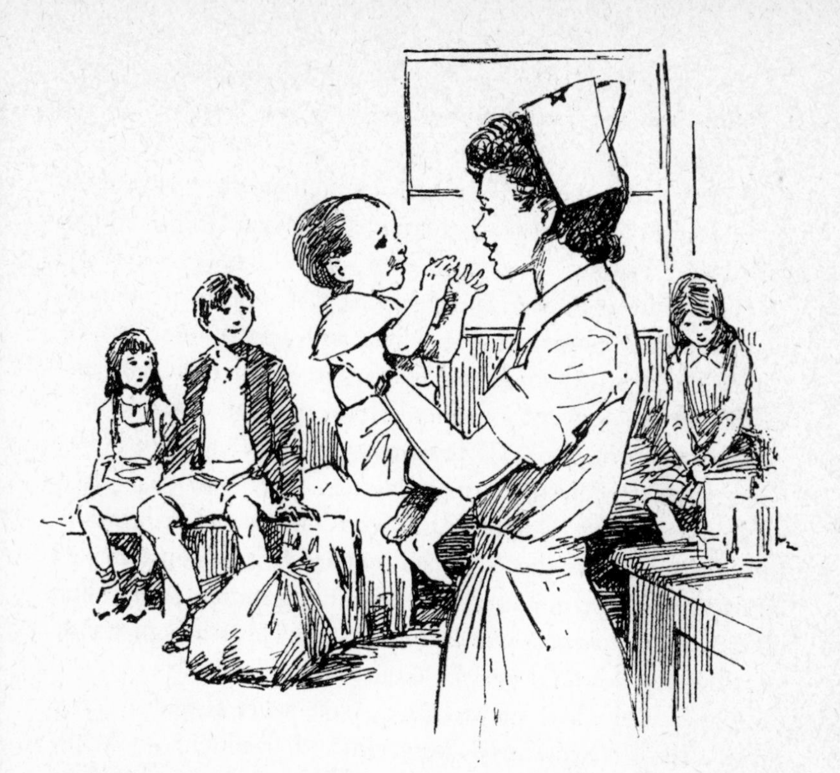

tration camps. This was done with the superb assistance of the intelligence units of the Jews of Palestine.

Youth Aliyah required enormous sums and superhuman effort. The project was first undertaken by the Hadassah and then joined in by other Zionist groups. To Hadassah goes the major share of credit for having saved about 17,000 children during the bitter war period.

Until the day of her death in 1945, Henrietta Szold personally led and directed the campaign to raise funds and to save lives through Youth Aliyah. It has continued to this very day. After the war, many orphaned children were found and brought to Israel. Others were brought from North Africa and the Arab-dominated countries. Through Hadassah, Mizrachi Women, Pioneer Women, and many other organizations, 62,000 children were rescued by 1954.

Why was the Yishuv unable to help the Jews?

The Jews of the Western Hemisphere could do very little to help their brothers in Europe. The only real and effective assistance could be made by the Jewish settlement in Palestine, called the "Yishuv."

The Yishuv had seen and accepted as one of its major purposes the creation of a home where any Jew would be welcome. The Yishuv, small and poor as it was, would have accepted all the Jews of Europe, if it were at all possible. For example, as many as 62,000 Jews, mostly from Poland and Germany, came to Palestine in 1935 alone.

But the British Mandatory Power controlled immigration. In order to appease the Arab landowners, Britain continued to increase its restrictions against Jewish immigration to Palestine. The Arab landowners were afraid that the Jewish high standard of living would show the Arab worker in Arab countries the poverty in which he was kept. They were also afraid that the Jews might become too powerful in Palestine. As a result, they used their influence on Britain to curtail immigration. As Hitler stepped up his war against the Jews, the British limited Jewish immigration even more. Finally, they tried to close off immigration completely.

What was the White Paper?

In the very year that Hitler invaded Poland, and after he showed that he was determined to fulfill all his threats to destroy the Jews of Europe, the British Government issued what was called a White Paper. The White Paper was a government decree which proposed to limit Jewish immigration to a maximum of 75,000 for the following five years. After that time, no further Jews would be permitted to enter the land. At the same time, severe restrictions on the acquisition of land by Jews would also go into effect. In this way, the number of Jews in the Yishuv would be kept permanently at about one-third of the population of Palestine, and would be allowed to own only a small portion of the land. After that, the country was to be made completely independent with a preponderant Arab majority. In this way, of course, there would never be a Jewish state.

England was, in effect, playing into the hands of the German murderers by closing the one small door of escape that still remained open to the Jews—the door to Palestine. It seemed as if all at once the last hopes for Jewish survival would be extinguished.

Things to Remember

1. What was the Johnson Act? How did it affect Jews?
2. What was the Nazi theory in regard to the Jewish people? How did they carry out this theory?
3. What was the Warsaw Ghetto Uprising?
4. How did Youth Aliyah help the Jews to survive?
5. How were the hands of the Yishuv tied?

Things to Think About

1. Do you think immigration to a country should be limited? How? When? When not?
2. Do you think England dealt honorably with the Yishuv of Palestine? Give reasons for your answer.
3. How can Christians explain their behavior and attitude to Nazi Germany when the Jews were being slaughtered? Do you see any excuse for it? What would you do, if you were in their place?

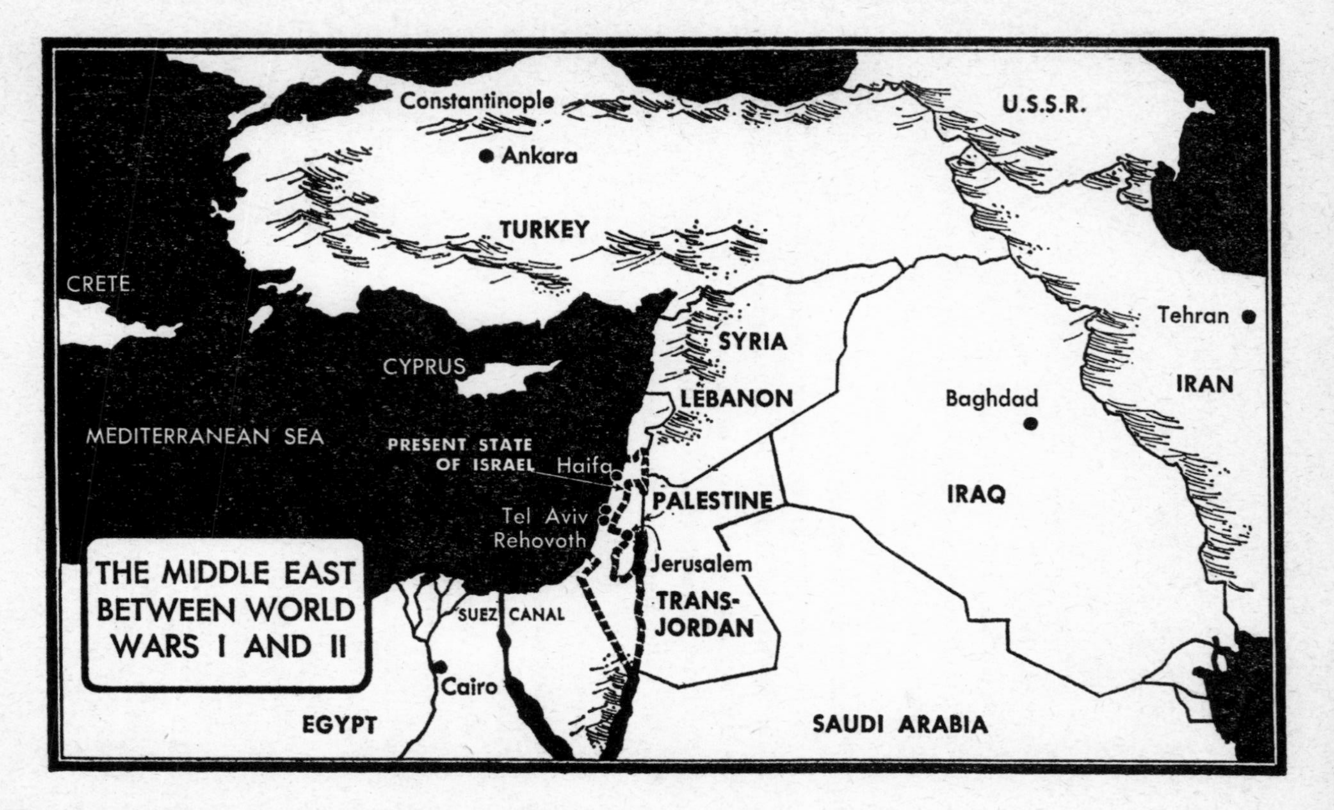
THE MIDDLE EAST
BETWEEN WORLD
WARS I AND II
Constantinople
Ankara
TURKEY
U.S.S.R.
CRETE
CYPRUS
MEDITERRANEAN SEA
SYRIA
LEBANON
PRESENT STATE
OF ISRAEL
Haifa
PALESTINE
Tel Aviv
Rehovoth
Jerusalem
TRANS-
JORDAN
SUEZ
CANAL
Cairo
EGYPT
SAUDI ARABIA
Baghdad
IRAQ
Tehran
IRAN

UNIT FOUR:

IN ISRAEL

In the Book of Genesis we read how the Lord pledged to Father Abraham that the land of Palestine would be given to him and his children forever. This promise has burned itself indelibly into the Jewish heart and soul.

For centuries after they were exiled from Palestine, the children of Israel dreamed of returning to their land. With the smoke still rising from the burning ruins of the First Temple, they pledged that they would "not forget Thee, O Jerusalem." In the torture chambers of the Spanish Inquisition, in the poverty of the ghettos of Europe, in the happy free air of America—in every moment of their history—they kept alive the dream of the Return, the Return to the Promised Land. It was only after our people went through the fires of the concentration camps, the horrors of Auschwitz and Buchenwald and Maidenek, that the dream became a reality and the new State of Israel was born.

Today, the promise made to our forefather Abraham has been fulfilled once again. Our people are now living in the Holy Land, tilling its soil, building its cities, and reestablishing it as a nation among nations. This great miracle it has been our privilege to behold!

In this unit we will study the historic events that led up to the miracle of the creation of the State of Israel. We will take pride in the achievements of the people of the State of Israel, their great progress against almost insurmountable odds. We will be able to follow the current events in Israel with greater knowledge, understanding, and appreciation.

CHAPTER FIFTEEN

BRINGING A PEOPLE HOME

In the years between the wars, the Yishuv in Palestine had been steadily growing. Before World War I there were 55,000 Jews living in Palestine. By the time World War II broke out, this number had jumped to 475,000.

The earth was being tilled and made productive as many new farm settlements blossomed forth. The "chalutzim," pioneer settlers, were not dismayed by the heat or the mosquitoes or the marshlands. Enthusiastic over their return to the Land, they were willing to suffer any hardship.

New cities like Tel Aviv, Haifa, and the new section of Jerusalem had been built. Hospitals were developing medical techniques to eliminate trachoma, the dreaded eye disease which was so prevalent among the Arabs. Malaria, as swamps were drained and marshes reforested, disappeared almost entirely.

The Hebrew University in Jerusalem, the Daniell Sieff Research Institute, later to be known as the Weizmann Scientific Institute at Rehovoth, and the Technion at Haifa stood at the summit of a growing network of schools. More books were published, in proportion, than in any other country of the world. Theater, painting, music, scientific research—every aspect of national culture was developing at an amazing rate.

But the settlers of the Yishuv were not contented. They wanted their land to become a free Jewish State.

How did England violate the terms of the Mandate?

By the terms of the mandate, England was only an agent for the League of Nations. She was supposed to carry out all the directives of the League and the terms of the mandate which were ratified by the League in 1922. These terms stated clearly and simply that England was to administer Palestine until the Jewish State could be established.

England, however, acted not as if she were agent of the League of Nations but as if Palestine were a crown colony and she its sole owner. For years England had been hampering Jewish immigration into the land and had put obstacles in the way of its development. England had encouraged Arab terrorists and made Jewish life miserable. England's interest in Arab oil lands, her desire to have the Arabs on her side, a measure of anti-Semitism, and a fear of upsetting her colonial empire by creating a new Jewish state turned England against the Balfour Declaration, and the resolution of the League of Nations which confirmed it.

As a result, England used none of her powers to help the Jews, as the Mandate required. She permitted the Arab peasants to be goaded by their religious leader, the Mufti, and the wealthy landowners into attacks against the Jews. The Mufti, who wanted to retain his own great power and wealth, and the landowners, who wanted to keep their Arabs as impoverished slaves, spread false rumors that the Jews were taking Arab land and were desecrating Moslem holy places.

On these occasions, the Arabs, in wild frenzies, would riot against the Jewish settlements, killing chalutzim, their wives and infants, tearing up new homes and pipelines, and burning trees and orchards. Such riots took place in 1920, 1921, and again in 1929. It was in one of these riots that Joseph Trumpeldor met his death at Tel Chai.

In addition to the open riots, there were sudden ambushes, constant acts of vandalism and sabotage, and other acts of aggression against the Yishuv. England, hoping to discourage new Jews from coming and old settlers from staying, was blind to all this. When she did take notice, it was only to blame the Jews.

Why was the White Paper withdrawn?

But the major restriction on the Yishuv that Britain was able to exercise was through the control of immigration. In 1929, shortly after the anti-Jewish riots of that year, the first White Paper reducing Jewish immigration was issued. Coming as it did so soon after the Arab riots, Britain seemed to have adopted a policy saying that if the Arabs could not destroy the Jews, England would at least limit their growth in the Yishuv.

When the White Paper of 1939 was issued, it caused a tumult and a furor in England and in America. While Germany was practicing wholesale murder against the Jews, England had heartlessly denied them the right of admission to the only country in the world that would take them! It was also a breach of faith, for England, through the Balfour Declaration, had promised the Jews their own homeland. At the same time, by decreeing restrictive laws against the Jews, England was also betraying completely the terms of the League of Nations' Mandate.

A speaker in England's Parliament, Herbert Morrison, referred to the White Paper as "a cynical breach of pledges given the Jews and the world, including America."

The Jews of America and of the Yishuv saw the White Paper for what it was. It was not an isolated case of British defiance of Jewish hopes. It was part of a calculated plan to discourage the creation of a national homeland.

American Jews refused to accept this plan. They agitated, demonstrated in mass rallies, wrote their senators, and wired their representatives. Finally, through great pressure of public opinion, Great Britain withdrew the White Paper.

But the British spirit of unfriendliness to a Jewish homeland still existed.

What was the purpose of the "Haganah"?

The members of the Yishuv, meanwhile, realized that England would never provide them the security which they needed to build and to grow. Especially were they faced with the immediate problem of continued self-protection against Arab terrorism. Out of this need, grew the famous "Haganah," which in Hebrew means "self-defense."

The Haganah was composed of thousands of men and women organized into a secret self-defense organization. Some of them had gained experience as soldiers in the Zion Mule Corps and in the Jewish Brigade during World War I. Others had served in the armies of other countries. These men with experience became the teachers for others. They instructed young men and women to carry arms and to serve as a protective police force.

The Haganah had several functions. They had to protect the fields and the orchards, defend the settlements, guard the

pipelines that carried water to isolated colonies, and stave off Arab attacks.

The Haganah had to work as an underground movement, in utter secrecy, because the British would not permit the Jews to carry arms even when they were attacked. Furthermore, the British did not want any powerful Jewish organization to exist. The Haganah knew that the British were seeking to destroy it, so the High Command developed a technique whereby each member knew only the limited few others of his particular unit. Nobody knew who the top leaders were, or where the main headquarters was located. In this way, even if a Haganah member were captured by the British, he was never able to reveal any helpful information. At the same time, the Haganah could be mobilized at a moment's notice.

What was "havlagah"?

One feature distinguished the Haganah from any other army that ever existed. This was the policy of "havlagah," of self-restraint. The Haganah never attacked; it only defended. The Haganah almost never went on reprisal attacks or counter-attacks. Even when its commanders knew an Arab attack was certain, they stood by ready for defense but never went out to attack first.

The rare time that the Haganah raided was when it had located the headquarters of an Arab band which had been making sneak attacks on individual Jews and isolated chalutzim. For the sake of these harassed pioneers, the Haganah quickly destroyed the headquarters and dispersed the gang. Even in these raids, they never attacked women, children, or peaceful Arabs, only military objectives. Never could they be accused of the terrorism which the Arabs practiced.

The Haganah was composed of settlers who normally were occupied with the peaceful chores of milking cows, planting seeds, building homes, and tilling the soil. They were like those early Jews who had returned to rebuild the Temple after its destruction by Babylonia. In one hand they held their tools, and in the other they grasped the weapons of defense.

The British hounded the Haganah day and night. They sought its supply depots, its caches of ammunition and guns, and above all, its leaders. But the Jews of Palestine were infused with a new kind of courage. They represented the new kind of Jew. They were not the passive Jews of the medieval ghetto or the Pale of Settlement, defenceless in the face of pogroms. They were devoted to their dream of a Jewish homeland, and in this devotion proved to be braver and cleverer than their hunters. The British could not break them down or penetrate their secrets.

With its experience and training as a police force, a border patrol, and a Jewish army all in one, the Haganah soon grew to be powerful, well-organized, and well-disciplined.

How did the Jews of the Yishuv help Britain in the war?

Three months after Britain's White Paper of 1939, World War II broke out. For the Yishuv, the major objective was not to fight Britain and the White Paper but to help destroy the Nazis, and at the same time, save as many Jews as possible from the roaring furnaces of Europe.

The Yishuv declared a temporary truce with Great Britain, at the same time repeating its refusal to recognize the White Paper. The Zionist Congress which met in Geneva shortly before the war, declared this intention in simple terms:

> We will fight beside Great Britain as though there were no White Paper, and we will fight the White Paper as though there were no war.

The Jewish Agency for Palestine, which was the Council authorized by the League of Nations to help implement the aims of the mandate, helped to facilitate Jewish land purchase, colonization, and immigration. Unofficially, it was also the Jewish government of the Yishuv. In this capacity, the Agency issued an immediate call for volunteers. In no time, thousands of men and women of the Yishuv were flocking to registration stations. All of these were volunteers. There was no need for a compulsory draft.

As in World War I, but with infinitely less hardship, a Jewish Brigade was authorized to serve in the British Army. This time, the brigade had Jewish commanders, in addition to its own Flag of Zion, and shoulder patches with the insignia of the Mogen David, the Jewish Star. The Mogen David, which the Germans had attempted to convert into a badge of shame worn by the inmates of the concentration camps, became a badge of heroism and glory worn by the people of Israel.

The Jews also served outside of their own brigade, in North Africa, France, Italy, Abyssinia, Syria, and elsewhere. They were especially brave in undertaking commando missions which often led them to certain death.

What side did the Arabs take in World War II?

While the British were pleased to use the Palestinian Jewish volunteers in their defense against the threat of the German armies in Africa and elsewhere, they still continued their appeasement of the Arabs. One might think that this was in reward for mighty Arab efforts against the Germans and on behalf of the British. Nothing could have been further from the truth!

The Arabs, for their part, saw no reason to fight against Germany, nor did they see any reason to battle for the British. They remained at home, playing one side against the other, waiting to see who the winner would be.

When the German Field Marshall Rommel was almost at the gates of Egypt in an effort to capture the Suez Canal, the Arabs actually carried on communications with him. They planned to help the German armies defeat the Allies.

The Mufti, the religious leader of the Arab Moslem world, made frequent trips to Berlin where he was pictured with Hitler, giving the Nazi salute. The Arabs felt that in helping the Nazis they would be destroying the Jews and the mandatory power in Palestine.

Who were the "shlichim"?

Meanwhile, under the direction of the Haganah, hundreds of trained Jewish commandos were sent from Palestine into Europe to establish contact with the Jews. They joined with Jewish partisan groups who were fighting guerrilla warfare against the Germans in the forests and mountains. They even penetrated into the concentration camps.

These "shlichim," or agents, as they were called, gave courage and hope to the decimated Jews, taught them self-defense, and prepared them for escape to Palestine. Secret headquarters and way stations were set up in Geneva, in Budapest, and in Istanbul to organize transports to Palestine.

Why is Hannah Senesch remembered?

The shlichim were also called upon by Britain to accept assignments which few others would accept. If it was necessary to parachute into enemy-occupied lands to destroy important military objectives, the shlichim volunteered. For the shlichim this meant certain death, for as Jews, they had no hope of even being treated as prisoners of war if they were captured by the Germans.

Men and women, boys and girls, volunteered. If they had any acquaintance with the land into which they would be parachuted, they were immediately accepted. One such heroic unit was dropped into the Balkans. Among the volunteers was a young girl named Hannah Senesch.

Hannah Senesch had come from Hungary to Palestine, possessed with the dream of building the Jewish homeland. She was already a fine Hebrew poet at the time of her mission. Her heart was broken by the news of what was happening to the Jews of Europe. She vowed to help save them and volunteered for the parachute team which was to take her back to her native Hungary.

Hannah Senesch knew the danger of her mission. In a most beautiful allegory, she compared her work and the work of others like her to a match. When the match is lit, it gives off a light which others use, but it itself is destroyed in the process of giving the light. The members of the Jewish fighting forces were like the match. They were ready to destroy themselves, give their lives, but in so doing would leave a light, a beacon of hope and security for others.

Before she left on the dangerous assignment which was to be her last, Hannah Senesch composed this allegorical verse. It is now part of the great heritage of the heroes of the Yishuv.

> Blessed is the match that is consumed in kindling flame.
> Blessed is the flame that burns in the secret fastness of the heart.
> Blessed is the heart with strength to stop its beating for honor's sake.
> Blessed is the match that is consumed in kindling flame.

Hannah Senesch was captured by the Germans and killed, but she left a light burning for others, and that light will never be extinguished.

Who were the "maapilim"?

There were many other spectacular exploits performed by members of the Yishuv during the war. The most important of these involved the smuggling of Jews across the borders of Europe and the expanses of the Mediterranean Sea to the shores of Palestine. These refugees came without certificates of immigration and without permission of the British. The British called them "illegal." The Yishuv called them "maapilim," those who dared to overcome all obstacles.

What were the "coffin boats"?

The British death hold on Palestine immigration did not lessen. It is strange to report that at the height of the war, when manpower and equipment were critically needed on all the major fronts, the British deployed troops and paratroopers, destroyers and cruisers, helicopters and warplanes, to patrol the shores of the Holy Land against Jewish immigration. These Jews were their own allies, victims of the Nazi war, and enemies of the Germans. If not as allies, then on the grounds of pity and compassion, they should have been extended every help! Instead, they were treated like enemy invaders.

The British had set up special units to trace all ships leaving Mediterranean ports in Europe to ascertain whether or not they were headed towards Palestine. Secret service men and intelligence officers, who could have been used to better advantage to fight the enemy, were detailed to follow Jewish movements in Europe, and to prevent the safe arrival of Jews in Palestine.

Out of desperation, because the Haganah could buy or charter no other ships, many of the refugees were placed on rickety, leaking cattle boats for the trip across the Mediterranean. These boats frequently made the trip to Palestine successfully. They would dock in the stealth of night, at some deserted beach point, and Haganah soldiers would row out to bring the passengers safely ashore and quickly disperse them over the length and breadth of the land. By the next day, most of the healthy maapilim either were already at work or in the Haganah, with false immigration papers. Others were effectively concealed, hospitalized, if necessary, and restored to good health.

But some of the leaky boats never even reached the shores

of Palestine, sinking somewhere en route. They were often torn apart by boiler explosions, heavy seas, and other maritime disasters. The poor refugees after managing to escape death at the hands of the Germans found it waiting for them, because of British persecution, on the very shores of the Promised Land. So many maapilim perished at sea, these boats came to be called "coffin boats."

What was the "Struma"?

But the worst fate was to be caught by a British patrol, and forced to turn back! One such ship, the *Struma*, was carrying 770 passengers. Even though she was known to be unseaworthy, the British patrol which caught her insisted that the *Struma* turn back.

Horrified, the Jews in America heard the news that the *Struma* was shuttling back and forth on the waters, searching for a port to dock. Britain refused to allow the 770 unfortunate Jews to enter Palestine. Certain death awaited them in Europe. Where could they go? In February, 1942, the tragic news came that the *Struma* had finally foundered and gone down in the Black Sea. World Jewry was shocked by this horrible and criminal catastrophe. Some had relatives on the *Struma*. Others wept for a world that could be so inhuman and cruel.

What battle was waged against the "Exodus"?

As late as 1947, two years after the war was over, an old American coastal steamer renamed the *Exodus* set forth from France for Palestine. The ship was built to carry 700 possengers. It carried 4500 refugees, who were broken in body but determined to get to the Holy Land.

A British patrol intercepted the ship and forced its passengers into three prison ships which were to take them back to Marseilles. The refugees refused to disembark. They would leave the ships only in a Palestinean port. Because they were being forced out of the ships, the French would not take them. Up until this time, the British had been interning refugees in internment camps which they had established on the island of Cyprus. These camps were surrounded by barbed wire, and were almost as filthy and primitive as the concentration camps from which the refugees came.

These internment camps in Cyprus were overcrowded, and there was no room for the 4500 *Exodus* refugees. For nearly a month the British Empire waged a war against these broken Jewish refugees. American Jews protested and used every means at their disposal to plead the cause of the 4500.

In the end, the British took them to a European occupation zone where they were herded into a Displaced Persons camp. It was only after the State of Israel was established that the surviving *Exodus* refugees reached home.

How did the British continue to fight the Haganah?

After World War II, the British were determined to rid themselves of the Haganah. Plan after plan was devised to capture its members, to find its leaders, and to destroy its arms.

The British placed Palestine under virtual martial law. Jews could not go out after curfew. Possessing weapons, even those used for defense against the Arabs, was punishable by death. Jail sentences were handed out wholesale. While Britain was waging its war against the Haganah, hundreds of thousands of Jews who had been liberated from concentration camps at the end of the war, were languishing in giant Displaced Persons camps in Europe, provided by the Allies. Their tragedy was that even after the war, they were still homeless and in concentration camps. Worse than that was the knowledge that no nation would accept them. The only land that would welcome them, Palestine, was surrounded by British armed forces.

The attempt of the British to disarm the Haganah, and their cruelty towards the refugees, tried the patience of the Yishuv.

Time and time again, they were brought to the brink of war against the British.

However, the Jewish Agency, which had by now actually become the Jewish government of Palestine, gave orders for the Haganah to continue to follow the principle of havlagah, self-restraint. Most of the Yishuv obeyed their leaders' request to be patient, but patience was a bitter pill to swallow.

What was the "Irgun Zvai Leumi"?

Not all Jews could master their anger and tolerate the shameful treatment dealt them by the British. As early as 1938, a small group of fighters had broken away from the Haganah to form the "Irgun Zvai Leumi," the National Military Organization. Their purpose was to fight British terror with terror. From them arose another offshoot called the "Stern Group," who were even more hostile to the British, and determined to drive them from Palestinian soil.

From 1944, these two groups terrorized the British, blowing up British supply dumps, wrecking radar, breaking into prisons and freeing their brothers in arms and assassinating British officers.

So effective were they that the British were forced to turn to the Yishuv and plead with them to reveal the members of these two groups. By the beginning of 1947, tension was mounting to feverish heights. Refugee boats were still being stopped. The Haganah was still confounding the British, and the Irgun and the Stern Group were destroying the morale of British troops. The Yishuv was like a keg of dynamite, ready to explode.

When did Great Britain leave Palestine?

Suddenly in a dramatic move which was also an admission of defeat, the British announced that they had decided to retreat from Palestine, and were referring the entire matter to the United Nations. The proclamation came in February, 1947, 25 years after the League of Nations had appointed Great Britain to administer the Mandate over Palestine. Technically, the British should have given up their Mandate as soon as the League of Nations had disintegrated. Instead, they held it, dealt with the Jews as with second-rate citizens, and tried to reduce Palestine to another territory in the British Empire.

Jews of the Yishuv rejoiced with the news of Britain's defeat. They had been waiting for 2000 years to acquire Palestine, and they felt their bloodshed and martyrdom had earned them the price of admission to the Holy Land.

At last, now, they would have the opportunity to build their own state.

Things to Remember

1. Why did England want to retain her mandatory powers over Palestine?
2. Why did England withdraw the White Paper of 1939?
3. How did the Haganah come into being? What was its achievement?
4. What was the policy of havlagah?
5. What was the British policy with regard to the maapilim?
6. What contribution did the Irgun and the Stern Group make?

Things to Think About

1. What admirable lesson does the policy of havlagah teach? Do you think the peoples of the world admired this policy when it was practiced by the Yishuv? Give reasons for your answer.

2. Do you think the shlichim were unusual people? Give reasons for your answer.
3. If you had to choose between the policy of havlagah as practiced by the Haganah and the policy of the Irgun and Stern Group, which would you choose? Why?

CHAPTER SIXTEEN

THE WAR FOR INDEPENDENCE

When the British government announced its decision in February, 1947, to refer the Palestine problem to the United Nations, the question of a Jewish homeland was returned once again to the powers of the world for decision.

The United Nations had taken the place of the League of Nations as an international council for peace. There were representatives of almost every country in the world sitting around the table to try to discuss and solve world problems in a just and peaceful fashion.

Hopefully, the Yishuv waited to see what would happen.

How did American Jewry organize to influence the UN decision?

The American delegation to the UN had a great deal of influence and weight among the other delegations and might conceivably control the decision of the world body. Recognizing this, the American Jewish community knew it had to obtain the moral and political support of the American people and the American government in favor of a Jewish national home. It also meant that the American Jewish community, which was the largest and wealthiest in the world, would have to organize itself to provide the necessary financial assistance to help in making the Yishuv into a state.

By this time, over a million American Jews were enrolled in Zionist groups. The Zionist Organization of America had at its helm inspired and dedicated men like Stephen Wise, Abba Hillel Silver, and Emanuel Neumann. Constant influence and pressure were brought to bear on the Jewish and non-Jewish public as giants like Chaim Weizmann, David ben Gurion, and Moshe Sharett were brought to America to explain the Zionist hope.

Even the right-wing Irgun had an American organization supporting it, called the American League for a Free Palestine. The League helped acquaint American public opinion with the British anti-Jewish policy in Palestine.

Through full-page ads in prominent newspapers, through films, mass meetings, rallies, letters, and notices, the American public was shown how important it was that a Jewish state be established.

At the very beginning of the war, almost all the various Zionist groups had established a united front through the American Zionist Council. The Council included thousands of prominent Christians as well, some of them state governors and senators. During the presidential campaign of 1944 between Franklin D. Roosevelt and Thomas E. Dewey, both Republican and Democratic parties had adopted pro-Zionist planks in their platforms. Through the work of the American Zionist Council, both Houses of Congress had also passed pro-Zionist resolutions. The political climate, as well as the feeling of the general population in America, seemed favorable to the establishment of a Jewish state.

What was the American Council for Judaism?

A very small minority of American Jews protested against the agitation for a Jewish state. They were united in the American Council for Judaism. The Council was made up of some Reform rabbis and laymen who were still being guided by the unreal and anti-Zionist principles of the Pittsburgh Platform. They were afraid of the charge of "dual allegiance." They dissociated themselves completely from Zionism. To this day they have not been able to accept the existence of the Jewish state.

What was the work of the United Jewish Appeal?

In 1938, when the financial needs of the Jews of Europe were so great, a broader fund-raising agency, which was called the United Jewish Appeal, or the UJA, was organized. The UJA represented three major agencies: the JDC, which served Jews all over the world, the United Palestine Appeal, which worked specifically in Israel, the United Service for New Americans, which helped rehabilitate refugees and settle them in the United States.

From 1947 on, the major concern of the UJA was the relocation of refugees in the Yishuv. In the critical year of 1947, $170 million was raised by American Jews. Half went directly to Palestine. Most of the other half went to rescue work in Europe and North Africa and for the resettlement of refugees in the United States.

With the exception of the insignificant membership of the American Council for Judaism, all the American Jewry was united on behalf of the Yishuv. Above and beyond the huge sums given to the UJA, Jews and Christians alike had contributed heavily towards the purchase of ships like the *Exodus*, arms for the Haganah, and other important projects needed by the Yishuv.

What was the recommendation of the UN committee?

All this outpouring of philanthropy, hope, and prayer hung in the balance as the United Nations undertook the task of solving the Palestine problem.

Despite the efforts of American Jews, the American delegation to the UN appeared neutral, their neutrality being inspired by the British.

The British were still more concerned with Arab oil than with Jewish blood. They argued that in the event of a Communist threat to the Middle East, the friendship of the large Arab populations would be necessary and helpful. The British had to justify their previous acts in the Yishuv, and clung to this theory even though the Arabs had hardly proved themselves as allies in World War II. The Arab nations spoke heatedly against the creation of a Jewish state. Their talks were steeped in anti-Semitism, hatred of the Jews, and threats of war.

With this agitation going on behind the scenes, the UN met in assembly. The first session on the Palestine problem resulted in the appointment of a fact-finding committee to investigate the situation at first-hand. The eleven-member commission held hearings in Jerusalem and Lebanon, and visited the refugee camps of Europe where they saw the survivors of German brutality.

At the end of August, 1947, the commission published its majority report, called the Partition Plan. Under this plan, Palestine was to be divided into two states, one for the Jews and one for the Arabs. Jerusalem was to remain an international city under the jurisdiction of the UN. Great Britain was to give up the Mandate the following year. Until she did so, however, she was to keep peace in Palestine.

How was the Partition Plan received?

The Arabs rejected the plan completely. They vowed they would never allow a Jewish state to exist in Palestine.

The Yishuv was disappointed. All of Palestine was not too large to begin with, and to cut it up into two parts made it seem very small indeed. Furthermore, partition meant giving up the hope of possessing all of the Holy Land. Partition also meant giving up the Holy City, Jerusalem.

LEBANON
SYRIA
ARAB
JEWISH
Haifa
Nazareth
JEWISH
Nablus
ARAB
Tel Aviv
Jaffa
Jericho
Jerusalem
Bethlehem
Gaza
INTERNATIONAL
ZONE
Hebron
JORDAN
Beersheba
ARAB
JEWISH
EGYPT
THE UNITED
NATIONS
PARTITION PLAN
FOR PALESTINE
1947

Nevertheless, the fact that the United Nations recognized the right of the Jews to establish an independent state was cheering and encouraging. Half a loaf was better than none. The Jews were willing to study, and perhaps accept, the plan.

But now it had to be accepted by the Assembly of the United Nations.

When was the Partition Plan passed?

All the persuasiveness, all the influence of the entire Jewish community of the free world, was enlisted in behalf of the Yishuv. Even the American Jewish Committee which had been lukewarm to the Zionist program, finally endorsed the Partition Plan.

From September to November, 1947, the United Nations debated the plan. Leaders of world Zionism spoke before the international organization. Dr. Chaim Weizmann, respected scientist and lifelong leader of world Zionism, Moshe Sharett, and David ben Gurion, bold and determined leaders of the Yishuv, firmly and realistically presented the Zionist cause. Unexpected support came from the Russian delegation, which wanted to remove the British from their dominant position in the Middle East. The Arab states, on the other hand, pledged a war of annihilation against any Jewish state that might be established.

The discussion continued to seesaw until the American delegation finally announced its intention to support the plan. It was undoubtedly owing to the great moral integrity of President Harry S. Truman that the cause of the Yishuv was recognized by the United States.

On November 29, 1947, the final vote was taken. The collective heart of world Jewry stopped beating as each country called out its "aye" or "nay." Jews all over the world sat glued to their radios, waiting, hoping, and praying. In the Yishuv, all business was at a standstill. There was an air of hushed silence.

The fate of an entire people was being decided by the nations of the world.

A two-thirds majority of those voting was required in order for the Partition Plan to become reality. Then the good news rang out. The General Assembly had accepted the Partition Plan by two votes more than the required two-thirds. The United States, France, and Russia had voted in the affirmative. Great Britain had abstained.

How did the announcement affect the Yishuv?

The two-thousand-year-old hope had at last come true. The United Nations had authorized the establishment of a Jewish state.

In America, men and women danced in the streets. Thousands of Jews came to rally in Madison Square Garden in New York City. Those who were unable to get into the Garden gathered in the streets and heard the program over loud speakers. Special prayers were offered in the synagogues. The Jewish people in America wept for joy that at last, at last, their dream would be realized.

In the Yishuv the rejoicing was mingled with watchfulness. There was much to be done, for they were surrounded by Arab enemies.

On the day after the United Nations decision, Arab forces began guerrilla warfare against the Jews. Palestinian Arabs and troops from the neighboring lands of Syria, Jordan, Iraq, and Egypt attacked outlying settlements. They sniped at road traffic, cut water lines, and firing from surprise ambushes, seized vital hill positions.

The British who were obligated by the UN decision to keep the peace until the two states were formed, did hardly anything to protect the Yishuv or stop the war. Instead, they helped the Arabs by interfering with Jewish defense efforts and by allowing the Arabs to occupy strategic positions.

But the Haganah had anticipated the British attitude.

Quickly, they moved against the major Arab cities of Jaffa, Haifa, Safed, and Tiberias. The blow was so sudden that Arab strategists ordered their people to flee from their homes to points across the partition line. Each fleeing Arab frightened another one into going until hundreds of thousands of Arabs had left the Jewish sections of Palestine to the Jews.

When was the Jewish state declared?

A serious complication took place when in a sudden about-face, the American government placed an embargo on the shipment of arms to the Middle East. The embargo was supposed to stop warfare by keeping weapons from both sides. In fact, it only hampered the Jews, who had no other sources to turn to. On the other hand, the British were supplying the Arabs with large quantities of all kinds of military equipment.

Since the Yishuv had not yet officially become a state, it could not receive recognition or help from other powers. Nor did any nation do anything to stop the Arab attacks or the malicious interference of the British.

To add to the problem, the British, on Friday, May 14, 1948, turned their forts and military supplies over to the Arabs and suddenly left Palestine. They probably thought that with their forces out of the way, the Arabs would swarm into Palestine from the neighboring countries and drive the Yishuv into the sea. Perhaps the British hoped that Jewish resistance would break down and that they would be called back to rule once again.

But the Yishuv had no such intentions. As soon as the British withdrew, the National Council of the Yishuv alerted the Haganah that a new state would be proclaimed. At least another day was needed to put everything in order. But since the following day was Sabbath, the 37 members of the National Council were hastily assembled that very day to meet in Tel Aviv.

So it was that on May 14, 1948, on the fifth day of Sivan

in the year 5708, David ben Gurion, chairman of the National Council, declared that the new state had come into being. As the sound of gunfire was heard from the hills, Ben Gurion in a choked and solemn voice read the proclamation fulfilling the historic dream of the people of Israel. Radios in all parts of the country, in Haganah barracks, in frontier settlements, and deep in the hills of Jerusalem, carried the significant words which brought the State of Israel into being.

> ...we, the members of the National Council, representing the Jewish people in Palestine and the Zionist movement of the world, met together in solemn assembly by virtue of the natural and historic right of the Jewish people and the resolution of the General Assembly of the United Nations, hereby proclaim the establishment of the Jewish state in Palestine, to be called Israel.

The one great moment of glory in the history of the people had finally come. After years of pain, persecution, struggle, and hope, the State of Israel had come into being. The six million Jews who had been killed did not live to see this day. For them, the miracle came too late. But their martyrdom had convinced the world of the need for a Jewish homeland. They, too, had built the Jewish state.

Which was the first country to recognize the new state?

Within two hours after the state was proclaimed, President Harry S. Truman, one of its greatest friends, extended formal American recognition of Israel. The Soviet Union followed soon after, as did many of the other great powers.

The first American Ambassador to Israel was James G. McDonald. The first Israeli Ambassador to the United States was Abba Eban, an outstanding scholar, brilliant thinker, inspired speaker, and firm advocate of the cause of his people.

When did the War of Independence break out?

The very first night of Jewish independence, on May 15, 1948, the armies of five Arab countries poured over the borders of the State of Israel. Among them was the crack Arab Legion of Jordan, which the British government had financed, trained, staffed, and directed. Brigadier General J. B. Glubb, a British officer and commander of the Legion, personally led the Jordanian attack. The other armies came from Syria, Egypt, Lebanon, Iraq, and later Saudi Arabia. Since Israel was surrounded by these countries, the attack came from all directions at once.

The Arabs also brought into play planes, long-distance artillery, tanks, and heavy equipment which they had been receiving for years from the Western powers. They soon proved their mechanical advantage in an Egyptian air raid on Tel Aviv in which 41 Jews were killed.

Israel did not own even one long-range cannon. She had no antitank guns. She had no navy, and her air force was almost nonexistent. It was no wonder then that the Arabs boasted at the time of their invasion that this would be a "war of extermination."

What was the policy of "Eyn Breyrah"?

But the Arab masses and their equipment could not overcome the Jewish determination to fight. The newly independent Yishuv had vowed that there would never be another massacre of Jews as had taken place in Germany. Nor would they give up an inch up of the free soil that they finally possessed. They entered the War of Independence with the unyielding determination that they would win or perish. This determination they captured in their slogan, "Eyn Breyrah," "There is no choice."

Eyn Breyrah meant that if you could not capture a hill by shelling it with heavy artillery, then you captured it by heroic hand-to-hand combat. It meant that if there were no antitank guns to stop the heavy Arab armor, then bottles were filled with gasoline and explosives and volunteers threw themselves under the treads of the tanks to wreck them. It meant that every boy and girl, man and woman, from the ages of 6 to 60 accepted an iron discipline and fought for his land. It meant that overnight factories were organized to produce rough tools of war. Eyn Breyrah meant that Israel had to survive. There was no other choice.

With Eyn Breyrah as its backbone, the Haganah, now the National Army of Israel, without any weapons for offensive, fought a holding war until it could find better equipment. For eight months, Israel's War of Liberation continued. The United Nations ordered several cease fires, which lasted for days at a time but were always broken by the Arabs when they thought they saw an advantage.

The colonies in the Negev, in the south of Israel, which were widely separated from each other and from the center of Israel, took terrible punishment. Many a settlement was leveled by Egyptian long-range cannons and planes until not a hut remained standing. But when the Arab foot soldiers approached in face-to-face combat, the settlements always remained in Israeli hands.

What was the "Davidka"?

Glorious chapters of Israeli heroism were written in almost every battle. The best-known was the Battle of Jerusalem.

When the war broke out, Jerusalem, which penetrates like a finger into what is now Jordan territory, was cut off from the rest of Israel. The Old City was captured by the Arabs, and the New City, where almost one hundred thousand Jews lived, was under heavy siege by Jordanian and Egyptian units. In addition, the one road that led to Jerusalem was dominated by hills which the Arabs had captured. No Jewish convoy could get through those hills. Soon shortages of water, food, and electricity began to plague the defenders of Jerusalem.

Under constant fire from the hills, the New City was running out of ammunition as well. There were only several mortars in all Jerusalem. They were handmade, rough, and impractical weapons mounted on wheels. These mortars were rushed from one corner of the city to the other, fired, and then rushed to another corner to fire again. The mortar was called the "Davidka." The Davidka made a terrifying sound, being more noisy than it was effective—and since it was fired from different parts of the city each time, the Arabs became so confused that they thought there was a great concentration of artillery in Jerusalem. They were afraid to rush in and attack.

What is the "K'vish HaG'Vurah"?

While the inhabitants of Jerusalem fired off the Davidkas, a daring plan was formulated by the Israeli General Staff. Through their archeological studies they knew that there was an ancient, abandoned road leading to Jerusalem. They searched until they found it. Then a magnificent plan was put in operation.

Thousands of soldiers and civilians, men and women, volunteered to lay a new road, following the track of the old one. The work could be done only under cover of night, not only because of fear of the enemy but also because the volunteers could not be spared from their daytime assignments at the front or in industry.

As each night fell, thousands of the workers gathered along the way of the road. By moonlight and by the sense of touch, they built a new road through the hills and cliffs to the city of Jerusalem. The heroic construction cracked the siege of the New City and enabled the Israeli Army eventually to capture Jerusalem and clean out the Arabs from the surrounding hills.

This road has often been called Israel's Burma Road. Today in Israel, it is known as "Kvish haG'Vurah," the Highway of Heroism.

How did Americans help the Israeli War of Independence?

While the furious fighting continued, the Jews of America realized that their future, as well as that of the Yishuv, hinged on the successful defense of Israel. Despite the United States embargo on the sale of arms, huge sums were raised to buy the necessary war materials and ship them to Israel.

Many American, Canadian, and South African Jews rushed to join the Israel Army of Liberation. They were the technicians and pilots that were so desperately needed.

Among the volunteers was Col. David Marcus, a West Point graduate and magnificent soldier. Colonel Marcus had a distinguished military record in World War II, having served on the staff of Gen. George C. Marshall and Gen. Douglas MacArthur and having accompanied President Roosevelt to Yalta when he met Premier Josef Stalin, of the U.S.S.R., and President Truman at the Potsdam Conference. At both these meetings, final plans were made for dealing with Germany at the end of the war. Colonel Marcus also helped draw up the surrender terms for Germany and Italy.

Colonel Marcus visited the Dachau concentration camp and realized the urgency of finding a home for the Jewish refugees. Almost immediately, he was smuggled into Palestine by the Jewish Agency, where he offered his services to the Haganah.

He began to work dictating the first military manual of the Haganah, set up officers' training schools, recommended the type of arms and weapons that the Haganah should buy and use.

"Micky" Marcus soon became one of the most beloved men in Israel, and one of its most brilliant defenders. He was put in charge of the Jerusalem defense ring, the most dangerous sector of the war. Unfortunately, he was killed just a few hours before the cease fire went into effect in June, 1948. There, like many hundreds of other Jews, Micky Marcus died a hero in the fight for freedom. His body was brought back to America where it was buried with full military honors at West Point.

Why was Israel opposed to an armistice?

With better weapons and with the beginnings of a modest Air Force, the Army of Israel slowly gained the initiative. The

quick victory which the Arabs had expected soon turned to humiliating defeat. The invaders were repelled. Egypt, the strongest of the Arab states, was itself invaded by Israeli units, and Cairo, its capital, was bombed.

The United Nations had done nothing to stop the war in its early stages when Israel teetered on the brink of defeat. But when the Arab states were driven from the Israeli borders, alarm set in. The United Nations now acted to bring about an armistice which the Arabs were entirely willing to accept.

The Israeli General Staff was against an armistice. Israeli troops would have to retreat from large stretches of Arab territory which they were now occupying. What was more important, the old city of Jerusalem was still in Arab hands. However, in the interests of peace and to show its good faith, the government of Israel indicated its willingness to negotiate.

Dr. Ralph Bunche, an American Negro, was appointed to lead the armistice talks. In January, 1949, they began, and after six months of discussion, the terms were finally agreed to. The boundaries of Israel were established. Armistice agreements were signed with Egypt, Jordan, Lebanon, Syria, and Iraq. Israel remained firm and free, the new Jewish homeland.

What problems did the armistice leave unsolved?

The armistice did not mean that peace had come to Israel. The Arab states determinedly refused to recognize the State of Israel, although it was recognized by almost all the world, including Great Britain. They refuse to this day to end the armistice and sign peace treaties with Israel. Since an armistice is only a temporary truce, technically, a state of war still exists between Israel and the Arabs.

These Arab countries are still boycotting, sabotaging, and blockading all Israeli efforts. Egypt, which controls the Suez Canal, still refuses passage to Israeli ships and to ships dealing with Israel. The Arab countries are also still publicly threatening Israel with a "second round" of war. They even make these threats in the halls of the United Nations. This blustering has caused continued Arab incidents along the borders between Israel and her neighbors. In 1956, Israel was forced to carry out a lightning-swift invasion of Egypt in order to end the border incidents.

Israel is also unhappy about the splitting of Jerusalem. The old city of Jerusalem, where the Temple stood and through which passes the road to the famous Hadassah Hospital and the Hebrew University, is in the hands of Jordan. Of all the Arab states, Jordan gained the most, because it annexed all the land which, according to the Partition Plan, was to have constituted a new Arab state.

Finally, there exists a problem of hundreds of thousands of Arab refugees who fled their homes in Israel on the advice of their leaders. These refugees are penned up in huge camps in the Gaza Strip, on the borders of Israel, and are supported by allowances from the United Nations.

After the war, Israel could not permit all the Arab refugees to return, because they were implacable enemies of the state, and would form a gigantic "fifth column." Instead, the government offered, and still continues to offer, to permit some to return and to pay the others for the properties they left. Israel has even offered to contribute towards resettling these Arabs in the vast, empty Arab lands. The Arab states, however, refuse to accept these offers and are using the refugees as an instrument with which to whip up public opinion against the Jews. In the many years since the war, the number of Arabs in the camps has continued to grow, and the problem is worse today.

When Israel's War of Independence was over and when the last shots of the war had been fired, even the most calloused Jew realized that the gallant Haganah and the courageous philosophy of Eyn Breyrah could not of themselves have sufficed to bring victory. The 650,000 Jews of Israel could hardly have been expected to win a war against six nations of almost 40 million people! It must have been a miracle given to the people of Israel by God!

Things to Remember

1. What was the Partition Plan?
2. What is the work of the UJA? Why is it important?
3. When was the State of Israel declared?
4. Why did Israel have to fight a War of Independence? With whom? What were the results of the war?

Things to Think About

1. How did the policy of Eyn Breyrah affect the thinking of the Israeli army and people? Do you think that same policy holds true today?
2. Your text says that six million martyrs who died helped build a Jewish state. How?
3. Israel has three main problems facing it today. How do you think these problems will be solved?

CHAPTER SEVENTEEN

THE NEW STATE OF ISRAEL

The United Nations machinery to arrange the Armstice between Israel and the Arab countries began to work on January, 1949. On February 14, the first meeting of the Knesset, the National Assembly of Israel, was held.

What is Israel's form of government?

Israel is a democratic republic governed by the Knesset, or Assembly. This legislature consists of only one house, the Chamber of Deputies. There are 120 members in the Knesset elected by the citizens of Israel. The first Knesset was elected in 1949. In the Knesset of 1959, 14 different political parties were represented. Among the 120 members were 4 Christians, 2 Moslems and 2 Druse.

In addition to making the laws, the Knesset elects the President, who serves for a five-year term.

What are the duties of the President of Israel?

The President has many duties, among them the concluding of international treaties, appointing the Commander-in-Chief of the Armed Forces, commissioning officers, and receiving foreign diplomats. He also has the power to pardon criminals and reduce their sentences. His functions, however, are mostly of an honorary nature.

The most important duty of the President is to appoint the Prime Minister and the heads of the various departments of state.

What is a coalition Cabinet?

The Prime Minister must have a majority of the Knesset. If he is a member of a political party which does not have a majority, the Prime Minister will often add members of other parties to his Cabinet, so that the Cabinet as a whole will have majority support. This is called a coalition Cabinet.

The Prime Minister is the most important officer in the state.

How does Israel practice democracy?

All citizens of Israel, whether Jewish or non-Jewish, have equal civic and political rights. Every citizen above the age of 18, regardless of sex, race, or religion, may vote in the election of the Knesset.

Hebrew is the official language of the land, but Arabic-speaking citizens are able to use their own language in the legislature and before the courts.

While the basic law of Israel decrees that the Sabbath and the Jewish Holy Days shall be days of rest, it adds: "The Holy Days of other religious denominations shall equally be recognized as legal days of rest for the members of such denominations."

What are the political parties of Israel?

The largest political party of Israel is the Mapai. It is one of several labor parties composed mostly of farmers and industrial workers. The Mapai believes in government control of production, and stresses the importance of labor in the new state. Through the Histadrut, the General Federation of Labor, the Mapai shows its great strength. David ben Gurion, Israel's first Prime Minister, was one of the organizers of Mapai and stands at its head. Another organizer was Yitzchak ben Zvi, the second President of the State of Israel. Other leading government figures in the first decade of Israel's existence were also members of Mapai.

After the labor parties, the religious parties are the next powerful group. They consist of the merged Mizrachi and Hapoel Hamizrachi movements known as the National Religious Party, the Agudath Israel, and the Poalei Agudath Israel. The purpose of the Religious Zionists is to influence the Jewish state to respect the religious traditions of Israel, and to observe them in all the functions of the state. The Mizrachi-Hapoel Hamizrachi have a strong following in the religious settlements which Orthodox Jews established.

Agudath Israel and its labor branch, the Poalei Agudath Israel, were for a long time opposed to Zionism. They believed that the return to Zion would become a reality only with the coming of the Messiah. They also refused to participate with nonreligious Jews in building the land. When the state was proclaimed, however, they became active politically, are represented in the Knesset, and have been in Ben Gurion's coalition cabinets at different times.

Among the other parties of Israel are the Mapam, the Cherut, and the General Zionists. The Mapam is another labor party which is critical of the policies of the Western powers. It blames Great Britain and her interests in Arabian oil for Israel's troubles, and fears that Great Britain's influence on the United States may still damage Israel.

The Cherut party is an outgrowth of the Irgun, and its name means "freedom." The head of Cherut is Menachem Beigen, who was the fiery leader of the Irgun. The Cherut party is still urging the Israeli government to extend the boundaries of the state to include all the land that lies west of the Jordan River, and part of what is now Jordan.

The General Zionists are related to the Zionist Organization of America and are a middle-of-the-road group. An offshoot of the General Zionists is the Progressive party, which is closer to the left, drawing some of its members from the Histadrut.

There are also Arab parties, an insignificant Communist party, and several splinter parties.

Who was the first President of Israel?

On February 14, 1949, the first meeting of the Knesset was held in the Holy City. It fell on Chamisha Oser B'Shvat, the Festival of the Trees. The Arab-Israeli war was at a standstill, and sunshine and peace seemed to prevail. The expectancy of spring bathed Jerusalem and all of Israel, and with that expectancy rose a new hope in the air, a hope for the new state itself.

When the Provisional Council had proclaimed the state in May, 1948, they had elected Chaim Weizmann as Provisional President. Of him Ben Gurion had said, "Weizmann may not need Israel, but Israel needs Weizmann." Now, as the formal and official government was taking over the guidance of the state, it was fitting that Weizmann should be called on again. On February 17, Dr. Weizmann was elected the first President of the State of Israel. As an honor guard led him to the dais of the Assembly, the diplomatic corps and delegates rose as one to honor the great scientist-statesman and servant of his people. In a solemn moment, broken only by the sounding of the shofar, there was a spontaneous outburst of the singing of Hatikvah.

Chaim Weizmann stood erect before the people who had loved him and chosen him to receive the highest honor they could bestow. At 75 years of age, tired, and suffering from waning eyesight, Weizmann represented a lifetime of devoted service and leadership to the people of Israel. As he stood there, he silently recalled the Zionist Congresses in Basle which he had attended more than half a century ago. The words of Herzl came back to him now as words of a prophecy. "If you will," Herzl had said, "it is no dream." The people of Israel had willed, and the dream was now reality.

His eyes turned moist, and in a low voice, Chaim Weizmann took the oath of office.

> I, Chaim, son of Ozer and Rachel Weizmann, undertake as President of the State, to maintain allegiance to the State of Israel and to its laws.

Three days earlier when Weizmann had opened the Knesset, he had expressed the feeling of Jews everywhere when he had said:

> This is a great moment in our history. Let us give thanks and praise to the God of Israel, who, in His mercy, granted us the privilege of witnessing the redemption of our people after centuries of affliction and suffering.
>
> It is our people who once gave the whole world the spiritual message fundamental to civilization. The world is watching us now to see the way we choose in ordering our lives, how we fashion our State. The world is listening to hear whether a new message will go forth from Zion, and what that message will be.
>
> Today is a great day in our lives....From this place we send fraternal blessings to our brethren throughout the world.

Now, as President of the State of Israel, Chaim Weizmann was ready to continue his service to his people. His first act of office was to call upon David ben Gurion to head the Cabinet and become the Prime Minister of Israel.

What was B.G.'s career as a Zionist?

Ben Gurion, or B.G., as he is fondly called, is one of the most remarkable men on the Jewish scene, a great orator and profound thinker and philosopher. His determination and personality more than that of any other man have influenced the nature of the Jewish state.

Ben Gurion was born in 1886 in Poland. In 1906, he came to Palestine, and together with Yitzchak ben Z'vi, founded the Poalei Zion movement. He studied law at Constantinople, was exiled by the Turks, and returned as a soldier in 1918. Before returning, both he and Ben Z'vi were active in recruiting soldiers for the Jewish Legion in the United States.

Ben Gurion is a Socialist who believes in the importance of labor and the laboring man. Together with Ben Z'vi, he helped found the labor movement, and the Histadrut. He was also active in the Jewish Agency during the years of the Mandate.

It was Ben Gurion who was a founder of the Haganah, the architect of Jewish resistance under the British, and the major strategist of the War of Liberation. Even though he is far from being a religious man, when his colleagues in the Cabinet were despondent over the bloody siege of Jerusalem and asked how he proposed to defend the city, Ben Gurion responded, " I believe in miracles."

Ben Gurion bolstered his faith in miracles by his faith in the people of Israel. At the United Nations deliberations, he had said firmly, "Jews will sacrifice themselves for Jerusalem no less than Englishmen for London, Russians for Moscow, or Americans for Washington."

He also applied himself with intense concentration to the study of military matters. At the age of 60 he began to study the functions of a supreme commander, surrounding himself with bright young men who had learned about strategy and logistics in the Haganah and in the British Army.

When B.G. became Prime Minister in 1949, however, much had to be done. The wreckage of war had to be cleared, a treasury and postal system had to be established, budgets had to be prepared, taxes levied, courts set up, schools built, new immigrants provided for. In short, a country had to be established. The Knesset, with Ben Gurion at its head, systematically went to work on all these problems.

When did Israel join the United Nations?

One of the most important achievements of the early days of the state took place when it became a member of the United Nations. On May 11, 1949, almost a year to the day after the state was proclaimed, the UN Assembly voted to accept Israel as its 55th member nation. Fifty-one nations made up the international body in October, 1945, when it was organized. Israel was the fourth nation to be admitted after the UN came into being.

What is Mount Herzl?

In all the bustling excitement and activity of the beginnings of the state, the people of Israel did not forget the one man who was most responsible for the dream of the homeland—Dr. Theodor Herzl.

Herzl was so sure that a state would be born that he had asked in his will that his remains be transported for burial in Israel as soon as the state came into being. In August of 1949, an Israeli plane brought the Herzl coffin back from Vienna. As the plane landed at Lydda Airport in Tel Aviv, Prime Minister Ben Gurion and his cabinet received the flag-draped casket on the soil of the Holy Land.

A burial place was chosen for Herzl on the peak of the highest hill near Jerusalem. There, as the body was lowered to its grave, hundreds of bags of earth, one from each of the hamlets, towns, and cities of the Holy Land, were deposited beside it. Herzl, in his eternal rest, was sheltered by earth from all the land of Israel that he loved so dearly. The guards presented arms and the multitude of reverent Jews recited the Kaddish. Herzl had come home at last.

The hill on which Herzl is buried is called Har Herzl, Mount Herzl. Other prominent Zionists have been buried near Herzl. And not far from him is Israel's National Military Cemetery with its hundreds of bodies of men and women, boys and girls, who died so that Israel would be free.

What is the Law of Return?

Nor did Israel forget the prime purpose of its existence, to create a home for the homeless. In 1950, the state proclaimed the Law of Return, enunciating one of the finest and noblest ideas of freedom. The law said that there would never be any bar against Jewish immigration to Israel. It said that all Jews, regardless of where they came from and what their condition was, had the right to return to Israel.

The Law of Return opened the door to all refugees, and soon the Yishuv was straining all its resources. In the first five years of its existence, Israel doubled its population. Today there are more than a million and three quarters Jews living in Israel, of which almost a million are immigrants who arrived since the establishment of the state.

What economic problem did the Law of Return impose on Israel?

The immigrants, like the original chalutzim, came from many lands. They came from the different countries of Europe, from the Western Hemisphere and most recently from the colorful lands of Asia and Africa. Today in Israel, there are Jews from Yemen and from Iraq, from Tunisia, and from Cochin, in southern India, from Iran and from Morocco, from Afghanistan and from South Africa. There are Oriental, dark-skinned Jews, as well as Ashkenazic and Sephardic Jews. All who have found persecution or unhappiness in the lands of the Diaspora have been welcomed in Israel on an equal basis with the original pioneers.

Most of the entering immigrants were ill and destitute. Those who came from Arab lands had been reduced to the state of beggars. Their property and possessions had been confiscated.

The survivors of the DP camps were utterly impoverished. In addition, many were suffering from malnutrition and disease and needed special medical care.

In 1957, several thousand Jews were allowed to emigrate from Poland; and towards the end of 1958, a trickle of immigration came from Rumania. They, too, had been left only the most limited and meager of possessions.

All these immigrants had to be fed, housed, clothed, and maintained until they could become self-supporting. The Jews who came from the Arabian countries had to be given expensive medical care. They also had to be taught a trade, since in the Moslem lands they had been allowed no opportunities for advancement or education. As immigrants still come to Israel, the problem continues to strain the country's resources. "The Ingathering of the Exiles" is complicated by the fact that Israel has an area of only about 8000 square miles, roughly the size of New Jersey. A large portion of this area is desert or hill country, which is most difficult to cultivate and cannot produce any harvest or support any settlements.

To take care of the immigrants means that every Israeli has to assume a tremendous tax burden, accept limitations in food and clothes, and do without even the least luxury. This sacrifice the entire nation has made, and continues to make today.

How does the United States help Israel?

The Yishuv was not alone in its determination to help every homeless Jew return to the Holy Land. In 1956, in the United States, almost 75 million dollars were raised through the UJA for Israeli needs. Similar amounts had been raised previously, and more has been raised since.

In addition, many millions of dollars were contributed directly to recognized institutions like the Hadassah Hospital, the Hebrew University, the Weizmann Institute of Science, the Technion, Bar Ilan University, Mizrachi Children's Villages, and countless other causes.

The American government, too, through its various aid programs, has made substantial contributions to the development of Israel. From 1950 through 1958, about 540 million dollars have been provided to Israel in loans and aid.

Like all young countries, Israel required this assistance. Perhaps by now, if it had only the original 600,000 Jews to provide for, Israel might already have become self-sufficient. But as a haven and a home for all Jewish refugees, its needs have been greater, and Israel will require continued help for some time longer in order to aid the "Ingathering."

What was "Operation Magic Carpet"?

The money raised by the UJA in America was given as a direct gift to finance individuals and to support needy projects. One of the most dramatic events which the UJA made possible occurred in 1956.

The entire Jewish population of Yemen, a Moslem state in Arabia, was threatened with annihilation by the Arabs. After many conferences, permission was finally granted for the Jews to leave within a specified period of time. Immediately, a fleet of airplanes was engaged to shuttle back and forth and transport the Jews of Yemen en masse to Israel. The airlift which carried them to Israel was appropriately entitled "Operation Magic Carpet." The tremendous transportation costs of bringing these Yemenite Jews to Israel and of settling them on the land was defrayed by the UJA.

What are Bonds for Israel?

In 1951, American Jews conceived of another way in which to provide financial assistance to Israel. An organization was formed to sell bonds guaranteed by the State of Israel, These bonds are like the government bonds sold in the United States. Each bond is a loan which is repaid with 4 per cent interest by Israel within 10 years after the date of purchase.

The money which the government receives from the sale of the bonds is used to build houses for the immigrants, to create factories, to finance agricultural projects, to increase transportation facilities, to develop the land. In all, $366½ million worth of bonds were sold in the years from 1951 to 1958.

How did German reparations help the new economy?

In 1952, after long negotiations, the present West German government signed an agreement with Israel to make some payment for the property that was stolen from the Jews of Germany by the Nazis. The amount agreed upon was about $715 million to be paid over a 12-year period. By the agreement, Germany has acknowledged its guilt in the mass murder of Jews by Hitler.

The payment of these funds has helped provide railroad cars, passenger and freight ships, and heavy industrial machinery so necessary in establishing Israel's economy. Under this agreement, individual Jews have also received additional reparations, helping them to resettle themselves without government help.

How have the refugees themselves helped the country?

The refugees have not meant only hardships for Israel. They have also brought with them many assets. During the years since 1948, many desperately needed doctors and scientists, technicians and engineers, have entered the Holy Land. They were immediately placed in vital areas all over the land.

Most important of all, the new refugees have brought added manpower and energy. They too, are "willing" Israel to become a reality, a state in which everyone will live happily and peacefully.

What are the Dead Sea Scrolls?

Israel is more than just another state. It is the cradle of the world's religion and civilization. Every day great archeological findings within Israel's borders cast more light on the early years of man.

In November, 1947, days before the Partition Plan was ratified by the United Nations, a Jerusalem dealer in antiquities showed Dr. E. L. Sukenik, renowned archaeologist of the Hebrew University, a fragment of a parchment scroll written in ancient square Hebrew script. The dealer claimed that Bedouins had found several scrolls in sealed jars stored in caves near the Dead Sea.

Dr. Sukenik was excited beyond belief at the thought that there might be more scrolls in the caves. Violence had already broken out between the Arabs and Israel, and the entire area was in Arab hands. Nevertheless, Sukenik was determined to learn more about the scrolls. Against the advice of his own son, Yigal Yadin, who was Chief of Staff of the Israeli Army, the archeologist entered Arab territory.

A dignitary of the Syrian Church now had the scrolls in his possession. Sukenik met with his dealer, who granted permission to study the scrolls. Microscopic examination proved to Sukenik that the scrolls were indeed authentic, and were a finding of the greatest importance. He purchased three scrolls for about $100, and a staff of Hebrew University scholars went painstakingly to work to unroll and identify them.

After Sukenik's death, more scrolls appeared. Four of these were acquired by Yigal Yadin, who, in addition to being an Army strategist, was an enthusiastic archaeologist in his own right. These four were bought for a quarter of a million dollars, which Yadin obtained from an American philanthropist. So much had their value risen since the day Sukenik first saw them!

What is the importance of the scrolls?

There are other scrolls still in the possession of the Jordan government, and when all of these will be understood and their secret told, a light will be cast on early days in Israel.

Scholars have taken years simply to unfold the rolled-up scrolls so as not to damage them. They are being studied under ultraviolet rays and submitted to all kinds of tests to determine their age.

Most scholars believe that the scrolls may be as much as 2000 years old. Several of the scrolls appear to be translations and commentaries on different books of the Bible. If they prove to be authentic, the scrolls will teach us a great deal about the Bible, the Jewish sect known as the Essenes, and some forms of Jewish life in the time of the destruction of the Second Temple, in the year 70.

Who was the second President of Israel?

On November 9, 1952, Chaim Weizmann died, at the age of 70. Mourned by all Israel, he left a heritage of achievement and dedication to a cause which they will never forget. Thousands visit his grave annually in Rechovot. Near the great Scientific Institute which bears his name, Chaim Weizmann lies at rest.

To replace Weizmann was no easy task. But the Knesset found the right man almost immediately. A month after Weizmann's death, they elected another great scholar, the ardent Zionist and chalutz, Dr. Yitzchak ben Zvi.

In his early years, Ben Zvi's life paralleled Ben Gurion's. He had come to settle in Palestine in 1907, helping to organize the Poalei Zion movement there. He, too, studied law in Constantinople and was among those Zionists deported from Palestine by the Turks during World War I. Like Ben Gurion, he was in the United States to recruit soldiers for the Jewish Legion and then returned to serve as a soldier in its ranks. He is also a member of Mapai.

For the 17 years prior to the establishment of Israel as a state, Ben Zvi was chairman of the National Council which decided policy for the Yishuv under the British Mandate. He was a member of the Knesset at the very time that he was elected by his fellow Zionists to succeed Weizmann.

Ben Zvi is President of Israel today. Like Weizmann he is a well-known scholar. He has written extensive studies in Jewish history. Ben Zvi was responsible for founding the Ben Zvi Institute at the Hebrew University, which specializes in the study of Jewish communities in the Near and Middle East. Whenever he can spare time from his presidential duties, Yitzchak ben Zvi can be found in his office at the Hebrew University.

Israel is the only country in the world whose presidents have been intellectuals and scholars rather than just politicians. They, in their lives, have upheld the Jewish tradition for learning and knowledge.

Things to Remember

1. How is Israel governed today? What is the Knesset? What are the duties of the President and Prime Minister?
2. Name three political parties in Israel and what they stand for.
3. What is the Law of Return? What problems did the law present?
4. How do American Jews help Israel in their Ingathering of the Exiles?

Things to Think About

1. How are Chaim Weizmann and Yitzchak ben Zvi different from presidents of other governments? How is this difference related to everything that Israel has stood for?
2. Your text says the Law of Return is a noble law. Do you agree or disagree with this answer? Give reasons for your opinion.
3. Do you think American Jews are doing enough to help Israel stabilize its economy? Explain.

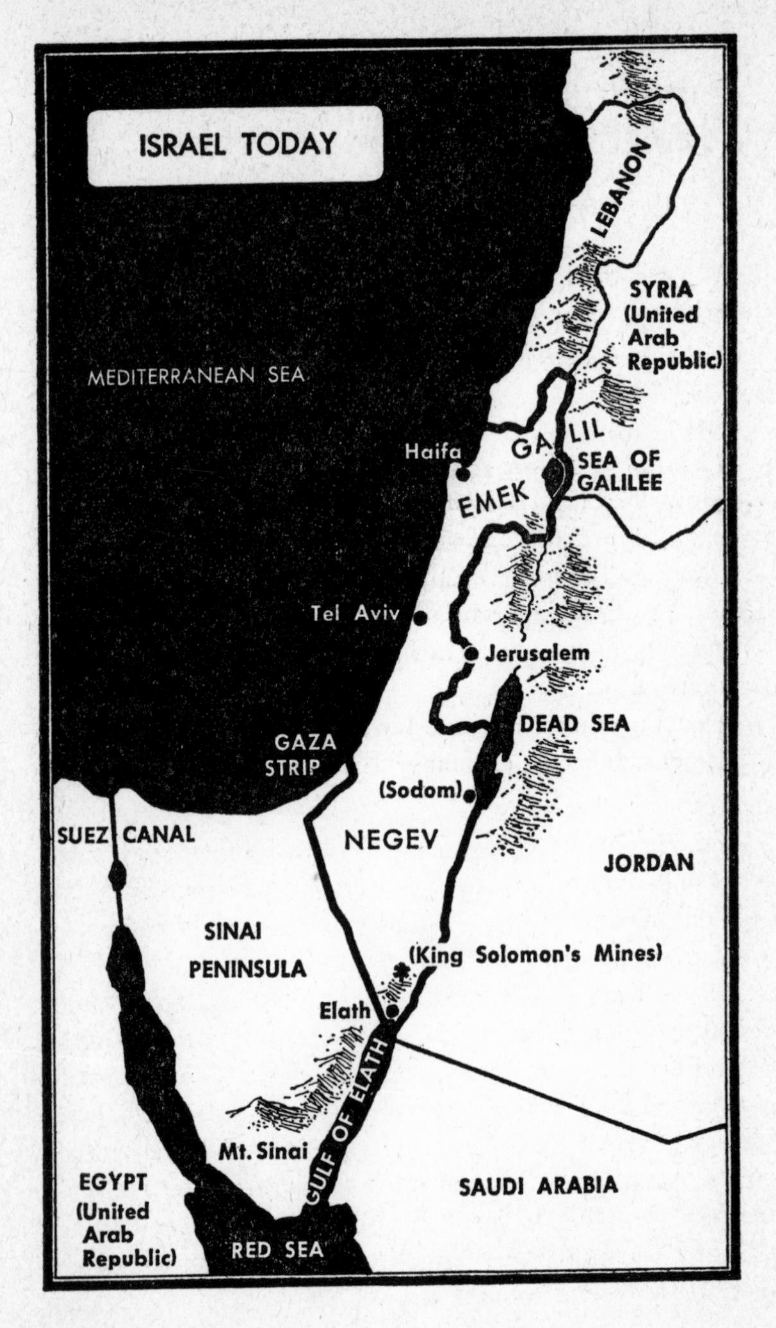
ISRAEL TODAY
LEBANON
SYRIA (United Arab Republic)
MEDITERRANEAN SEA
GALIL
Haifa
SEA OF GALILEE
EMEK
Tel Aviv
Jerusalem
DEAD SEA
GAZA STRIP
(Sodom)
SUEZ CANAL
NEGEV
JORDAN
SINAI PENINSULA
(King Solomon's Mines)
Elath
GULF OF ELATH
Mt. Sinai
EGYPT (United Arab Republic)
SAUDI ARABIA
RED SEA

UNIT FIVE:

ISRAEL AND AMERICA TODAY

Both Israel and America have been guided by the Biblical principles of human liberty, equality, and justice. In America, we have seen how recognition was given to the ethical teachings of the Torah by the founders of our Constitution. The fight against religious intolerance and political tyranny found inspiration and guidance in the Jewish Bible. As we watched the Colonies grow, we learned how the spirit of American democracy was shaped and molded throughout the years until it became what it is today.

Israel, too, has maintained this spirit of democracy. It is the only truly democratic republic in the Middle East. There is no other land in that part of the world that is so aware of the responsibility of man to his fellow man, and the need for fairness and justice in every aspect of national life.

This regard for brotherhood, for the principles of righteousness as opposed to tyranny, dictatorship, and oppression, has been the attribute of the Jewish people throughout the ages. In Israel, it is reaching its full expression.

As we bring Jewish history in America and Israel up to date, you will see that the two countries share in their great dedication to human rights and democracy. We have already emphasized the bonds that tie American Jews to Israeli Jews. We have also seen the common influence of the Biblical heritage on the American and Israeli forms of government. All these ties have roots in God and in the Torah. We Jews see here the effect of Torah and the Will of God on all history and on the destiny of every man and woman.

CHAPTER EIGHTEEN

ISRAEL TODAY

What are Israel's industries?

Since the War of Liberation, Israel has developed and grown. Farms and orchards, growing citrus and other fruits, and olive groves are covering what once were barren and wasted areas. Grains, peanuts, cotton, bananas, and vegetables also flourish. Backbreaking work is going on to drain swamplands, irrigate the dry land, and reforest as many stretches of land as possible. Israel's chief agricultural industries are wine making, oil pressing, and citrus growing.

However, Israel still is not self-sufficient. She must rely heavily on materials imported from abroad. The development of agriculture is one of the country's main interests. The Department of Agriculture has established many agricultural schools and a fishing school. Young men and women are sent abroad on scholarship grants to learn the latest methods and then to bring them home to Israel.

Although Israel has no significant heavy industry, it has assembly plants for automobiles, refrigerators, and other products. It is also manufacturing textile goods, cement, building materials, and some electrical products including a limited amount of machinery. Israel is already the second largest diamond cutting and polishing center in the world. Israel also has

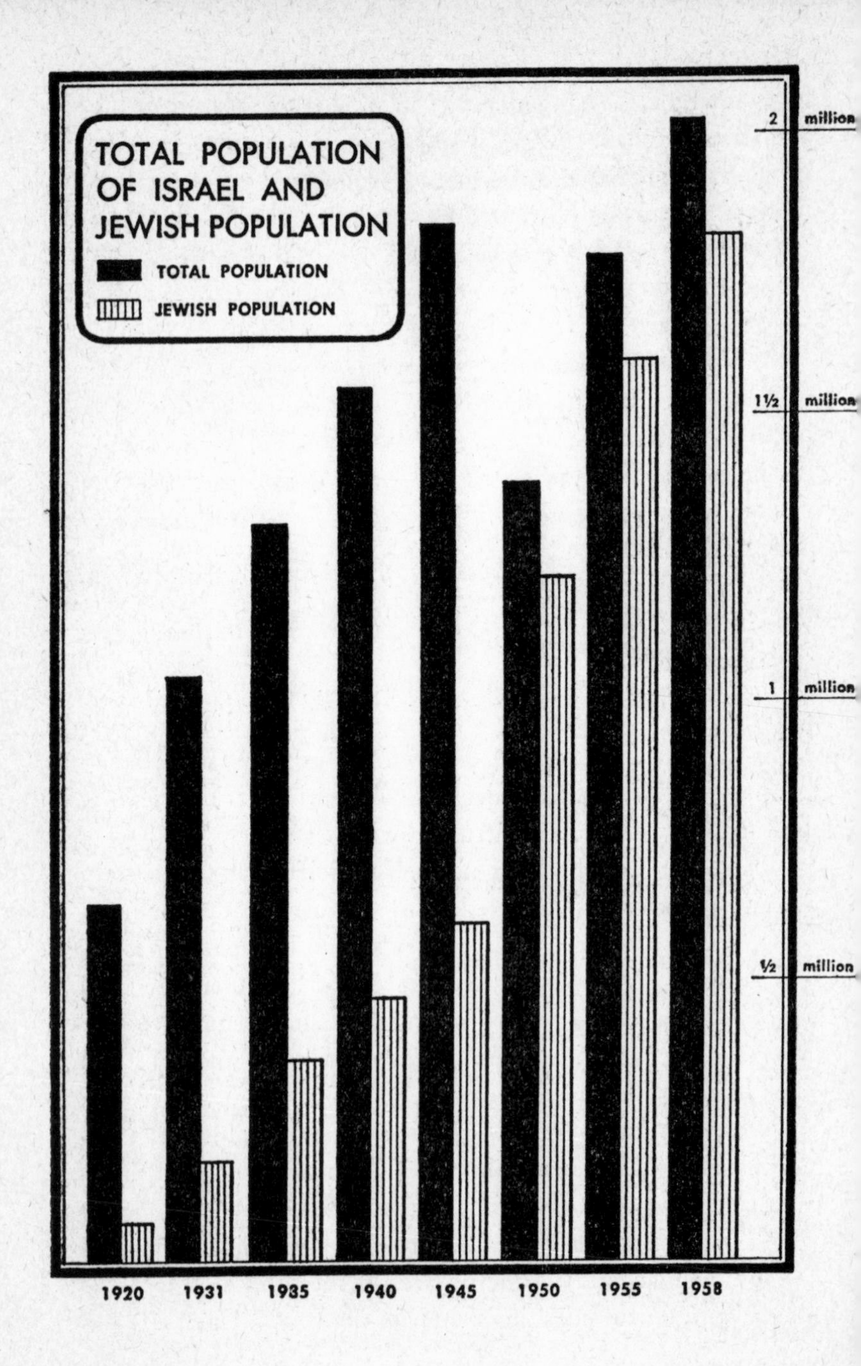
TOTAL POPULATION OF ISRAEL AND JEWISH POPULATION
TOTAL POPULATION
JEWISH POPULATION
2 million
1½ million
1 million
½ million
1920
1931
1935
1940
1945
1950
1955
1958

its own airline, El Al, which flies to all parts of the world, and a modest merchant marine. The government is striving to improve its industrial and production facilities in order to make more jobs available. Greater industry will also raise the standard of living and will reduce, as much as possible, the need to import from other countries.

What is the geography of Israel?

Israel can roughly be divided into three main areas. The north is called the Galil. The central and coastal plain is called the Emek, the Hebrew word for "valley." The southern part of Israel is called the Negev. The Jordan River and the Kingdom of Jordan bound Israel on the East, while the Mediterranean is its western border. Egypt is to the south and southwest of Israel, while Lebanon is on its northwest border. At its northeast lies Syria.

Its important bodies of water are the Sea of Galilee, or Lake Kinneret, which is at the upper part of the Jordan River in the Galil. The Dead Sea is formed at the southern end of the Jordan River and is 1300 feet below sea level. The Biblical city of Sodom is at the lower tip of the Dead Sea.

The southern part of Israel is wedged-shaped, like a triangle, with the narrow tip pointing south. Jordan continues along the eastern border, with Egypt on the western border. Actually the western border is nothing more than a geographic line drawn through the desert. On the Israeli side of the line, the desert is called the Negev. On the Egyptian side it is called the Sinai Peninsula. The peninsula was named after the mountain range which runs through it. On one of the peaks of this range, Mount Sinai, the Torah was given to the Jews.

The tip of the triangle ends at the Gulf of Elath, also called the Gulf of Akkaba, which empties into the Red Sea. Israel is developing a major port at this point, in the city of Elath. Elath is of great importance because it is the waterway to trade with Africa. In the event that the Suez Canal remains closed to Israeli shipping, this is the only port through which Israel can ship out merchandise and receive merchandise from the rest of the world.

The discovery of the ancient King Solomon's mines has led to the production of copper in the Elath area. More and more precious minerals such as potash, phosphate, uranium, sulphur, and glass sand are being produced in great quantities, both from the Dead Sea and from Elath.

What is the climate of Israel?

Because Israel lies between the sea and the desert, because it has high mountains and areas that are below sea level, it has only two seasons. Winter is the cold, rainy season. Summer is the hot, dry season. During hot weather there are occasional dry winds from the east. These winds are called by their Arabic name, "hamsin," and are very difficult and trying.

What was the threat of a "second round"?

While the struggling new state was trying to develop its resources, to bring in its exiles and to stabilize its economy, the threat of another Arab war hung over its people constantly.

The Arabs, since their defeat in 1948, had been threatening a "second round" of war against Israel. Colonel Gamal Abdel Nasser, who had been among those captured in a Negev battle during the War of Liberation, was now the President of Egypt. One of Nasser's objectives was to build up enough Arab strength to attack Israel again and to defeat it. Because the Soviet Union was interested in creating unrest in the Middle East, Nasser was able to negotiate a gigantic arms shipment from Russia, which included the most modern jet planes, tanks, and guns. At the same time, Nasser made an agreement with Syria and Jordan to join him in the attack. Together, the three countries could practically encircle Israel.

Who were the "Fedayeen"?

One of the Egyptian bases was in the Gaza Strip, a tongue of land about 22 miles long and 8 miles wide, between Israel and Egypt. The Gaza Strip was the area in which hundreds of thousands of Arab refugees were living. From among these Arabs and from his own troops, Nasser had trained units to cross the border and attack Jews. These special troops were called "Fedayeen." Their job was to blow up houses, burn fields of grain, orchards, and olive groves, break water lines, and kill from ambush.

What was occurring along the Gaza Strip was also taking place along the Israeli borders. Nasser, with the tremendous military supplies behind him, with Syria and Jordan by his side, and with the possible encouragement of the Soviet Union, was laying the groundwork for war.

Israeli intelligence forces had long known of the military build-up. They were aware that with its Russian jets, Egypt could attack Tel Aviv, Jerusalem, and Haifa before the alarm could even be sounded. Furthermore the Fedayeen attacks were taking many lives, destroying much property, terrifying some settlers, and endangering road travel. These attacks were also an invasion of Israeli territory by what were, in effect, foreign troops. If Israel remained silent now, total invasion would certainly follow.

What was the Sinai campaign?

On a Thursday, late in October, 1956, Ben Gurion carefully consulted with Chief of Staff Moshe Dayan and Yaakov Herzog, his political adviser. His decision was made. The army began silent mobilization. Men and women all over Israel suddenly disappeared without their whereabouts being known to anyone. True to its reputation as the quickest army in the world to mobilize, Israel had its units assembled by Sunday.

On Saturday night, Ben Gurion assembled some members of his Cabinet and told them that the Sinai campaign was ready to begin. He explained that the attack had three objectives: to destroy Egyptian bases in the Sinai Peninsula, to expel the Egyptians from the Gaza Strip, and to safeguard Israeli navigation and shipping in Elath, at the south of Israel.

Not even Abba Eban, the Israeli Ambassador to the United States and Israel's Chief Delegate to the United Nations, knew what was about to happen. Nor of course did the Egyptians.

The Israeli attack startled the entire world when news of it was broadcast on Monday morning. Israel, which had so often been attacked, was now retaliating. At 9 o'clock on the following Tuesday morning, the first Israeli communiqué was issued:

> Israel forces have struck into the heart of Sinai and are more than half way to Suez.

Who is Shlomo Goren?

By daring use of paratroopers, the entire campaign was over in several days. Chief Chaplain Shlomo Goren, himself a paratrooper and one of the greatest Talmudic scholars in Israel, led the attack as one of the ranking army officers. Holding a Sefer Torah aloft, he led the soldiers on, giving them faith and courage.

The Egyptians, terrified, fled before the Israeli troops, leaving valuable equipment, tanks and guns. There was enough equipment to supply an army, hundreds of tanks and artillery pieces, and 6000 frightened prisoners. Israel had also captured an Egyptian destroyer and towed it in triumph to Haifa.

On the same day, France and Great Britain took advantage of the Israeli action and attacked Egypt, destroying almost her entire force. By Friday, Gaza surrendered to Israel and the war was over.

What were the results of the Sinai campaign?

Israel now held the Gaza Strip, all of the Sinai Desert, and the Egyptian coast of the Gulf of Elath. Her forces were within 10 miles of the Suez Canal. Then came a political barrage: a threat from Premier Bulganin of Russia, threats from the United States, including a radio and television address by President Dwight D. Eisenhower, and threats from the United Nations. France and England were quick to withdraw. Israel could not help but follow.

Nevertheless, the results of the campaign were rewarding. A great amount of equipment was in the hands of the Israelis where it was sorely needed. The Fedayeen were almost completely cleared out. Egyptian arrogance and power were broken. The Port of Elath was secured for Israel's maritime needs. And finally, the Arab nations learned that the State of Israel meant to hold its land and that it was ready to defend itself at all times.

Since the Sinai campaign, Nasser's flirting with Russia has begun again. Because of the weak stand of the West, Nasser has also assumed complete control of the Suez Canal. Israel's ships, and ships carrying cargoes to and from Israel, are still barred from the Canal.

Public admissions have been made in the Western capitals that it was a mistake to have stopped Israel from toppling Nasser from his position of power. Time alone can tell what lies in the future.

Why did Ben Gurion resign?

Ben Gurion had become almost synonymous with the Jewish state. He was at the head of the Provisional Government which proclaimed the new state; he served it as Prime Minister, and was Minister of Defense during the time of the Arab invasion. Between December, 1953, and February, 1955, Ben Gurion had taken a much needed rest. He resigned from all government duties to assume a normal life as an ordinary settler in S'deh Boker, a primitive settlement in the Negev.

But his government needed him, and in 1955, he returned as Prime Minister. In July, 1959, Ben Gurion resigned again, this time over one of the most bitterly contested issues in the history of the state. A year before he had suffered a rebuke because of his instigation of the "Who is a Jew?" controversy, an argument which we will soon consider. But this time, a more severe rebuke was administered to the 73-year-old Prime Minister.

News had leaked out that Ben Gurion had concluded an agreement, involving millions of dollars, to sell Israeli-made grenade throwers to the West German Republic. Public indignation ran high. How could Israel openly and callously trade with a nation that had destroyed almost half of the Jewish people? Jewish blood was still fresh on the hands of the Germans, they said. How could Jews even sit at the same table with a nation of murderers, let alone sell them instruments of war?

Ben Gurion's reply was that Israel needed to export as much of her production as she could for economic survival. He also pointed out that Germany was helping Israel through the payment of reparations. Germany, he said, would become a good customer for Israeli goods, as well as a good source of supply for vital materials.

Both sides of the debate seemed to have some merit. But the moral issue of dealing with the Germans remained unanswered. Ben Gurion probably would have been supported in the Knesset. But he was enraged that members of his own Cabinet had revealed what they had decided should be kept secret. He therefore resigned, only to become Prime Minister again after the subsequent elections.

What was the controversy over "Who is a Jew?"

In July, 1958, the Minister of Interior, Bar Yehudah, ruled that children of mixed marriages could be registered as Jews if both parents desired it. This ruling was strenuously opposed by the Orthodox religious parties. Their representatives maintained that not the state, only Jewish religious law, can determine who is a Jew. The National Religious Party resigned from the Cabinet to show its protest against the decision. All religious Jews suppored their stand, and letters poured in from all parts of the world. The controversy soon became known as the "Who is a Jew?" controversy.

Ben Gurion sent a letter of inquiry to 61 of the outstanding Jews of the world to poll their opinions. This included non-Orthodox rabbis and important Jews in the legal profession, in various fields of scholarship, literature, and the arts. More than

90 per cent of the answers agreed with the Orthodox point of view, pointing out, thereby, that the question of "Who is a Jew?" must be decided by Torah Law.

What have the religious parties accomplished?

The religious parties were succesful in many more areas than in the "Who is a Jew?" controversy. They have actually breathed a religious quality into the state. Under their urging and prodding, the Sabbath was adopted as the official day of rest. Most city buses do not operate on the Sabbath. All public offices are closed. The mail is not delivered on the Sabbath, either.

The religious parties in Israel were successful in having kosher food served in the Army. Marriage and divorce are enforced according to Orthodox law, and a system of rabbinical courts has been established.

Its most important accomplishment was to create a network of secondary schools and yeshivoth to give religious instruction throughout the country. Through the fund raising of Mizrachi throughout the world, a new university called Bar Ilan, patterned after Yeshiva University in America, was established.

The religious parties are also the strongest supporters of the Chief Rabbinate and the Armed Forces Chaplaincy Service. In most of these programs, the National Religious Party had the cooperation of the Agudath Israel and the Poalei Agudath Israel.

Among the outstanding members of the National Religious Party are Rabbi Judah L. Maimon, the first Minister of Religious Affairs, Moshe Shapiro who had succeeded him, and Joseph Burg who was Minister of Posts. These men were almost consistently members of the Cabinet from the time of its formation in 1948.

The leaders of the Agudath Israel parties are Rabbi Yitzchak Meir Levin, Binyamin Mintz, and Rabbi Menachem Poresh.

What is the chief rabbinate?

Under the British Mandate, two chief rabbis were appointed for the Yishuv. One represented the head of the Sephardic community, and another represented the entire Ashkenazic community. When the new state was declared, this policy remained. The purpose of the Chief Rabbinate is to unify religious practices and to encourage authoritative decisions on religious issues.

These two chief rabbis are at the head of the Rabbinical Court System. They also maintain religious councils in different sections of the country. They certify which rabbis may act in a religious capacity to perform weddings and divorces.

Since 1955, the Sephardic Chief Rabbi has been Rabbi Yitzchak Rachamim Nissim of Baghdad. Rabbi Nissim is a distinguished authority on Jewish law and an author of many Responsa and Talmudic studies. He is revered and respected throughout Israel.

Who was Rabbi Herzog?

The Ashkenazic Chief Rabbi, Rabbi Isaac Halevi Herzog, died in July, 1959. He had been Chief Rabbi for 23 years, since 1936. Rabbi Herzog was born in Poland, the son of a rabbi. He began his distinguished career as a rabbi in Leeds, England. He received his master's degree and doctorate at London University, so that he was qualified both in secular studies and in religious matters.

Before coming to Palestine, Rabbi Herzog had been the Chief Rabbi of Ireland for 17 years. He was noted for his great Talmudic learning. He wrote many articles and books in Hebrew, and his five-volume edition of *The Main Institutions of Jewish Law* received wide acclaim. He took a vigorous part in the struggle for Jewish Independence and was active in saving Jewish lives in Nazi-occupied lands during World War II.

Rabbi Herzog's death left a vacuum in Jewish life. For years visitors to Israel had been served Sabbath "kiddush" and welcomed graciously in his home. Israelis throughout the land mourned a great leader.

Rabbi Herzog's family continued the tradition of service which he set for them. One son, Yaakov, himself a rabbi, is a distinguished member of Israel's foreign service, having served at one time as Minister to Washington. Another son, Chaim, is a brigadier general in the Israel Army and commander of the vital Negev defenses.

What has Israel shown to the world?

Israel is now firmly established in the eyes of the world as a free, independent, and sovereign state. It is fulfilling its pledge to accept all Jewish exiles who wish to return. The Jewish people have shown that, given the opportunity, they can be good farmers, engineers, scientists, and soldiers. The native-born Israelis, called "Sabras," are proud and unafraid. They have shown what Jews who are not brought up in the shadow of fear can be!

The accomplishments of Israel have brought pride to all Jews and have gained respect from the peoples of the world. With its great institutions of secular learning, with its widespread yeshivoth for the study of Torah, Israel is becoming the center of Jewish study and thinking. As it grows and flourishes, the words of the Bible will yet be fulfilled:

From Zion shall go forth the Law
And the Word of the Lord from Jerusalem.

Things to Remember

1. What were the results of the Sinai campaign?
2. What was the "Who is a Jew?" controversy?
3. What are the achievements of Israel's religious parties?
4. What is the function of the chief rabbis of Israel?

Things to Think About

1. Why do you think it was a mistake for Western capitals to have stopped Israel in her Sinai campaign?
2. How do you feel about Ben Gurion's resignation over the sale of arms to Germany? Are you for it or against it? Give reasons for your answer.
3. Do you think it would be possible to have a chief rabbi in America? Give reasons for your answer.

CHAPTER NINETEEN

AMERICAN JEWS TODAY

The American Jewish Community since the end of World War I has undergone many complex changes and assumed many great responsibilities. The first change it underwent was to become a fully integrated part of the American community. The limitation of immigration has eliminated almost all foreign influences on American Jews. Their language, their interests, their clothes, their way of thought, all are like those of their Christian American neighbors.

Even the differences among Jews themselves which once seemed so important have vanished almost completely. The difference between the East European and the Sephardic, or German, Jew is no longer marked. These were differences that existed for the immigrants because of the different traditions and customs of their various places of origin. These differences, however, have long been forgotten by the children and grandchildren of these immigrants, most of whom are American born.

How do we distinguish American Jews from their neighbors?

There are two major differences that generally still distinguish Jews from non-Jews in America. One is the intense inter-

est felt by most Jews for the land of Israel. This devotion is also shared by many Christians who, because of a sense of righteousness and fairness, are enthusiastic about the existence of a Jewish homeland. But love for Israel is predominantly a Jewish quality.

The second mark of the Jew is his identification with Judaism, the faith, the culture, the history, and the hopes of the people of Israel throughout the ages. In 1959, there were 5¼ million Jews in the United States. More and more of them are identified with congregations, Jewish centers, Jewish organizations and institutions, and Jewish philanthropies.

The religious institutions and congregational buildings of early Orthodoxy, Reform, and Conservatism have grown and expanded as the number of Jews increased and as they became better able to support them. In 1954, it was estimated that there were about 460 Reform congregations, 473 Conservative congregations, and about 3000 Orthodox congregations. Almost 3½ million of the 5¼ million Jews of America are in some way connected with a Jewish House of Worship.

How Has Reform Judaism grown?

In the Reform wing there has been a consistent increase of interest in Israel, and a corresponding increase in the use of religious schools and religious services. In their Seminary, the Hebrew Union College–Jewish Institute of Religion, there is now a greater emphasis on the learning of Hebrew and the study of the Bible for their rabbinical students.

The Reform rabbis through their organization, the Central Conference of American Rabbis, have almost entirely rejected the anti-Zionism of the Pittsburgh Platform. The President of the HUC–JIR, a famous archaeologist, Dr. Nelson Glueck, himself is greatly interested in Israel. His many archaeological findings in the Holy Land have helped a great deal to reconstruct our early history in Palestine.

Many Reform rabbis have been urging a more intense celebration of the Jewish holidays, a return to more tradition and the acceptance of more rituals. There has also been a growing demand for a more definite guide or code for Reform practices. In 1958, the President of the Union of American Hebrew Congregations, in urging the adoption of such a code, pointed out the confusion that exists in Reform observances. The following is part of what he said:

> Hats on, hats off:...one day of Rosh Hashonnah and two days likewise; kosher kitchens in Reform social halls—all this and ham and bacon too; Bar Mitzvah encouraged, Bar Mitzvah barred; confirmation at thirteen, at fourteen, at fifteen, at sixteen....Some may call this the "free development of the religious idea"....I....call it "anarchy and utter chaos"...A guide, a standard...is needed.

How has Conservative Judaism grown?

The Conservatives, too, have announced plans to intensify the study of Bible and Talmud for rabbinical students in the Jewish Theological Seminary. The emphasis on these studies is necessary because of the poor preparation in the subjects that most Conservative rabbis have, unless they come from Orthodox homes, or homes where they had the opportunity to have a yeshiva education.

The JTS has also established a branch in Los Angeles, California, called the University of Judaism. Its purpose is to educate Conservative laymen and to promote Conservative Judaism.

The Conservative movement has accomplished much in the field of public relations. "The Eternal Light" radio and television programs have reached millions of Americans, bringing Jewish ideas and the history of Jewish personalities to their attention.

The head of the Conservative movement is the president of JTS, Dr. Louis Finkelstein, the son of an immigrant Orthodox rabbi and himself a great scholar and writer.

As with the Reform, Conservative rabbis are becoming increasingly aware of confusion among their laymen as to what their religious duties are. For example, they are told to revere the Torah and yet are permitted and even urged by some of their rabbis to ride to the synagogue on the Sabbath. On the other hand, some of the Conservative rabbis feel that "the only way to preserve Judaism is through the binding character of Jewish law." The wide differences in religious practices between the rabbis themselves, and between different congregations, has made it almost impossible to define what Conservative Judaism really represents.

What is Reconstructionism?

An extreme left-wing position in the Conservative rabbinate was created by Dr. Mordecai Kaplan, of the Jewish Theological Seminary. He is the founder of a movement called Reconstructionism.

Reconstructionism speaks of Judaism as a "civilization" in which religion is only one factor, although a major one. Other factors are Jewish art, music, literature, and devotion to Zionism and the State of Israel. Reconstructionism has denied the sacredness of the Torah, the Revelation at Mount Sinai, and consequently all the mitzvoth. In a sense, it has denied the existence of God as Jews throughout the generations have thought of Him. In fact, according to Reconstructionism, strange as it may seem, one can become a rabbi even if one does not believe in God.

The Reconstructionist movement is strongly Zionistic and works ardently for the continued welfare of Israel. It represents a small portion of the Conservative movement.

Both the Conservatives and the Reform groups have summer camps, national youth organizations, a national men's club, and a national union of sisterhoods. All these groups help them to communicate the philosophy of their movements.

How has Orthodoxy grown?

The Rabbi Isaac Elchanan Theological Seminary and Yeshiva College have shown the greatest growth among Jewish educational institutions in the United States. Under the dynamic and inspired leadership of its president and world-famous Torah scholar, Dr. Samuel Belkin, a vast program of development has taken place at Yeshiva College. The most remarkable achievement was the elevation of the college to university status. Yeshiva University has graduate schools in Semitics, mathematics, social work, education, and related fields. The graduate school in Semitics is named after RIETS' first president, Dr. Bernard Revel.

Yeshiva University has also added a college for women, called Stern College, and a medical school, called the Albert Einstein College of Medicine. The medical school, in its short period of existence, has already become one of the foremost in the United States, attracting great teachers and brilliant students.

What started out as a modest rabbinical seminary is now one of the leading universities in the country. It is a pride to all Orthodoxy that Yeshiva University created and maintains the first high school, the first college, the first university, the first graduate schools, the first women's college and the first medical school under Jewish auspices in the Western Hemisphere. More than 4500 students are studying in its schools.

Who are the leaders of Orthodoxy?

Dr. Belkin, like Dr. Revel before him, is a scholar renowned in secular and Talmudic studies. Ordained by the greatest rabbinical scholars of Europe and educated at Brown University in America, Dr. Belkin embodies the highest combination of religious and general knowledge.

Dr. Belkin gathered together and inspired an excellent faculty for the many schools under his direction. The most outstanding teacher on the faculty of RIETS is Dr. Joseph B. Soloveitchik, a descendant of a renowned family of great rabbis. Dr. Soloveitchik succeeded his father, Rabbi Moses Soloveitchik, as the head of the rabbinical school faculty. He is also professor of philosophy, a brilliant orator, and a human encyclopedia of rabbinic scholarship.

Dr. Belkin and Dr. Soloveitchik are recognized to be among the most profound and most influential religious leaders in the Orthodox world.

What other Orthodox rabbinical schools exist?

Several other rabbinical seminaries have also been established by Orthodox Jews since the launching of RIETS. Among them is the Hebrew Theological College of Chicago. Under the presidency of Rabbi Oscar Z. Fasman, the seminary has grown and expanded. It has built a magnificent new campus in Skokie, Illinois, which will include a college for men and women.

In addition, there are a number of other yeshivoth which, like RIETS and the Hebrew Theological Seminary, educate Orthodox leadership for American Jews. Some, like the Yeshiva of Telshe and the Mirrer Yeshiva, have been transplanted on American soil since the war. Others, like the Mesifta Torah Vo-Daath, the Chofetz Chaim Yeshiva, Yeshiva Rabbi Chaim Berlin and the Lubavitcher Yeshiva, were organized in America. Hundreds of rabbis are ordained annually by these institutions.

What is the work of the Orthodox rabbinical bodies?

There are three major Orthodox rabbinical groups. The Union of Orthodox Rabbis has about 600 members, mostly of European origin. The Rabbinical Alliance has approximately

500 members. The largest group is the Rabbinical Council of America, which has a membership of more than 750.

All of these rabbinical groups have devoted their energies to reviving and strengthening Jewish living in America. They have been carrying out a program to maintain the separation of the sexes in the synagogues, as required by Jewish law, and to teach the Torah and its mitzvoth to the members of their congregations.

How have American Jews organized for educational purposes?

American Jewish religious schools for children fall into three main classifications. The Sunday Schools meet for a few hours on Sunday morning. Because of the limited time, little subject matter can be covered.

The weekday Hebrew Schools, or Talmud Torahs, are slightly better, since the boys and girls enrolled in them receive between five and ten hours of instruction every week, and the instruction is spread over several days of the week.

The best type of Jewish education is the yeshiva, or day school. In 1920, there were perhaps a dozen of these yeshivoth, all in New York City. At that time, these schools served only a handful of students who came from religious homes and whose parents were, for the most part, new immigrants.

Since then yeshivoth have spread all over the land. Yeshiva students are found in second- and third-generation American families. There are 180 elementary yeshivoth in the United States, with more in Canada, Mexico, and South America. Some 42,000 students attend yeshivoth, with more and more registering each year.

In higher education, besides Yeshiva University and the rabbinic seminaries established by the Reform and the Conservative groups, American Jews support other colleges too. Brandeis University at Waltham, Massachusetts, and Dropsie Col-

lege for Hebrew and Cognate Learning at Philadelphia are both major institutions. Brandeis University, the youngest Jewish sponsored university, maintains a college of liberal arts and sciences and offers graduate instruction in certain areas. Dropsie College is a graduate school which offers advanced degrees in all branches of Jewish learning and in Semitic studies.

Another educational institution is the Hillel Foundation, sponsored by the B'nai B'rith. The Hillel Foundation has branches in the universities. These branches generally have a rabbi at their head to direct the religious, social, and spiritual welfare of Jewish students on the campuses, creating a Jewish environment for them and serving their needs.

What two meanings lie in the phrase, "the People of the Book"?

Mohammet, the founder of the Moslem religion, called the Jewish people the "People of the Book." By this he meant that the Jews lived by the Holy Book, the Bible.

Today, that phrase takes on an added meaning. Not only do Jews live by the Bible, but they express their love of learning and reading by buying and publishing many books. Israel, small as it is, has published and sold more books in ratio to its size than any other country.

American Jews, too, have shown their love of books by founding many publishing houses that specialize in bringing out books of Jewish interest. The three largest of these are the Jewish Publication Society of America, Bloch Publishing Co., and Behrman House in New York City. There are also a number of Jewish libraries and museums which have excellent collections of Jewish, Anglo-Jewish, and Hebrew books, and objects of art.

In addition to the Yiddish newspapers, such as the *Day-Morning Journal* and the *Forward*, which still exist, there are a large number of Anglo-Jewish periodicals, and some Hebrew.

The best-known Hebrew weekly is *Hadoar*, the *Post*, but there are others as well.

How has Yiddish fared in the United States?

Yiddish has unfortunately lost its popularity, and fewer and fewer and Jews speak it.

The Yiddish theater is almost completely gone. Of the many Yiddish newspapers, only two are still published today. The Yiddish schools, under the auspices of the Arbeiter Ring, are very few in number.

When the Nazis so brutally exterminated all of European Jewry, the Jewish Scientific Institute, called YIVO, moved its offices from Europe to New York City. The YIVO sponsors important publications in Yiddish about Jewish life and history. The Yiddish-speaking groups, in addition, support the Jewish Teachers Seminary and Peoples University in New York City.

The Yiddish schools are still secular in outlook. They emphasize Yiddish language and literature and do not teach Hebrew or religious subjects.

Who are some famous American Jews?

Jews, like non-Jews, have been active in every aspect of American life—in business, industry, literature, science, philanthropy, and politics. They have never held a monopoly in any particular field but have contributed as individual human beings through their talents or their services to society.

We saw how Jews were instrumental in building up the clothing industry of America and organizing its workers. In the moving-picture industry Jews like William Fox, Adolf Zukor, Samuel Goldwyn, and Dore Schary have made great names for themselves. David Sarnoff is one of the pioneers in radio and television.

The Guggenheim family contributed to the development

of copper mining in the West. By his grants on behalf of aeronautic education, Daniel Guggenheim helped the aviation industry to advance.

In the field of physical science and invention, Albert Michaelson was one of America's most distinguished physicists. He was the first American to win a Nobel Prize, receiving the award for his work in measuring the speed of light. There have since been other Jewish winners of the Nobel Prize. Among them are Victor Hess, who discovered the nature of cosmic rays and Otto Stern, who pioneered research in the properties of atoms. Albert Einstein, who escaped from Nazi Germany and became an American citizen, was one of the greatest scientists of all time.

The field of atomic science and electronics is dotted with names of illustrious Jews. Albert Einstein of course leads the list. Others include Enrico Fermi, Niels Bohr, Lise Meitner, Robert Oppenheimer, Edward Teller, Isador Rabi, Admiral Hyman Rickover, and Admiral Lewis S. Strauss, who is a past chairman of the Atomic Energy Commission.

These and many others engaged in every form of atomic research did not originate their studies in order to develop more powerful instruments of war but rather in the interest of pure science and greater understanding of the universe.

Their hope, like that of all good peoples of the world, is that the powers they have helped create will be used for healing of the sick and as instruments of peace.

In the field of medicine and biology, many Jews made lasting contributions. Joseph Goldberger's studies of malnutrition led to the naming of Vitamin G after him. Bela Schick discovered the test for immunity against diphtheria that is known as the Schick Test. Selman Waksman discovered streptomycin. Jonas Salk discovered an inoculation against polio. Dr. Alfred B. Sabin later discovered a vaccine against polio that can be given orally. The U.S. Public Health service was quoted as saying that the availability of these two vaccines would eliminate polio in the United States.

There have always been leading Jewish jurists. Three Jews have served on the bench of the highest court in the land, the United States Supreme Court. Louis D. Brandeis, Benjamin Cardozo, and Felix Frankfurter helped to shape the legal thinking of more than two generations of Americans. Other Jews have served with distinction in lower federal, state, and municipal courts.

There have been many Jewish writers and editors. Adolph Ochs, the founder of *The New York Times,* and Joseph Pulitzer, the founder of the *New York World,* after whom the Pulitzer Prize is named, were both Jews. The present publisher of *The New York Times,* Arthur Hays Sulzberger, is also Jewish. Jewish American writers like Joseph Auslander, Fannie Hurst, Edna Ferber, Herman Wouk, Charles Angoff, Bernard Malamud, and Meyer Levin have been outstanding in the field of literature.

Finally, in the entertainment arts–in music, movies, and the theater–Jews have become beloved by millions of Americans. To mention just a few, George Gershwin, Aaron Copland, Leonard Bernstein, and Ernest Bloch became famous as composers. Bruno Walter and the late Serge Koussevitsky, both Jewish, won renown as two of the greatest conductors in the world.

Violin virtuosos like Jascha Heifetz, Mischa Elman, Efrem Zimbalist, and Nathan Milstein–and great pianists like Vladimir Horowitz, Artur Rubinstein, and Rudolf Serkin–have thrilled the nation and the world with their musical abilities.

The song writer, Irving Berlin, represents many more Jewish men in the field of popular music. More recently there have been Frederick Loewe, who wrote the score for *My Fair Lady* and Alan Jay Lerner, who wrote the book and lyrics for this same hit musical. The famous composer, Richard Rodgers, is also Jewish. Rodgers and Hammerstein's *South Pacific* set a record for the American theater. And even that was in some ways surpassed by their following musical *The King and I.*

Jewish actors and actresses are too numerous to mention—Edward G. Robinson, Eddie Cantor, Paul Muni, Sylvia Sidney, Joseph Schildkraut, Jerry Lewis, Luise Rainier—all these and many more have helped to "hold, as 'twere the mirror up to Nature," bringing power, compassion, color, and sparkle to the American stage.

Among American Jews who have distinguished themselves in the fields of industrial design and engineering are Raymond Loewy and Albert Kahn, the latter of whom designed Ford's River Rouge plant near Detroit.

Chaim Gross, the sculptor, Max Weber, the painter, and Arthur Szyk, the illustrator, painter, and book designer, are among the American Jews of modern times who have made significant contributions in the fine arts.

What is the challenge to American Orthodoxy?

But the most important contribution that American Jews make is the contribution that they make as Jews, to something specifically Jewish. To be born a Jew is an accident of fate; to live as a Jew is an exercise of choice.

Throughout the formative years of America's growth and development, the choice of the American Jew was to live as a Jew. The early settlers like Asser Levy, who fought for citizenship privileges, were fighting for the Biblical concept of equal rights for all men. The antislavery Abolitionists were fighting for the Torah's holy principle of man's equality before God. The Socialists, who took up the cudgels on behalf of the workingman, were inspired by the Bible's teachings of fairness and consideration in dealing with one's fellowman. Even the tragic martyrdom of six million European Jews in the flames and fire kindled by the madman Hitler taught the world the holiness and dignity of human life and the unspeakable evils of dictatorship.

More and more the American Jew has chosen to live as a Jew. By building yeshivoth and day schools, by establishing more synagogues, by spreading the word of the Torah, American Jews are marching on the road of their ancient faith and the way of their forefathers.

Because European Jewry has been almost completely wiped out, American Jews have to look to their own resources for future leaders. They can no longer rely on great rabbis, teachers, and scholars coming from Europe and offering their leadership to the American Jewish community. The American Jewish community must renew itself from within and develop its own leaders from native American ranks.

This great need Orthdoxy in America is fulfilling. It has also moved into many other cultural avenues, as testified by the founding of a medical school and of graduate schools in almost every field of scholarship.

Orthodoxy has proved its ability to harmonize with all the streams of American culture, to produce an American Jewish community that will be reverent of God, obedient to His mitzvoth, and steeped in His Torah.

Things to Remember

1. How do American Jews identify themselves as Jews?
2. How have Reform, Conservatism, and Orthodoxy grown in America?
3. What educational institutions have Jews provided in the field of elementary Jewish education? In higher Jewish education?
4. Name some Jews who were or are prominent in:
   a. science
   b. law
   c. literature
   d. music

Things to Think About

1. Your text says: "To be born a Jew is an accident of fate; to live as a Jew is an exercise of choice." What does this mean? Do you agree or disagree with this statement?
2. Do you think these are special causes that have brought out Jewish talent in certain fields?
3. How does Jewish life in America today differ from Jewish life here at the time your grandfather or great grandfather came to America?

UNIT PROJECTS

The following class or individual projects are suggested for each unit in the textbook.

UNIT ONE: FROM COLUMBUS TO LINCOLN

1. Discuss religious influences in colonial America and their contribution to civil rights laws.
2. Pretend that you are Asser Levy. Write a diary, keeping a day-by-day account of the Jewish community's struggle with Peter Stuyvesant, of life in the early settlement, etc.
3. Make up a short story about Mordecai Sheftall *or* Francis Salvador. Make it an exciting blood-and-thunder tale.
4. Write the story of a person who sails from Holland for the New World. At the beginning of your story, draw a map tracing the route that person might have taken.
5. Draw a huge poster *or* make a giant scrapbook of prominent Jews in the time between Columbus and Lincoln. The scrapbook can include pictures, stories, poems. The poster can show the time in which each person lived, his contribution to America, his contribution to Judaism.
6. Make a class mural of the contributions of Jews in the period between Washington and Lincoln.
7. Draw a painting of the founding of Ararat *or* write an eyewitness account of the event.
8. Write to the Touro Synagogue in Newport, Rhode Island, and ask them to send you all the pictures, data, and historical information that they have. Then present this information in a report to your class.

9. Prepare a pictorial time line of the period from "Washington to Lincoln." Place the great Jews of this period in their proper time.
10. Make up a play about Judah Benjamin, choosing important events in his life for each episode.

UNIT TWO: THE DEVELOPING AMERICAN JEWISH COMMUNITY

1. Make up a debate on the Pittsburgh Platform, choosing pro and con arguments.
2. Draw a cartoon strip depicting the life of Isaac Mayer Wise.
3. Write to the HUC, JTS, and RIETS asking them for pictures, information, and data that they can send you. Then make a scrapbook of the Reform, Conservative, and Orthodox seminaries in America.
4. Ask your rabbi if he would like to visit your class and tell you about the school he came from and what he had to study to become a rabbi.
5. Dramatize a story about the "greenhorns."
6. Ask your parents if they ever belonged to a landsmanschaft. Perhaps one of your parents or grandparents could come down and speak about the landsmanschaft, how it was organized, and what it does.
7. Draw a picture of the new immigrants and their first sight of the Statue of Liberty.
8. If possible, take a trip to a port of entry or immigration station.
9. Make some illustrations of life in a tenement house.
10. Pretend you are a new immigrant from Russia. Write a letter to your friends at home, telling them about the new life in the "Goldenne M'dinah," how it differs from the old country, and what you miss the most.

11. Draw a picture of the first meeting of students in the home of Rabbi Moses Matlin.
12. Make a movie on "Jewish Organizations and How They Began."
13. Write a "folk song" or poem about the life of the peddler in early America.

UNIT THREE: THE WORLD AT WAR

1. Draw a cartoon strip showing how one of the Congressional Medal of Honor winners won his award in World War I.
2. Illustrate the Zion Mule Corps at work in World War I.
3. Do some research on Jabotinsky or Trumpeldor. When you have all the material assembled, prepare a report to the class.
4. Pretend you are Theodor Herzl. Write a series of articles for your newspaper on the Dreyfus case.
5. Write an eye-witness account of the First Zionist Congress.
6. Pretend you are a "roving eye" reporter. Interview each of the following and ask his reaction to the creation of a Jewish state.
   a. A Munich Reform Rabbi
   b. A Chassidic Rabbi
   c. Ahad Ha'Am
   d. Israel Zangwill.

   Television—Make a skit out of your interviews.
7. Write a play about any one of the following:
   Eliezer ben Yehuda
   Chaim Weizmann
   Theodore Herzl
8. Make a giant scrapbook on the death of the six million Jews in Europe. Call it "We Will Not Forget." Include pictures, articles, stories, poems.

9. Keep a diary of the Warsaw Ghetto Uprising. Pretend you are one of the last defenders. This diary will be the only record of what has happened. Your diary should be concise, full, and accurate. People it with people who might have died in the Warsaw Ghetto Uprising.
10. Draw a painting of a Youth Aliyah child leaving her or his parents.

UNIT FOUR: IN ISRAEL

1. Write a play about the life of Hannah Senesch.
2. Write a letter to the editor protesting Britain's action against the *Struma*.
3. Paint a mural depicting the shlichim at work. Show how they help bring the maapilim to the Holy Land. Show how they get them off their boats in the dead of night.
4. Write a "folk song" about an Israeli soldier who lost his life in Israel's War of Independence.
5. Invite a United Jewish Appeal representative to come to your class and tell you about the UJA, what it does and how it got started.
6. Dramatize the UN voting on the partition plan through a "You Are There" radio script.
7. Draw an illustration of Operation Magic Carpet.
8. Do some research on the Jews of Yemen. What do they look like? How do they dress? How many Yemenites are in Israel today? Where, in Israel, do they live?
9. Draw a cartoon strip of the day when Chaim Weizmann became President of Israel.
10. Write a newspaper account of the finding of the Dead Sea Scrolls.

UNIT FIVE: ISRAEL AND AMERICA TODAY

1. Write to a national Zionist organization and ask if you can get a film on Israel from them. Show the film in class. Discuss the things you see in the light of what you have learned.
2. Draw a picture map of Israel. Show its borders, its neighbors. Put in its chief industries, main cities. Show its three big divisions.
3. Pretend you are a soldier in Chaplain Goren's division. Keep a day-by-day account of the Sinai campaign.
4. Arrange a Knesset meeting when the "Who is a Jew?" controversy is being discussed. Different children in the class should take different parts of Ben Gurion, Joseph Burg, Moshe Shapiro, etc.
5. Write a column about the passing of Rabbi Herzog, what he has meant to Israel, and what he stood for.
6. Make a scrapbook of famous living American Jews.
7. If you live in New York City or near it, arrange for a trip to Yeshiva University.
8. Or write to Yeshiva University and ask for information and pictures about it. Then discuss this information in class.

IMPORTANT DATES TO REMEMBER

1492	Columbus discovers America.
1654	First Jewish settlement at New Amsterdam.
1730	First synagogue building in New York City.
1776	New York State grants Jews full rights.
1791	France grants Jews full citizenship rights.
1815–1820	"Second Wave" of Jewish Immigration to U.S. begins.
1824	Reform movement in U.S. begins at Charleston, S. C.
1881	"Third Wave" of Jewish Immigration begins.
1885	Pittsburgh Platform.
1886	Yeshiva Etz Chaim established.
1886	United Hebrew Trades founded.
1887	Jewish Theological Seminary established.
1896	Rabbi Isaac Elchanan Theological Seminary established.
1897	First Zionist Congress called by Theodor Herzl.
1914	The world at war.
1917	Balfour Declaration.
1917	Russian Revolution.
1921	Johnson Act limits immigration to the U.S.
1933	Hitler seizes power in Germany.
1939	World War II begins.
1940	Warsaw Ghetto uprising.
1941	U.S. enters war after Japanese attack.
1948	State of Israel proclaimed.
1949	Israel becomes 55th member of United Nations.
1956	Israel launches Sinai campaign.

MILESTONES IN JEWISH HISTORY

(Early dates are approximate)

1800 B.C.E.	Father Abraham, the first of the Patriarchs, introduces monotheism to the world and receives God's promise that the children of Israel will inherit the land of Canaan. These two ideals become the basic principles of the people of Israel.
1440 B.C.E.	The Exodus from Egypt and the Revelation at Mount Sinai provide national independence and a religious constitution for the people of Israel. The conquest of Canaan completes the initial experience of Jewish national fulfillment.
1000 B.C.E.	King David begins the Davidic dynasty, and under King Solomon the Temple is built.
515 B.C.E.	The destroyed Temple is rebuilt by the remaining tribes of Israel, ten having been exiled and lost. Ezra, the Scribe, introduces the religious leadership of the Knesset Hagdolah, which is the forerunner of the Talmudic Age.
165 B.C.E.	The Maccabean revolt brings the rededication of the Temple and the first Hanukah. Hillel and the tannaim follow shortly thereafter.
C.E. 70	The Second Temple is destroyed, and with its destruction Palestine is weakened as the central force in Jewish life.
200	The Age of the Tannaim comes to a close with the writing of the Mishna by Rabbi Judah-ha-Nasi.
500	The Babylonian Talmud is completed, marking the end of the Age of the Amoraim.

500–1000	The Age of the Gaonim flourishes in Babylonia, after which that region ceases to be the center of Jewish life.
950–1280	Spain becomes the center and source of Jewish learning and creativity. In this Golden Age flourish ibn Gabirol, the ibn Ezras, Judah Halevi, the Rambam, Ranbam, and countless others.
960–1200	Simultaneously, brilliant scholars in the Rhineland, Rabennu Gershon, Rashi, and Rabbi Meir of Rotenburg, create a new form of intensive Talmud study.
1096–1492	The Crusades introduce organized terror against the Jews of Europe. They are climaxed by expulsions from England and France and by the Inquisition in Spain, ending in the expulsion from that country.
1555	A Torah milestone is reached with the compiling of the *Shulchan Aruch* by the Ramo. Talmudic learning and religious observance continue at a remarkable pace in Poland and East Europe.
1654	Jews settle in New Amsterdam.
1700–1790	Baal Shem Tov introduces Chassidism, which is disputed by Mithnagdim. The latter's outstanding figure and greatest scholar of all time is the Gaon of Vilna.
1789	The French Revolution and Napoleonic Wars introduce emancipation to Western Europe and are followed by German Haskalah and Reform, and by the Haskalah in Russia.
1861	Rabbi Kalischer founds colonization groups in Palestine. Jewish nationalism begins to grow,

reaching its peak in the work of Herzl and the Zionist Congresses.

1881–1882 The May Laws in Russia set off large-scale East European emigration to the United States.

1885 Pittsburgh Platform crystallizes American Reform, followed by founding of Jewish Theological Seminary and Rabbi Isaac Elchanan Theological Seminary.

1914 World War I brings agony to Jews in Europe. Relief agencies founded in America. Zionism encouraged by Balfour Declaration. Russian Revolution dooms Jews in Russia.

1921 Rising anti-Semitism in Europe and restriction on Jewish immigration to U.S. and Palestine create prison for Jews on continent.

1933 Hitler comes to power in Germany and begins war against Jews.

1939–1945 World War II brings almost all of Europe under Hitler domination. During the war six million Jews are killed in German concentration camps.

1948 The State of Israel is proclaimed to the accompaniment of an Arab war. Israel proves victorious and furnishes a home to all Jews who seek its sanctuary.

BIBLIOGRAPHY ON ISRAEL

Bein, Alex, *Theodor Herzl*, Jewish Publication Society, Philadelphia, 1940

Berg, Mary, *Warsaw Diary*, L. B. Fischer, 1945

Dunner, Joseph, *The Republic of Israel, Its History and Its Promise*, Whittlesey House, McGraw-Hill Book Co., Inc., New York, 1952

Herzl, Theodor, *The Jewish State*, Scopus, Inc., New York, 1943

Hirschman, Ira *Life Line to a Promised Land*, Jewish Book Guild of America, 1946

Joseph, Dov, *The Faithful City, The Siege of Jerusalem, 1948*, Simon and Schuster, Inc., New York, 1960

Learsi, Rufus, *Israel, A History of the Jewish People*, World Publishing Company, New York, 1950

Lehrman, Hal, *Israel–The Beginning and Tomorrow*, William Sloan Associates, Inc., New York

Levin, Meyer, *My Father's House*, Viking Press, New York, 1947

Potar, Raphael, *Israel between East and West*, Jewish Publication Society, Philadelphia, 1953

Revasky, Abraham, *Jews in Palestine*, Bloch Publishing Co., Inc., New York, 1945

Samuel, Maurice, *Harvest in the Desert*, Jewish Publication Society, Philadelphia, 1944

Syrkin, Marie, *Blessed Is the Match*, Jewish Publication Society, Philadelphia, 1947

Van Paasen, Pierre, *The Forgotten Ally*, Dell Publishing Co., Inc., New York, 1943

Vilnay, Zev, *Israel Guide*, Central Press, Jerusalem, 1958

Weizmann, Chaim, *Trial and Error–The Autobiography of Chaim Weizmann*, Harper & Brothers, New York, 1949

GENERAL BIBLIOGRAPHY

Antin, Mary, *The Promised Land*, Houghton Mifflin Company, Boston, 1912

Edidin, Ben M., *Jewish Community Life in America*, Hebrew Publishing Co., New York, 1947

Freund, Miriam K., *Jewish Merchants in Colonial America*, Behrman House, Inc., New York, 1939

Friedman, Lee M., *Pilgrims in a New Land*, Jewish Publication Society, New York, 1948

Friedman, Theo-Gordis, Rbt., *Jewish Life in America*, Horizon Press, Inc., New York, 1955

Goodman, A., *American Overture: Jewish Rights in Colonial Times*, Jewish Publication Society, Philadelphia, 1947

Gottschalk, Max, and Duker, Abraham G., *Jews in Post-war World*, Dryden Press, Inc., New York, 1945

Grayzel, Solomon, *A History of the Jews*, Jewish Publications Society, Philadelphia, 1947

Grinstein, Hyman B., *The Rise of the Jewish Community of New York 1654-1860*, Jewish Publication Society, Philadelphia, 1945

Janowsky, Oscar I., *The American Jew—A Composite Portrait*, Harper & Brothers, New York, 1942

Lebeson, Anita, *Jewish Pioneers in America*, Behrman House, Inc., New York, 1938

Levinger, Lee J., *A History of the Jews in the U.S.*, Union of American Hebrew Congregations, New York, 1935

Levitan, Tina, *The Laureates*, Twayne Publishers, New York, 1960

Marcus, Jacob R., *Memoirs of American Jews—Vols. 2 and 3, 1775-1865*, Jewish Publications Society, Philadelphia, 1955

——, *Early American Jewry, Vols. 1 and 2*, Jewish Publication Society, Philadelphia, 1951

Pilch, Judah, *Jewish Life in Our Times*, Behrman House, Inc., New York, 1944

Roth, Cecil, *The Jewish Contribution to Civilization*, Union of American Hebrew Congregations, New York, 1940

Schappes, Morris, *Documentary History of Jews in the United States 1654-1875*, Citadel Press, New York, 1950

Sachar, Abraham L., *Sufferance Is the Badge*, Alfred A. Knof, Inc., New York, 1940

INDEX